THE BREAKFAST WAR

THE BREAKFAST WAR

by

RUPERT FURNEAUX

THOMAS Y. CROWELL COMPANY

New York · Established 1834

CONTENTS

MAPS

ILLUSTRATIONS

Following page 64

The Bashi-Bazouks at bay
The July Assault from the southeast
Death of Colonel Rosenbaum of the Archangel
   Regiment
Osman Pasha, The Defender of Plevna
General Michael Skobeleff of the Russian Army
The Great Assault
Attack on a redoubt
A Turkish family in Plevna

Following page 192

The Correspondents' camp attacked by wolves
Storming the Grivitza redoubt
In the captured Grivitza redoubt
General Radetzky's Dragoons to the rescue
General Skobeleff resting in the forward trenches
The Turkish sortie from Plevna
Osman Pasha on his way to be received by the Czar
Osman Pasha en route to Kharkoff

FOREWORD

"PLEVNA! Plevna!" You may exclaim, "Where is Plevna? And why Plevna? Was its siege so famous? One of the decisive battles of the world perhaps?"

Plevna was, and still is as far as I know, a sleepy, rather smelly, utterly dull little Bulgarian town, of no conceivable importance in itself, which for a brief moment of time became the focal point in the last great struggle between Cross and Crescent. Its heroic defence by the Turks, and the no less heroic failure of the Russians to take it by storm, caught the imagination of the newspaper readers of the civilized world to whose breakfast tables, day by day, the corps of international war correspondents brought their eye-witness stories of assault and siege.

In the summer and winter of 1877 Plevna was front page news. Now its great siege is forgotten history, but a story perhaps which may still set our blood atingle as we watch from the Radishevo ridge with Archibald Forbes, or stand with Skobeleff and MacGahan on the Green Hills, as wave after wave of Russian infantry shatter and break on those impregnable Turkish redoubts.

This is the story of Plevna and its bulldog defender, Osman Pasha, the Victorious, and it is the story, too, of an Englishman, an American and a Russian, two of them newspaper correspondents and the other a soldier, who loved each other as comrades, as the one fought and the other two wrote amidst the four months' carnage which made the siege of Plevna a landmark in the evolution of man's ability to slay other men in even greater masses.

CHAPTER ONE

THE WAR CALLED HOLY

"WE shall dine in Plevna tonight," exclaimed Forbes to his friend Frederick Villiers as the two newspaper men peered through the swirling cannon smoke at the flaming redoubt across the valley. As they watched, their blood tingling with the excitement of the fray, wave after wave of grey-clad Russians poured over the parapet and a great shout, half yell, half cheer, was wafted back on the breeze. From the pall of smoke rose a chaos of noise, the clash of steel on steel, the sharp crackle of the rifle fire, the whine of bullets, the deep boom of the cannon and the shouts of reckless men bent on victory or death. An almost irresistible craving comes to the watchers to throw themselves into the fray, to do something, no matter what. The full fury of the battle reaches its maddest paroxysm. In the distance lies Plevna, snug in its valley, quiet and serene like a sleeping babe amongst a pack of wolves, the sun glinting on its spires and minarets. Behind them, the Russian cannon belch fire and noise. In front, in a gigantic horse shoe the battle rages in all its splendour and horror. But the toll of blood is too great. From the Turkish redoubt the Russians fall back, shattered by the terrible hail of fire, and the ground is strewn with dead and dying, the wounded to be butchered by the terrible Bashi-Bazouks, for this is a Holy War between Cross and Crescent in which no quarter is given.

For once Forbes, the 'incompatible Archibald' as his colleagues called him, the veteran observer of wars, was wrong. A hundred and forty days would go by before a Russian foot trod the tortuous streets of Plevna, the little Bulgarian town which Forbes and his colleagues were to make famous. All that night and the next Forbes galloped, through the ruck of the defeated Russian army, to the nearest telegraph point in neutral Hungary to tell the readers of the London *Daily News*, "The Russian defeat is utter: the whole plan of campaign is changed. Plevna must be taken."

Only a few weeks before, the Russian army, 180,000 strong, watched by the Great White Czar himself, had crossed the Danube confident in a speedy victory over the despised Turks, and a triumphal march to Constantinople, the age-old Russian goal on the Bosporus. In Bulgaria, they had been welcomed as liberators of the Christians from the yoke of the Moslem Turk. Bearded priests in long white petticoats held up wooden crosses for the soldiers, generals, grand dukes and princes and the Czar himself, to kiss. Pretty girls threw flowers in their path and kissed the soldiers' hands. The Bulgarian peasants waved a welcome and cheated the Russians right and left. To the Russians the war was a Crusade, a Holy War, to drive the Turks from the provinces they had despoiled. Even the Czar believed the cause a righteous one, although the perfidious British declared that the wrongs of the Christian subjects of the Sultan were no more than an excuse for a war of aggression in which the Russian goal was an outlet on the Mediterranean.

In the previous summer of 1876, the civilized world had been shocked by the stories of the Bulgarian atrocities of the unspeakable Turk. At first only rumours percolated out of the Turkish Balkan Provinces. By Disraeli, the British Prime Minister, anxious to preserve the Near Eastern *status quo* and to keep the Colossus of the North from interfering, these stories of murder and rapine were pooh-poohed. A few Bulgarian insurgents had been killed, no doubt, but that was their own fault for rising in rebellion against their overlord the Sultan who was doing his best to bring about the reforms Turkey had long promised. But, as the rumours grew, disquiet deepened, and the London *Daily News*, commissioned J. A. MacGahan, an American newspaper man who had made himself famous by his ride across the burning wastes of Central Asia to report the Russian campaign against the Khan of Klokhand in 1873, who was

then in Constantinople, to go to Bulgaria and investigate
the truth of these stories.

MacGahan's telegrams from Batak and Philipopolis fell
like a bomb in England in August 1876, and caused a wave
of indignation and horror which brought a cry of fury from
the aged statesman, Gladstone, who declared that the Turks
must be thrown out 'bag and baggage' from the provinces
they had desecrated and pillaged. In a pamphlet which sold
50,000 copies and netted him £12,000, Gladstone told the

J. A. MacGahan
Daily News, with the Russians

people of England: "Five million Bulgarians, cowed and
beaten down to the ground, hardly venturing to look up-
wards, even to their Father in Heaven, have extended their
hands to you."

From Batak, MacGahan, who was accompanied by
Eugene Schuyler the American Consul-General in Turkey,
described how on approaching the town they found a number
of skulls scattered about, and one ghastly heap of skeletons:
"I counted from the saddle a hundred skulls, picked and
licked clean: all of women and children. We entered the
town. On every side were skulls and skeletons charred among
the ruins, or lying entire where they fell in their clothing.

They were skeletons of girls and women with long brown hair hanging to their skulls. We approached the church. There these remains were more frequent, until the ground was literally covered with skeletons, skulls and putrefying bodies in clothing. Between the church and the school there were heaps. The stench was fearful. We entered the churchyard. The sight was more dreadful. The whole churchyard for three feet deep was festering with dead bodies partly covered—hands, legs, arms and heads projected in ghastly confusion. I saw many little hands, heads and feet of children of three years of age, and girls with heads covered with beautiful hair. The church was still worse. The floor was covered with rotting bodies quite uncovered. I never imagined anything so fearful. There were three thousand bodies in the churchyard and church. . . . In the school, a fine building, two hundred women and children had been burnt alive. All over the town there were the same scenes. . . . The man who did all this, Achmed Aga, has been promoted and is still Governor of the district. The newspaper accounts were not exaggerated. They could not be. No crime invented by Turkish ferocity was left uncommitted."

This appeared in the *Daily News* on 7 August. On the 16th MacGahan wrote: "I fear I am no longer impartial, and I certainly am no longer cool. . . . I have already investigated enough to feel convinced that, except from a purely statistical point of view, further investigation would be unnecessary. . . . When you are met in the outset of your investigation with the admission that sixty or seventy villages have been burned, that some fifteen thousand people have been slaughtered, of whom a large part were women and children, you begin to feel that it is useless to go any further."

Then came a long letter from MacGahan in elaboration from Batak: "We asked about the skulls and bones we had seen up on the hill upon first arriving in the village when the dogs had barked at us. These we were told were the bones of about two hundred young girls, who had first been captured and particularly reserved for a worse fate than death. They had been kept till the last: they had been in the hands of their captors for several days—for the burning and pillaging had not all been accomplished in a single day—and during this time they had suffered all that it was possible that poor, weak, trembling girls could suffer at the hands of brutal savages. Then when the town had been pillaged and burned, when all their friends had been slaughtered, these poor young things, whose very wrongs should have insured their safety, whose very outrages should

JAMES DOW
Sheffield Daily Telegraph, with the Turks

have insured their protection, were taken, in the broad light of day, beneath the smiling canopy of heaven, and coolly beheaded, then thrown in a heap there and left to rot."

He then described the fate of the village of Panagurishte where, he said, "the scene of pillage, violence and massacre equalled that of Batak. Women, young girls, children, infants were ruthlessly slaughtered. These Turks have no pity, no compassion, no bowels. They have not even the generosity, the pity of wild beasts. Even the tiger will not slay the young of its own species. But these Turks, these strong, bearded men, picked infants up out of their cradles with their bayonets tossed them in the air, caught them again and flung them at the heads of their shrieking mothers. They carried little babes about the streets on the points of their bayonets, with their poor little heads and arms drooping around the barrels of their guns, and the blood streaming down over their hands. . . . Not a woman in the place seems to have escaped outrage. . . . Outrages were committed so publicly, so generally, that they feel it would be useless to try to hide their shame and they avow it openly. These acts were committed not only in the houses, but in the streets, in the yards, in the courts: for the Turks have not even the decency which may accompany vice. They have not even the modesty of vileness; they have not even the shame of nature. Mothers were outraged in the presence of their daughters; young girls in the presence of their mothers, of their sisters and brothers." And he concluded: "And you say, O Statesmen of Europe, that the *status quo* must be maintained: that this must last. I tell you it will not last. You must find another solution to the Eastern Question, or another solution will find you. It will not last, or civilization is a delusion, justice a mockery, and Christianity a farce and a failure."

In London, Benjamin Disraeli, now Lord Beaconsfield, tried to minimize MacGahan's disclosures; 'picturesque journalism', they were called. But Disraeli was being cautious, not callous. British interests demanded that the Russians be kept from the Eastern Mediterranean, where Britain had recently acquired the Suez Canal shares from the Khedive of Egypt. The Crimean War had been fought to prevent Russia from establishing herself as the Protector of the Balkan Christians, and Disraeli feared that the Czar would now raise the same cry, this time with right on his side.

The Balkan unrest had been carefully fostered by the Russians. The Turks, well intentioned but ineffective, had long been trying to put their house in order. For centuries Turks and Bulgarians had lived together amicably. Atrocities were almost unknown until, in 1860, the Sublime Porte in a fit of misguided zeal imported sixty thousand Circassian settlers from Asia Minor into Bulgaria. These Circassians, the Bashi-Bazouks or guerilla troops of the Turkish army, ordered to quell a disturbance occasioned by the rise of Bulgarian

THE WAR CALLED HOLY

nationalistic aspirations, proceeded to massacre every Bulgarian they could lay their hands on. The Turkish Government proved powerless, or disinclined, to stop them. Influenced, perhaps, by the Circassian ladies of the harem, the most beautiful women of the Ottoman Empire, the viziers and pashas at Constantinople turned a blind eye to what was going on.

When no satisfaction could be obtained by the statesmen of Europe from the young Sultan, Abdul Hamid, the Russians seized their opportunity, well knowing that, after MacGahan's disclosures, no hand would be raised in defence of Turkey. Declaring Turkey to be the 'sick man of Europe', the Czar set out to become his heir. To his demands for the independence of the Balkan provinces, Abdul Hamid, relying on the divisions amongst the Powers, and on the belief that Britain would never allow the Russians to take Constantinople, remained obdurate.

In April, the Czar declared a Holy War and for the tenth time the Russians set out for Constantinople.

.   .   .   .   .

Across the smiling fields a long wave of dust slowly advances, rising and darkening the summer sky: faintly comes the boom of thunder, followed by a curious rushing sound, ending in a flash of fire. A lone pine tree, its branches shattered, reverberates like a giant tuning-fork as the earth trembles. The ancient streets of a dozen little towns echo with the clatter of hoofs, the clang of gun-limbers and the tread of marching feet. As night falls a thousand watch-fires twinkle across the plain, marking the line of march. Nearer still, the sky is lit by the burning villages of the fleeing population, choking the roads with their bullock wagons piled with their household goods, their flocks of sheep and their droves of cattle, as they toil painfully along in the vain hope of escaping from the doom of war.

On the highway of death the first shots of the Holy War have been exchanged as Christianity and Islam meet in their last great struggle. As Cross and Crescent battle to the death in the mountains and valleys of the Balkans, vibrating telegraph wires will make millions in every city of the civilized world ringside spectators as the corps of international war correspondents gallop to the sound of the guns. Never before has a war been so fully described: never would it be again, for after 1877 the heavy hand of the censor clamped down on the vivid eye-witness stories of the men who brought news of war to the suburban breakfast-table and to the enemy intelligence system.

With the Russian army rode Archibald Forbes, the veteran war correspondent who had beaten all his rivals with his scoops in the Franco-Prussian War, and his inseparable companion, Frederick Villiers, the war-artist of the *Weekly Graphic*. With Forbes for the London *Daily News* and *New York Herald* were J. A. MacGahan, world famous for his ride to Khiva and for his atrocity disclosures, and Frank Millet who was to become famous as an artist. Between them, Forbes and MacGahan were to make the name of Plevna ring round the world. More than seventy newspaper correspondents followed the Russian armies, and a number attached themselves to the Turks. On the Russian side, censorship was not strict, the correspondents being asked only to give an undertaking that they would not report information likely to be useful to the enemy. The Turks, on the other hand, would not allow criticism, and only the pro-Turkish newspapers, the *Daily Telegraph*, the *Standard* and the *Pall Mall Gazette* got their men to the front.

CHAPTER TWO

THE PEN AND THE SWORD

"I BECAME a war correspondent," says Archibald Forbes, "from listening to a lecture on the Crimean War delivered by William Howard Russell (the famous correspondent of *The Times*, the 'father' of war correspondents) in 1857." Russell's description of the charge of the Light Brigade at Balaclava ("They swept proudly past, glittering in the morning sun in all the pride and splendour of war") fired young Forbes to become a soldier, and a propensity for scribbling turned him into a war correspondent. On the strength of some barrack room sketches, Forbes went to France in 1870 to send back reports of the war with Prussia for the *Morning Advertiser,* but, with the débâcle of Sedan, the paper found no further need of his services. Out of a job and with only a few guineas in his pocket, Forbes stood disconsolate in Fleet Street. He was determined to return to the war where the Germans were besieging Paris, but with which popular paper should he try his fortune? The *Daily News,* the *Telegraph* or the *Standard*? The *Daily News* had once paid him ninepence for a paragraph nine inches long, but that hardly constituted a claim for favour. Forbes decided to toss a coin to decide which paper should have the offer of his services. The *Daily News* won and to Bouverie Street Forbes turned his feet. To Mr. Robinson, the manager, went a note: "Left German lines before Paris three days ago, possessed of exclusive information." "Would Mr. Forbes write an article?" Mr. Robinson asked.

Hurrying back to his lodgings, Forbes wrote like a whirlwind, the faster he wrote, the better. "As I wrote," he says, "the picture breadthened on the canvas. I caught the details with alert colour: I had that flow and sense of power that come to a man with the consciousness that he is doing good work." In three hours he was back in Bouverie Street. "We'll take as much of this kind of stuff as you care to write," the assistant editor told him. Next day Forbes was at the office with more. He was taken up to Mr. Robinson. "You've come for your cheque, I suppose," said he, as it seemed to Forbes, rather shortly. Forbes explained that he had been asked to submit further contributions. "I don't think we will trouble you," replied Mr. Robinson.

ARCHIBALD FORBES
Daily News, with the Russians

Forbes lost his temper, used strong language and was away up the street before the manager could stop him. "Don't be a fool," Robinson shouted in pursuit, "I want you to start for Metz tonight."

The rapidity with which Forbes got his news and stories home from France amazed his rivals. His success lay in his power of organization. He learned that every night a train ran from the German lines round Paris to Saarbruck, a journey of fifteen hours. After gathering news all day he sent his despatch to the telegraph office manager at Saarbruck with whom he had deposited a substantial sum of money. From there it was wired to London. His most notable scoop was the story of the bombardment of St. Denis.

THE PEN AND THE SWORD

Some days before Forbes secured from the Crown Prince
of Saxony a description of the operations that would take
place. This he sent to the *Daily News* where it was set up
in type. The moment the bombardment commenced, Forbes
wired to London, "Go ahead", and the presses started
turning. On another occasion, or so the story goes, learning
that *The Times* had chartered a special train to carry the
news of the German entry into Paris, Forbes disguised
himself as a fireman and went along too.

Seven years have now gone by and Forbes is dining
with MacGahan at Broffts Hotel in Bucharest. The Russians
have not yet crossed the Danube and he found himself
fascinated by his new colleague in the service of the *Daily
News*. Although both newspaper men had covered the
Franco-Prussian war, the Paris Commune and the Spanish
Civil War, they had never met. MacGahan died too soon
to record his opinion of Forbes, but Forbes lived to write
of MacGahan, the man he learned to respect as a colleague
and love as a comrade.

MacGahan, says Forbes, was the hero of that most
remarkable and daring exploit in all the annals of war
correspondence, his ride through the great desert of Central
Asia in pursuit of the column with which General Kaufmann
was marching against Khiva. In this tremendous venture,
MacGahan, to use his own phrase, 'took his chances', with
singular recklessness, and those chances included, not alone
death in half a dozen shapes, but the risk of punishment
by the Russians for his daring violation of the sweeping ban
against war correspondents. For four long weeks of constant
travel, MacGahan and his friend Eugene Schuyler, journeyed
across the frozen steppes of Russia and the broad snowy
plains of Turkestan, enduring a cold ranging from twenty
degrees to thirty degrees below zero. Kayala he reached to
find that the Russian column was long gone, and to catch
it up 300 miles of hostile desert had to be travelled. Evading
the vigilance of the Russians, MacGahan pressed on alone
into the wilderness of the Kyril Khum desert. Seventeen
days' ride through the land of the fierce Kirghis tribesmen
brought him to Khala Alta, to learn that Kaufmann was still

far ahead. Again dodging the Russian officials MacGahan 'plunged into the darkness', as he later wrote in his book *Campaigning on the Oxus,* with the Oxus for his goal and the knowledge that he would have to run the gauntlet of the hostile Turkomans.

The Cossacks sent from Tashkend to intercept him and bring him back, failed to catch him and they dared not follow where he had gone. After many days of hard riding sustained only with black bread and scant water, the glittering Oxus lay at his feet, its valley echoing to the roar of Kaufmann's guns. "As I sat on horseback watching the contest," MacGahan wrote, "there was a sense of difficulties overcome and dangers past, which, with the exciting scene before me, was well calculated to put a war correspondent in good humour." General Kaufmann accepted MacGahan cordially and hailed him as *molodyetz,* 'brave fellow', for his reckless performance. The Czar sent him the Order of St. Stanislaus, and to every Russian officer and soldier he became a comrade. "Do you know MacGahan?" Forbes was often asked in the war to come. "Ah, indeed he is *molodyetz,*" and Forbes found that in Bulgaria it was next best to being MacGahan himself to be MacGahan's friend.

When travelling with MacGahan in Bulgaria, Forbes found it touching to see how the people thronged about him, fondly treating him as their liberator and kissing his hands with devotion, and many of the principal Bulgarians were agitating that MacGahan should be offered the chiefhood of the future Bulgarian national state. Although MacGahan was by then in his grave, such a preposterous idea was firmly quashed by a special clause in the Treaty of Berlin, which laid down that the chosen ruler should belong to a princely family.

With his prestige as the man who had told the world of the Turkish atrocities in Bulgaria, which proved so convenient to the Russians, MacGahan was made welcome in St. Petersburg where he went to report on the preparations for the war which the Russians declared in April 1877. The stiff reserves of Russian bureaucracy dissolved before him. "How much better the American newspaper correspondent gets on with continental functionaries, both civil and military, than do the British," Forbes remarks. The habitual attitude of the British official, says Forbes, makes it impossible for the non-official person to have any accord with him. The official occupies an entrenched position, and, for the non-official to achieve anything, the advantage must be won at the point of the bayonet. When the British newspaper correspondent comes into contact with foreign officialdom, he cannot easily forget his insular experiences. He goes into a foreign bureau with the same sensation he was wont to have on the Whitehall threshold, of being about to struggle with the beasts of Ephesus, expecting to be slighted and treated with discourtesy.

But the happy child of the West, Forbes finds, suffers from no such inhibitions, and he arrives in Europe expecting to find officials, not enemies, but friends: never had he seen such a fellow for making himself at home with officials as MacGahan. When some difficulty was raised about MacGahan's authorization as a war correspondent, he said in his quiet and imperturbable way, "Oh, well, then, I shall claim to be an ambassador of the English Opposition." In Bulgaria, Forbes found, MacGahan could do anything he liked with the Russian generals and officials, patronizing some and "nodding affably to the Grand Duke Nicholas".

When he learned that he and MacGahan were to be colleagues, Forbes wondered how they would get on. The most whole-hearted co-operation was needed for the production of an adequate record of the great campaign. Nothing tries the temper like war correspondence, Forbes knew, nor was any pursuit so prone to engender jealousy and ill-feeling. War correspondents are essentially rivals, and their rivalry is, equally essentially, of the keenest and quickest kind. They are torn constantly between their comradeship and their duty to their paper. It is not in the nature of things, Forbes knew, for the energetic ones to be beloved by those over whom they score, and friction may result. How would he and MacGahan get on? he asked himself. In a conflict of opinion he had been given the right to decide, but Forbes did not disclose this to MacGahan. "We never

had a moment's friction," Forbes says. "Often we differed.
Then we argued the points out, and the one whom the other
convinced loyally gave in. From the first there was a strong,
close affinity, between MacGahan and myself, as ever, I
believe subsisted between two men, and I do not believe
that any two men loved each other more than MacGahan
did me and I did MacGahan."

MacGahan and Forbes met for the first time at the
railway station at Jassy in Moldavia, on their way to the
headquarters of the Russian army. Forbes was in difficulty
with the Moldavian porters, "When a shortish, thick-set
man, with calm, clear eyes, short dense brown beard, and
singularly small hands and feet, came up to me with a limp,
and asked in a singularly pleasant voice whether I was not
an Englishman, and whether my name was not Forbes."
Forbes replied that it was and the other introduced himself
as MacGahan. "We confronted each other for a short space
in silence," says Forbes, "looked each other deliberately
over, gazed steadfastly into each other's eyes, and then, as
if by simultaneous impulse, clasped hands. The grip was a
symbol of a friendship that was never to falter."

MacGahan, Forbes learned, had broken a bone in his
ankle when his horse had fallen on him. After such a mishap
at the start of a campaign, Forbes would have fretted himself
to death but MacGahan, Forbes says, did not know how to
fret. "His nature was of the sunniest serenity. I never saw
him ruffled, although once I heard him threaten to shoot a
man. He announced his intention in a bland drawl: he pulled
out his revolver with a sweet smile; and when the hulking
ruffian backed down, he resumed the thread of the inter-
rupted conversation with a calm deliberation in which there
was not so much as the quiver of the voice."

Although provided with a waggon and a team of horses,
and a driver, loaded with supplies, MacGahan preferred to
ride alone, with a clean shirt in his saddle-bag and the
knowledge that he was welcome always at the stewpot of the
Russian soldiers in their bivouac or with the general in his
tent. His wretched coachman, Forbes says, was a standing
joke amongst the correspondents, a forlorn wandering Jew,

ever in vain searching after his meteoric master. At all sorts
of unlikely places Isaac would turn up with the melancholy
question, "Have you seen my master?" followed by a request
for a little money to keep himself and his horses alive. Yet,
despite his lack of wardrobe, MacGahan always looked clean.
Other men, says Forbes, scorched by the sun, and caked with

MR. SUTER
Daily Telegraph, with the Turks

layers of Bulgarian dust, looked disreputably dingy and
travel-soiled, but MacGahan seemed exempt from the sun
blisters that gave most people the aspect of suffering from
smallpox, and it seemed as if the dust would not clot on him.
Forbes often saw him standing amongst the privates supping
soup out of the company kettle with a huge wooden spoon
one of the men had lent him, and when nothing to eat came
his way, he went without with a light heart. On one occasion
before Plevna, MacGahan, Frank Millet and Prince Shakofsky were eating together under the shade of a tree within
range of the Turkish fire. There was about enough food for
one and all were hungry. A shell burst among the branches
of the tree, and Millet and the general left off eating. Then
came a spattering of bullets that brought the leaves down
about their ears. Millet and Shakofsky hurriedly jumped up

and sought a safer spot; MacGahan sat still and serenely
finished his victuals.

MacGahan's theme at the dinner at Broffts Hotel with
Forbes was a certain heroic young Russian general named
Skobeleff, an old Khivan comrade of his, of whom Forbes
had barely heard. MacGahan predicted in his confident,
emphatic fashion, that as he had been the hero of the Khivan
campaign, so Skobeleff would prove himself the hero of the
far more stupendous struggle that lay ahead across the
Danube. Skobeleff was only a colonel and barely thirty
years old when MacGahan first met him in Central Asia.
Kaufmann had reached the city of Khiva and was training
his cannon on the ramparts and preparing to assault the
walls, when, suddenly on the fortress above the gate Kaufmann was threatening there stood displayed against the
skyline the tall figure of Skobeleff. With a handful of Cossacks
he had quietly ridden round to the rear gate of Khiva,
carried it after a flicker of resistance, taken the town by
surprise, and was now beckoning to Kaufmann to limber up
his batteries and countermand the detachments told off for
the assault of the place that had already been won.

On another occasion, of five Russian columns which had
set out on the desert march from different points with the
common objective of reaching Khiva, only four had made
good their destination. Markosoff's column had not yet
arrived when the time approached for Kaufmann to evacuate
Khiva. It could not be left to its fate and it was necessary
to ascertain whether, thwarted by bad conditions, it had
turned back, or, whether it was struggling on through the
hordes of Turkomans who infested the region through which
lay its line of route. For this hazardous enterprise Skobeleff
volunteered. With three friendly Turkomans, himself disguised as a Turkoman, Skobeleff rode away in to the desert
on his perilous task. After ten days, he was given up for
lost, and Kaufmann, unable to tarry longer, reluctantly made
preparations for departure. The day before Kaufmann's
evacuation, Skobeleff returned, alone, on foot, and half
dead. He had lost his companions and his horse; he had
run the gauntlet of the marauding Turkomans time after

time, but he had accomplished his mission. He had struck the point at which Markosoff had for want of water been forced to turn back, and he had solved the mystery of his non-appearance.

At the end of the Khivan campaign, 'General' Skobeleff as he had been promoted, was made Governor of the Khanate of Khokana which he had conquered and annexed after a three months' campaign. But his quick promotion drew upon Skobeleff the jealousy of rivals who called him the Victor of 'Asiatic Dressing-Gown Makers', and the hatred of the contractors whose recognized evil practices he would not tolerate. He was charged with ruthless cruelties and of having stolen millions of roubles. He was disgraced and superseded. Skobeleff, with witnesses and vouchers to disprove the charges against him, hurried to St. Petersburg, and he tarried there until the official auditors had gone through his accounts and had cleared him of the accusation of peculation. Skobeleff with the proofs of his honesty in his hand, hurried after the Czar who had already left for Rumania at the start of the Russian-Turkish war, but the Czar's mind had been poisoned against him and Skobeleff was refused a command. He was, however, allowed to act as chief of staff to his father, also a general, to whom had been assigned the Command of a Division of Cossack cavalry, with a sort of tacit understanding that he should be at liberty to risk his life in any hazardous adventure he might choose.

As they gossiped over a flagon of Pilsener, Forbes chanced to notice two men enter the garden restaurant in which they sat. The two men were arm in arm. One was dressed in the ugly plain blue uniform of a private of dragoons, a small, slight, swarthy man, whose face was not unfamiliar to Forbes. His companion, tall, stately, and blond, was dressed in spotless white, and wore the insignia of a general. Forbes called MacGahan's attention to this curious spectacle. MacGahan sprang to his feet, with the exclamation, "Why, it's the very man—it is Skobeleff himself", and he ran to greet his friend. As Forbes watched Skobeleff standing on the garden path, the cynosure of every gaze, his fine face glowing with pleasure as he returned the greeting of his old friend, he thought that he had never looked on a finer man. Six feet tall, straight as a pine, the head carried high with gallant debonair fearlessness, square across the broad shoulders, deep in the chest, slender of waist, clean of flank, the muscular, graceful, supple figure set off to perfection by the white frock-coat with the decorations and the gold lace on it, Skobeleff, with his frank high bearing, looked a genial king of men.

Skobeleff and his companion, Prince Tserteleff, joined Forbes and MacGahan at their table. The Prince, Forbes recalled, had been attaché to the Russian Embassy at the Court of St. James; his sister was the morganatic wife of the Czar. Throwing up his appointment he had volunteered for the army and he was soon to distinguish himself in the Shipka Pass where, disguised as a Bulgarian, he led General Gourko's advance through the Balkans. The excitement of the war overturned his mind and not long after it he died in a private madhouse.

As he talked to Skobeleff, Forbes looked into his face. Except for MacGahan, Forbes says, he never knew a man so winning. It was impossible to know Skobeleff, to have him smile on you with that sweet grave smile of his, and not to love him. Writing years later, he could see before him the broad, lofty forehead shaded with chestnut curls, the clear, frank, manly blue eyes that met his so staunchly; the long, straight, decisive nose, the kind of nose Napoleon said he looked for amongst his officers when he wanted to find a general; the beautiful mouth with its wonderful mobility of expression; the well turned compact chin, with the deep dimple in its centre. Spellbound by Skobeleff's talk, Forbes could not fancy that the man who sat talking, in the purest idiomatic English, of common English friends was a foreigner. To Forbes he looked an English country gentleman, such as Miss Braddon depicted in *Lady Audley's Husband*. This young man, he was barely thirty-five, Forbes found, had been every-where, seen everything, done everything and read everything. He was familiar with Forbes' professional career; he had carried a flying reconnaissance from Khokand over the Pamir Steppe, right into the flanks of the Hindoo Kush:

he quoted Balzac, Herbert Spencer, Hamley's *Operations of War*, and the *School for Scandal;* he had no belief in the first favourite for the approaching Derby; he thought Madame Chaumont very *chic*, and considered the British household cavalry rather under-horsed; he imparted the information that the upper fords of the Oxus were dangerous because of quicksands; and gave it as his opinion after deliberate consideration that you could get as good a *supreme de volaille* at the Café Royal in Regent Street as either at Bignons or the Café Anglais. In the music room after dinner, Skobeleff, to his own piano accompaniment, sang songs in French, German, Russian, Kirghis, Italian, English and wound up with 'Auld Lang Syne' in unimpeachable vernacular, according to Forbes, himself a Scotsman. But with all this, Forbes observes, he had not yet seen Skobeleff's most striking attribute. He had yet to see him fight but that experience was soon afforded him.

Born in 1843, the son of a general, Skobeleff won his rank by his own sword and he delighted in telling his soldiers that his grandfather had been a sergeant and his great-grandfather a peasant. "Are you going to be a general?" he would ask some young private. "Never, Excellency," would be the reply. "What never?" Skobeleff would retort, "That's a bad sign. My old grandfather was a peasant like you, yet I am a general and so may you be, if you are brave." One correspondent, Sir Edwin Pears, declares that Skobeleff told him he was descended from a Scotsman who had emigrated to Russia. But whether he was of pure Russian or half Scottish descent, the English newspaper correspondents, who watched his heroic gallantry in the assaults on Plevna, accorded Skobeleff the highest compliment that it is possible for an Englishman to bestow, when he has exhausted all his praise, on a foreigner. "He might be taken for an Englishman," they said.

Skobeleff was always in the forefront of the battle, leading the charge, dressed in a white uniform and mounted on a white charger. He dressed conspicuously, not to show off, but to show his men that he was with them, and he went into battle always with colours flying and bands playing to give a bloody assault the air of an afternoon parade. He dressed in his best uniform and put on fresh underclothing for, he said, "we must all be prepared for death, and go to meet it as we are when going to take Holy Communion." But Skobeleff was far more than a merely courageous man. "This first essential to a general, or to any officer," he declared, "is the habit of being accustomed to danger and the responsibility of command under fire," an essential to which most of the other Russian generals at Plevna showed themselves singularly unaccustomed. "It is not enough for a soldier to be brave," Skobeleff said, "he must be intelligent too." He had made a study of all recent campaigns and he devised his own tactics to defeat the impregnability of earthworks and magazine rifles.

To his men, Skobeleff was both a leader and a friend. "Come," he would say—not "Go," and he always explained the situation to them and told them what they had to do. He demanded unhesitating, unflinching, unquestionable obedience, but his men knew that he would not ask them to do anything he could not or would not do himself. He punished his men for the slightest depredation on the local inhabitants, but he saw to it that they were the best fed and clothed soldiers in the army. All his salary went to provide comforts for his men and no hard luck story could fail to move him. Finding a young soldier in tears, Skobeleff learned that he had heard from home that the cow had died and the family were without support. He gave the boy fifty roubles to telegraph home. At the end of the campaign he spent 15,000 roubles of his own money chartering a steamer to take the wounded and sick back to Russia. When his friends expressed their admiration, he replied, "I owe everything in the world to these men, and the least I can do is to spend a few thousand roubles to help them." "Thank you, brothers," he would say to his men after a battle, "it is you who have done all this! The orders I wear are yours by right, they have been given me for your brave deeds."

CHAPTER THREE

THE LOCK OF THE DOOR

On 22 June, in face of feeble Turkish resistance, the Russian Army, 100,000 strong, commanded by the Czar's brother, the Grand Duke Nicholas, and watched by the Czar himself as an august spectator, crossed the Danube from Rumania into Bulgaria at Sistova. For days Forbes and MacGahan had been trying to learn the place and date of the crossing. On the night of 21 June they came across Skobeleff, but not even to MacGahan would he pass the slightest hint. "Haven't the slightest idea," he replied as he bolted from his embarrassing questioners to assist a lady out of her *calèche*. Thirty hours later, hiding amongst the willows on the river bank, Forbes discerned in the gloom of the night, a familiar figure in a white coat jump into the leading pontoon, and he heard a voice he knew well call his 'brothers' to get aboard, as Skobeleff led the Danube crossing as a volunteer under General Dragomiroff. Skobeleff was the first man to spring ashore on the Bulgarian bank, and from the northern bank Forbes watched him lead the attack on the opposing Turks. Skobeleff had shown the way to all and sundry including the Czar and he very naturally expected that his behaviour would have wiped out even the most inveterate disfavour.

After the Russian Army had established itself across the Danube, those that had led the way were paraded for the Czar's inspection. In front of the long impressive line stood Generals Dragomiroff, Yolchine and Skobeleff. Dragomiroff, the Czar embraced in true Russian fashion and decorated with the Cross of St. George; with cheery little Yolchine he shook hands and he also received the St. George. Then the Czar came to Skobeleff. For a moment the two, tall, proud, soldierly men confronted each other. On the Czar's face, Forbes could trace the struggle between prejudice and

appreciation. It was over in a moment, the wrong way for
Skobeleff. The Czar frowned, turned short on his heel, and
strode resolutely away, without a word or gesture. It was a
flagrant insult, a gross injustice in face of the whole army.
Skobeleff bowed, flushed scarlet, then turned pale and set
his teeth. But Forbes never heard him allude to the slur,
and within two months he heard the Czar, at his own dinner
table in the Imperial marquee at Gorni Studen, beg his
guests to pledge him in the toast of "Skobeleff, the hero of
Lovtcha".

With the passage of the Danube, the first Turkish line
of defence had been breached. Between Constantinople and
the Bosporus, and the Russians, lay 250,000 Turks and the
mountain barrier of the Balkans. Another Russian army
under the command of the Grand Duke Michael had already
invaded Turkey from the Caucasus. With the reserves left
behind in Rumania, the Russian army of Bulgaria consisted
of 180 battalions of infantry, 200 squadrons of cavalry and
800 guns, in all about 180,000 men.

The Turkish armies opposing them were distributed thus:

In the Western Provinces (Bosnia to Thessaly and in Montenegro)	85,000
On the Upper Danube (on the west at Widdin)	60,000
In the quadrilateral of fortresses to the east (Rustchuk, Silistria, Varna and Shumla)	50,000
Minor detachments along the Danube	15,000
South of the Balkans (at Sophia, Philippopolis, Adrianople and Constantinople)	40,000

Two hundred and fifty thousand men,
comprising 360 battalions, 85 squadrons and
450 guns. Of these, 165,000 were immediately
available for operations in Bulgaria.

The Russian plan of campaign was delightfully simple,
a *blitzkrieg* sixty-three years before Corporal Hitler thought

of it. Two armies, the 'Eastern' army of the Czarewitch and the 'Western' army of General Krudener, would mask or neutralize the Turkish armies of the Quadrilateral and of Widdin. While the Russian right and left flanks were thus protected by walls of steel, General Gourko would thrust southward, through the corridor thus made, over the Balkans, defeat Suleiman Pasha's army of the south and march triumphantly to Constantinople. The plan was based on the expected inertia of the Turks, and it was capable of success had the Russians double the number of men. As it was, there were insufficient troops to conduct all three operations simultaneously, and the plan suffered from the serious military defect of being designed to overcome geography rather than to achieve the annihilation of the enemy's armies in the field. It was brought to a headlong stop at Plevna.

Compared with the army that had been defeated in the Crimea twenty-three years before, the Russian army of Bulgaria was a modernized fighting force but, nonetheless, it suffered from the ineptitude that characterized all things Russian prior to 1917. It was a strange mixture of barbaric splendour and modern inefficiency. Forbes speaks of its champagne-loving under-officers and MacGahan of its card-playing old generals, who knew war only as a somewhat gentlemanly affair of infantry drawn up in squares and muzzle-loading muskets, but of the Russian common soldier both have the highest praise. Stolid, passive, devoted, responsive to good leading, but singularly lacking in initiative he was a ruthless fighting man, gallant and heroic in action, capable of almost unlimited physical endurance. "Small-eyed, pug-nosed, stalwart, hardy, well built, hard as nails, brown as a berrie, of vast energy and gaiety, but strong of odour," Forbes calls the Russian fighting man. He and the other correspondents speak frequently of the gallantry and kindness of the Russian soldier to those in distress: on the march to battle they would give all their precious food and their few pennies to some starving Bulgarian or Turkish family, to friends and foes alike. Forbes' view of the officer class is recorded later.

All male Russians, out of a total population of 90,000,000, were liable to military service, and each year 150,000 young men were conscripted for six years with the colours, nine years with the reserve and five in the militia. Over the Turks, the Russians had a vast superiority in manpower, for only Moslems, of whom there were 16,000,000 in the Empire, were liable to military service. The Christians paid a head tax and remained at home to benefit in trade, commerce and agriculture from their neighbours' absence and perhaps death.

The Russian army was cursed with the system of 'influence' by which promotion to commissioned rank depended on 'protection' rather than efficiency. It was possible, but unusual, for a man to rise by his own efforts. Forbes records meeting a lieutenant aged seventy-three, and the majority of the generals were decrepit dug-outs who could only be dismissed with a loss of face which the Czar would not countenance in respect to his old retainers. Field and regimental officers, if they lacked nothing in bravery, were singularly deficient in military knowledge and skill but, of all the burdens the army of Bulgaria had to bear, the greatest was its commander, the Grand Duke Nicholas, who, fearful of committing himself to any definite action, dissipated his forces by trying to cover every possible eventuality. The Russian high command underrated and despised its enemy and gave the Turks no credit for initiative, for which, except in the case of Osman Pasha, they apparently had some excuse. After the reverses at Plevna, the Russian generals complained bitterly that no one had told them that the Turks could fight so well.

No army suffered more than the Turkish from muddle and corruption in high places, and from sloth and procrastination amongst its generals who were afraid to back each other up lest the hated rival, by his victory, should gain the coveted Grand Vizierate. Physical activity was looked upon by the pashas as against the Moslem tradition and the other generals disapproved of Osman's energetic dash to Plevna. The magnitude and barefacedness of corruption in Turkey is illustrated by the story of the Minister of Marine who was indignantly accused by the Sultan of pocketing £200,000 on a contract. He replied, just as indignantly, that the sum was £300,000. The Turkish soldier proved himself as good, or better, a fighting man as the Russian although he had none of the creature comforts of his enemy. Their pay was never less than a year in arrears, and they were ill provided with clothes and food, and in the care of the wounded. But the Moslem soldier was actuated with a burning zeal to kill the hated infidel for death in battle was a passport to paradise. Put a Turkish soldier in a ditch with a bag of biscuit, a jug of water, a magazine rifle and a quantity of ammunition and he was invincible. Properly led, he was as brave in attack as the Russian.

The great difference in the two armies lay in their armament. The Turks were equipped with Krupp steel breech-loading guns of eight and nine centimetres calibre which in quality of metal, range, accuracy and lightness were far superior to the bronze pieces of the Russians. In small-arms the majority of the Turks were armed with the Peabody-Martini rifle, calibre ·45, initial velocity 1,349 feet per second, made by the Providence Tool Company of Rhode Island, U.S.A. Five hundred thousand of these breech-loading rifles had been bought and paid for. The Russians were equipped with both the old Krenck rifle, a breech-loader of ·60 inch calibre, initial velocity 1,082 feet per second, and the better Berdan of ·42 inch calibre and 1,450 feet per second velocity. The magazines of both had a habit of jamming and we hear of General Skobeleff sitting down in a trench, taking a rifle apart and putting it together again, a capability which demonstrates his attention to detail, and after the fall of Plevna, much to the displeasure of the High Command who considered his action derogatory to Russian dignity, he equipped his men with the captured Peabody-Martini rifles of the Turk.

In dress, both armies marched to war in clothes designed for comfort rather than elegance. The Russian soldier wore blue trousers tucked into heavy top boots, a white blouse, a blue tunic and was provided with a thick overcoat of duffel blanketing and a cap which fitted over the ears. His greatest lack was entrenching tools with which each company of infantry was very poorly supplied. The Turkish soldier wore a foot high turban, a silk shirt beneath a short, embroidered jacket, short breeches, cloth leggings, leather shoes, with an immense sash round his waist, stuffed with weapons.

Both armies relied on, and were ill served, by irregular cavalry. Both the Russian Cossacks (the Caucasian Cossacks and the Don Cossacks) and the Circassians of the Turks (the 'Bashi-Bazouks,' as they were called, a term meaning 'irregular soldiers', men who were farmers one day and fighting men the next) committed excesses which neither army seemed capable of preventing. Plunderers and brigands, the Cossacks and the Bashi-Bazouks were ruthless fighting men, lacking in discipline, and they were employed chiefly as scouts and as dispatch riders. Both sides accused the other of appalling atrocities, the slaughter of the wounded and the massacre of Bulgarian and Turkish civilians who fell in the path of the armies. Undoubtedly such atrocities occurred, and they were committed almost entirely by irregular troops which on both sides were Asiatics. Neither the Turkish nor the Russian regular soldier killed needlessly, and by both Russians and Turks wounded prisoners were often treated with consideration equal to that accorded their own men.

The Cossacks and the Bashi-Bazouks not only behaved alike: they looked alike and the similarity of their dress often led to confusion. The Turkish irregular horseman, the Circassian, wore a long coat, with a row of cartridges across the breast, a fur cap, a belt full of daggers and pistols, and as well as his Winchester rifle, he often carried the old family matchlock, an heirloom embellished with silver. There were two types of Cossacks, the Christian Cossacks of the Don and the Moslem Cossacks of the Caucasus. Both wore enormous overcoats and boots to the knee and were armed to the teeth, "more than any man of his size in Europe", Forbes declared. Cossacks and Circassians were small wiry men, mounted on tough little ponies, one looking exactly like the other, so that Forbes wondered if they had not all been made to order from one mould, with, in case of accidents, interchangeable heads, arms and legs.

Many Englishmen, and hosts of European soldiers of fortune, fought with the Turkish armies, and the Turkish medical corps was largely staffed by European doctors.

Colonel Valentine Baker, the guardsman who had been cashiered and sent to prison for kissing a girl in a suburban railway carriage, became a Turkish pasha, and another, Hobart Pasha, became an admiral in the navy. In Plevna we shall find Dr. Charles Ryan, a young Australian, and Lieutenant William Herbert, a German of British descent.

Whether or not the Turks had a 'plan' by which to resist the Russian advance, cannot be decided: at the start of the campaign they stood on the defensive on three sides of a square, east, south and west of the Danube but, having overcome their initial surprise at the Russian crossing, which had been apparent for months, the armies of Mehemet Ali in the Quadrilateral on the Russian left flank and of Suleiman south of the Balkans made some attempt to act on the offensive. The battles in the Quadrilateral, though they tied up considerable man-power, had little effect on the siege of Plevna. Suleiman's offensive in the Shipka Pass in August is referred to in due course.

With the Russian army established south of the Danube, General Krudener, with the IX Army Corps, was sent to occupy the line of the Vid with the object of neutralizing Osman Pasha's army at Widdin. His first objective was the town of Nikopoli, twenty miles north of Plevna, to which he laid siege, its easy capture on 16 July inspiring the Russians with a fatal contempt for Turkish fortifications. Krudener's second objective was the little town of Plevna, an important road junction on the river Vid. But Krudener delayed too long at Nikopoli. By the 20 July when his advance guard reached Plevna, it was already occupied by the Turks.

Meanwhile General Gourko had set out with a small mobile force to capture the passes through the Balkans, by which the main army could follow on its triumphant march to Constantinople. By a brilliant coup, one of the romances of warfare as Forbes was to call it, General Gourko burst open the lock of the door which protected Turkey from invasion.

With Gourko rode MacGahan, though lame with a broken ankle. Forbes, by mutual arrangement, remained at headquarters to receive MacGahan's reports as they came back by dispatch riders and to transmit them to London by telegraph, which necessitated a ride to Bucharest, the telegraph offices in Bulgaria being unable to transmit Roman letters. In the difficult defiles of the Balkans, MacGahan's horse slipped on a bank and his ankle was injured again and he was forced to complete the journey strapped to a gun-carriage.

"We are deep in a gorge of the Balkans," MacGahan wrote on 15 July, "in a dark, narrow little dell, whose sides are so steep that the dozen houses which make up the village seem to be holding on with hooks and claws, to keep from slipping down into the ravine beneath them. It is night, and a thick veil of darkness covers mountains, trees, rocks and forests. Almost perfect silence reigns, and the occasional cry of some bird, startled in its slumbers, echoes fearfully distinct and alarming. Other sounds may be heard if one listens closely; an occasional hum of voices, the impatient stamp of a horse's hoof, and the rattle of harness."

Extending for three or four miles in the dark, crooked valley, lies an army asleep on its arms, without fire or supper, waiting the first rays of daylight to resume its march. "It would be madness," MacGahan explains, "to attempt taking the artillery along this road in the darkness, and there are artillery and cavalry as well as infantry trying to make their way over this almost impassable road. We are in one of the most difficult defiles of the Balkans, at the entrance to a pass which the Turks have left unguarded, a pass which we hope to get through early in the morning, and this is the reason for our secrecy and silence, the absence of camp-fires and supper, and the usual sights and sounds of bivouac."

The glare of camp fires reflected on the sky, and seen from the other side of the mountains, might give the alarm to the Turks who have no inkling of the Russian cavalry raid, by a small force of less than ten thousand men. "Should the Turks get word of our advance, they could concentrate and cut us off in detail as we come out, as easily as you catch water coming out of a bunghole," warns MacGahan. "It is a hazardous undertaking," he declares, "but one which, if successful, will ensure the passage of the Balkans to the main army. Tomorrow we shall be over and will pour out of the mountains to the great surprise of the Turks who are watching for us in a very different place."

Led by the Russian Prince Tserteleff, disguised as a Bulgarian peasant, Gourko's advance guard reached the summit of the Shipka Pass on 19 July, MacGahan writing: "We are two hundred Cossacks drawn up on this ridge, with our horses' heads turned South, looking away over the interminable labyrinth of mountains, hills, ridges, valleys, hollows and gorges, through which we still have to bore our way to the valley of the Tundja before our passage can be assured. The first streak of day is just growing visible in the east, and a long flash of rosy light is climbing slowly up the sky. Before and beneath us is a dark narrow gorge, still a pool of blackness into which we slowly descend. We are soon down to the depths of the dark defile. The first three or four hundred feet are very steep, but at the end of that time we have come fairly into the little hollow, and the descent the rest of the way is gentle and easy, although the road is rough. The hollow is narrower even than on the other side, and the trees here are large, their branches completely uniting overhead, making it as dark as a cavern. We move on as silently as we can, for, to tell the truth, it is, for aught we know, a most perilous adventure. The Turks might choose to lay an ambush for us, to let us pass, and place a small force in the road behind us, and a hundred or even fifty infantry would quite suffice to bar the way and render retreat impossible. So we push on cautiously, watching for any indication of the presence of the enemy."

The Turks were completely taken by surprise and the passage of the Balkans, as MacGahan says, one of the most formidable bulwarks ever raised for the defence of a country, was secured for the main army with hardly a shot fired, and the loss of six men wounded. The news of the capture of the Balkan passes caused consternation in Constantinople; Hannibal was at the Gates. Abdul Kerim, the commander-in-chief of the Turkish armies in the Balkans, was dismissed, and Mehemet Ali appointed in his place, and the Sultan seriously contemplated flight to Brusa in Asia Minor.

By Disraeli the British fleet was ordered to the Dardanelles.

Confident of success, the main Russian army prepared to set out to cross the Balkans and march to the Bosporus.

CHAPTER FOUR

THE RACE FOR PLEVNA

UNKNOWN to the Russians, Osman Pasha, the Military Governor of Widdin, higher up the Danube, was advancing by forced marches at the rate of twenty miles a day, in the direction of Plevna with 12,000 men and fifty-four guns.

After the Russian crossing of the Danube, Osman had suggested to Abdul Kerim, the Turkish commander-in-chief, that he should cross the Danube and strike at the Russian rear. Kerim, anxious to keep Osman's army of 60,000 men at Widdin to overawe the Servians, who might take it into their heads to support the Russians, ordered him to remain there.

Osman then proposed that he should advance south-westwards with part of his army to make junction with Hassan Hairi, the commander at Nikopoli, who would quit the town without waiting for the enemy's attack, and he and Hassan would march to Tirnova, upon which the army of the Quadrilateral would advance westward, thus cutting across the southern advance of the Russians. The combined armies could then strike at Sistova, the Russian bridgehead across the Danube. Abdul Kerim opposed this plan also, and by the time he was overruled by the Sultan it was too late for Nikopoli was already invested. Given a free hand by the Sultan, Osman determined to move in the direction of Plevna and Lovtcha to effect a junction with Suleiman's army of the south instead.

Osman Pasha, Osman 'Ghazi', the Victorious, as he was soon to become, is the pivot of this story, yet we know little about him except that he was a general who saw his chance, took it, and, having taken it, hung on like grim death. The bulldog defender of Plevna, the name of Osman Pasha rang round the world as, week after week, he flung defiance at

the hosts of Russia. A fanatical Moslem, Osman disliked
foreigners and hated war correspondents, and except when
he admitted the correspondent of the *Daily Telegraph* at the
command of the Sultan, he refused to allow them in his
camp. As a result, and probably much to his relief, Osman
missed the pen-picture which might have turned him into
a man of flesh and blood like Skobeleff. A soldier's general,
Osman was satisfied to do his job and he was concerned
to do it well, if only for his own gratification. Born about
1837, and therefore forty years or so of age in 1877, Osman
was a veteran of the Crimean campaign, in which his defence
of Kalafet cost the Russians 20,000 lives, and he had won
two decisive victories against the Servian insurgents in 1876.
Short, but of commanding presence, dignified, taciturn,
grave and abrupt of speech, Osman was now to wreck the
whole Russian plan of campaign.

After a breakfast of hot meat and rice had been served
to the men, Osman's little army set out on its 120 mile
march to Plevna on Friday, 13 July, at sunrise, the men
being in fine fettle and eager to get to grips with the enemy
after months of inactivity. Every soldier carried eighty rounds
of ammunition and a week's ration of hard biscuits, each
the size of a soup plate, which had to be broken with a
hatchet and soaked in water before they could be eaten.
Behind the army followed a number of marauders, hoping
to plunder those who dropped from fatigue, but they were
chased away and some were killed. Marching through Vidpol
on the Danube, the column, which was ten miles long, was
shelled by the Rumanians from the opposite bank but without casualties.

In Osman's army are two foreigners, Charles Ryan, a
young Australian doctor who had joined the Turkish Medical
Corps, the 'Red Crescent', as a volunteer, and Lieutenant
William Herbert, a young German of British descent who
threw up a job in a merchants' office to join the Turkish
army.

Reaching the village of Artzar by sunset, the army
bivouacked for the night, Dr. Charles Ryan, to whom the
sights and sounds of campaigning were strange, watching,

40

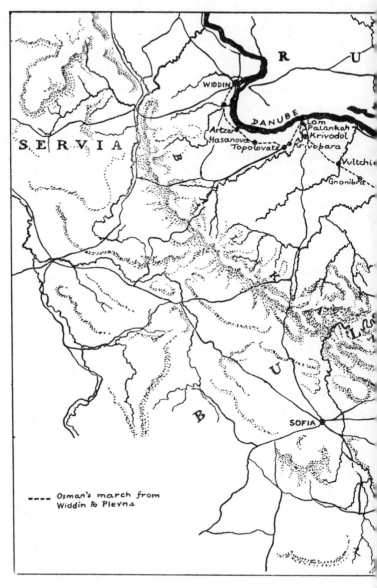

Osman's march from
Widdin to Plevna

BULGARIA.

as he tried to sleep, the lights of a thousand camp-fires dancing on the quiet waters of the river, and to his ears came through the soft night breeze the hum and laughter of 12,000 men lying around him. Gradually, one by one, the lights died down as the men, tired after their long and dusty march through the heat of a summer's day, wrapped themselves in their great-coats and sank into slumber.

On the second day the army struck away from the river along by-roads, footpaths and bridle paths, so precipitous in places that the horses and oxen were taken out of the carts and gun-carriages and they were pulled to the summit by men with drag ropes, across bare, shelterless, waterless country through which they marched in intense heat, choked by dust. During the day six men fell out suffering from sunstroke and they were left by the side of the road.

Reaching the village of Krivodol at 4 p.m. Osman found a telegraph message awaiting him from the Sultan, who implored him to push on to Plevna with the utmost dispatch, as the Russians had unexpectedly appeared south of the Balkans. The Turkish Empire was between life and death, the Sultan declared. When Osman told his troops of General Gourko's raid through the Balkan passes, they could hardly believe that the great mountain barrier had been lost without a fight.

In the little picturesque village, which lay in a sheltered valley watered by a stream, Dr. Ryan was intrigued by a number of curious mounds of earth and he was told that they were the tombs of Greek settlers in Byzantine days. Excavating one he found an old stone coffin containing bones, which he was careful to leave undisturbed, and a number of pretty Greek vases and some Byzantine coins, which he wrapped up in his saddle-bags.

On Osman's orders, the march was resumed at midnight and all through the night and all next morning, the army stumbled on, footsore and weary, forbidden to sing or even to speak lest their presence be betrayed to the Cossacks who were reported in the vicinity. "Oh, the monotonous horror of that march," Dr. Ryan was to recall many years later. Sick for want of food and faint from lack of water, the men struggled on until at noon they were permitted to lie down and "fall into a death-like slumber", according to eighteen year old Lieutenant Herbert who found the night march "interesting and romantic". Many men fell out and were left by the wayside, as were the pieces of Dr. Ryan's Greek vases which were broken when his horse stumbled into a hole.

At the village of Vultchiderma on the river Chibritza, another telegram from the Sultan was waiting Osman, urging him to make the utmost speed if he was to save Plevna and Lovtcha from the Russians. Knowing that at the best his army, encumbered with a baggage train and artillery, could not reach Plevna before the 19th Osman despatched an advance guard of three battalions to push ahead and hold off the Russians until he could come up with the main army. Allowing his men but a few hours rest, Osman started them off again at 4 a.m. on the 16th. A stage of twenty-four miles across arid country lay ahead. Hour after hour the men trudged on in silence, many dropping by the way, until Altimir on the river Skit was reached at midnight, after twenty hours of almost continuous march.

Next morning the soldiers were too exhausted to move and the start was delayed until 4 p.m. When the army reached Kenieja at midnight, the men heard that Nikopoli was being furiously attacked by the Russians and that Lovtcha had been occupied. After only six hours' rest Osman's army was on its way again, reaching and fording the river Isker at midday. As the soldiers struggled up the bank, after wading through water as high as their shoulders, Osman told them Nikopoli had fallen and that their country was in its death agonies and only they could save it. Osman knew that the Russians, now freed from the siege of Nikopoli, would push on to Plevna. It would be a race to see who got there first. At 6 p.m., 18 July, the army arrived at Gorna Netropole, ten miles west of Plevna, to learn that the Russians were approaching Plevna from the east.

That night, the order of Osman Pasha to expect to meet the enemy the next day was read out and the men lay down arrayed in battle order and slept with arms in hand.

The last stage of the fearful march was started at 5 a.m.

As Osman's army crossed the ancient stone bridge spanning the river Vid, the men could hear the sound of guns in the east. At a bend in the road the troops caught their first glimpse of Plevna, lying deep in a fertile valley, and presenting to William Herbert a striking picture with its minarets and domes, its white houses, and its patches of foliage against the background of hills. As they marched into the town, all was peaceful. There was no sight of the enemy. They had won the race. Osman's advance guard and the small force of Turks which had been in Plevna for some time, were out on the northern and eastern hills, replying to the Russian fire.

Two days previously, on the 17th, Russian pickets had reported that a large Turkish force was moving west of Plevna. The Grand Duke apparently attached little importance to this information for it was not until the 18th that he telegraphed General Krudener at Nikopoli "to occupy Plevna as promptly as you can", and even then no great sense of urgency was shown. On receiving this message, Krudener ordered General Schilder-Schuldner to move south and occupy Plevna. Although Schilder-Schuldner started at once he advanced only ten miles, or half-way to Plevna, before bivouacking for the night. As he approached Plevna soon after midday on the 19th his force of 6,500 men and forty-six guns was halted by the fire of the Turks from the heights above the village of Grivitza. Without cavalry to scout ahead, he was unaware that the town had been occupied by Osman's army from Widdin. Falling back, Schilder-Schuldner prepared to oust the Turks next day.

Plevna (Turkish) or Pleven (Bulgarian) was in 1877 a town of 17,000 inhabitants, of whom 10,000 were Bulgarians. Between the Russian crossing of the Danube and 20 July, 4,000 Bulgarians had fled and 2,000 Turks had taken refuge in the town, so that the Turks now outnumbered the Bulgarians. Alongside the main street, flowing across it in one place, ran the Tultchenitza stream, serving as the town's main drain, and the Grivitza brook skirted the town's northern margin, the two streams uniting north-west of Plevna to flow together into the Vid at Opanetz.

William Herbert thought Plevna better built than other

Turkish towns he had seen, but he found the ruined and deserted houses, the palsied hovels, and the waste spaces full of rubbish, which were a feature of the country. He speaks of filthy streets, badly paved or unpaved, and in wet weather impassable, the absence of sanitary arrangements, the heaps of offal, and the thousand-and-one stenches of urban Turkey. Dr. Ryan says that the streets were paved with cobble-stones and the main street formed the principal bazaar, while sundry evil smelling lanes ran off to right and left. Here and there he noticed a Turk civilian dressed in the long, loose caftan and the wide trousers tucked into high boots, which formed the universal dress of the Turks, while the scowling Bulgarians, who looked as though they would have cut his throat with the greatest of pleasure, wore sheepskin caps and suits of coarse yellow frieze. In the Tultchenitza brook (the main drain) the townswomen were washing their clothes. At the lower end of the town he came across a collection of dirty huts occupied by gipsies who, seeming to recognize that the arrival of the troops heralded the horrors of war, set up a prolonged howling and they wrung their hands with gestures of the deepest grief.

Herbert found many good buildings in Plevna: the Konak or official building, was he learned erected on the site and built with the materials of a Roman ruin. Many of the dwelling-houses, both Turkish and Bulgarian, were pretty and charmingly situated in well kept gardens. The town contained a civil hospital, presided over by a German doctor, two khans (inns), a clock tower, eighteen mosques, two Christian churches, a military elementary school, and eight Turkish and five Bulgarian schools. Places of amusement or of public recreation did not exist.

Plevna, when Osman reached it on 19 July was unfortified. How its natural features contributed to make it impregnable to assault is explained by the combination of ridges and valleys which radiated outwards on its north, east and south. The west of Plevna was naturally protected by a great hill, the Namasgula Bair, covered with vineyards and orchards, and by the river Vid, and no Russian assault was launched from that direction. The most northerly of these ridges, the Janik Bair, rising to 1,300 feet above sea level and 350 feet above the Plevna valley and four miles long, extended to the north-east in the direction of the village of Grivitza. Between it and the south-eastern ridge, facing the village of Radishevo, ran the valley of the Grivitza stream. The south-eastern ridge, which is shaped like a claw, was separated from a low range of hills or knolls, south-west of Plevna, by the valley of the Tultchenitza, deep, narrow and rocky. These natural ramparts afforded splendid opportunities for defence and their strength was enhanced by the valleys and deep ravines which provided protected interior lines of communication, and made the lateral communication of the attacking force difficult.

The importance of Plevna lay in its position on the intersection of the main roads from Orkhanie and Sofia, from Lovtcha and the road eastward to Bulgareni. Its possession was vital to the Turks if they wished to attempt a conjunction of the armies of Widdin and the Quadrilateral, and the loss of the Shipka Pass increased its importance inasmuch as Plevna and Lovtcha now represented the only route, bar the recapture of the Shipka, by which the army of Widdin and that of Suleiman to the south of the Balkans could link up. To the Russians its importance was two-fold. It pushed a wedge into the line of the Vid, which they wished to hold as their right flank, and its possession would enable them to advance south-westward to Sofia and onward to the Bosporus. The great significance of Plevna to the campaign lay in Osman's presence there with, as time went on, a powerful army which the Russians could not leave at large on their right flank while they advanced southward through the Balkans to Adrianople.

The following distances from Plevna need to be stated:

Lovtcha	..	20 miles (and Troyan Pass 38)
Orkhanie	..	55 miles
Sofia	..	83 miles (via Orkhanie)
Bulgareni	..	23 miles
Rustchuk	..	73 miles (the nearest point in the
Nikopoli	..	23 miles Quadrilateral)

The villages in the immediate environs of Plevna which figure in the battles and siege, were as follows:

North:	Opanetz	..	4 miles distant
	Bukova	..	2 miles „
East:	Grivitza	..	4 miles „
South-East:	Radishevo	..	3 miles „
	Poradim	..	9 miles „
South:	Brestovitz	..	5 miles „
	Krishnin	..	3 miles „

Soon after the Danube crossing on 8 July, a party of Cossacks appeared in Plevna and forced the small garrison of gendarmes to retreat. When the Cossacks left on the following day, Atouf Pasha was sent from Nikopoli with three battalions and four guns and he held the town until Osman arrived.

It is now 19 July; Atouf's men and the advance guard sent ahead by Osman are lying out on the northern ridge, the Janik Bair, holding with their fire the stumbling advance of General Schilder-Schuldner. Behind them, Osman's army is streaming into Plevna.

Shortly after his arrival, Osman and his staff rode out to the hills on the north and east to select points for his troops. Dr. Ryan, who was one of the first to reach the town, was overjoyed to discover a European doctor and he promptly called and introduced himself. Dr. Robert, he found, had come from Switzerland ten years before, but why he had chosen an obscure Balkan town in which to practice, Ryan never learned. He had a good practice amongst the Bulgarians and was evidently a fashionable physician who commanded his own price. He lived in the best house of the town and drove the finest team of cobs Ryan had ever seen, and he had a menagerie in his garden containing a collection of storks and herons, a tame animal which appeared to be a jackal and four deer which Ryan assisted Dr. Robert to eat later on. Dr. Robert who had not seen any European for ten years, was pleased to see Ryan, and his Viennese house-keeper cooked them an excellent dinner and, after they had

eaten it, Dr. Robert sat down at his piano and roared out
convivial ditties in French, German and Bulgarian until the
whole house shook. Even the housekeeper, who came in with
a threatening aspect, failed to quieten him, and as Ryan
made his way to his quarters Dr. Robert was still chanting
the praises of 'Wein, Weib, und Gesang'.

On their way into the town, William Herbert's sergeant
had spotted some deserted houses in the northern suburb and,
as his regiment had not been ordered to the hills until dawn
the next day, the door of one of these houses was battered
down and the house commandeered as his company quarters.
After seven days forced march, the feet of many of the men
were one ghastly wound; several, on removing their socks,
tore off skin and flesh. When a supper of boiled mutton and
rice had been eaten, biscuits, cold coffee and ammunition
were issued and the men were warned that they would get
no breakfast and probably no dinner next day. Fatigued by
their march some of the men flung themselves down to
sleep on the furniture and beds of the well appointed house,
and the rest slept in the hall, in the cellars, on the landing
and even on the stairs. Just as Herbert was about to fall
asleep, he was disturbed by a brother officer, "an extra-
ordinarily hardy man", who had found a set of chess-men
and insisted that Herbert should join him in a game.

At 9.30 p.m., the captain, who had been writing letters
for hours to his wives at home, Herbert imagined, for he had
noticed that polygamy did not appear to soften a man's love
for those belonging to him, came and told him, "Tomorrow,
you will be under fire for the first time; there is every prospect
of a serious engagement. I trust you will do your duty."
On his way to rest Herbert looked into the kitchen where
one man was dozing over the Koran and others were
whispering of the coming fray. At the end of the garden
the sentries paced to and fro. Outside it was a beautiful
starlit summer night. Within a few square miles, Herbert
knew, 15,000 men lay ready to slay or be slain on the morrow.
Occasionally the silence was broken by the tramp of a patrol,
the neighing of a horse, or by the change of guard. In the
distance he could hear the bark of a watchdog, which

reminded him strangely and sadly of home. He lay down and tried, vainly, to sleep but thoughts of the morrow crept through his mind like ugly phantoms. He was but eighteen years old, and the thought that twenty-four hours later, and for all eternity, his bed might be the soil, unnerved him and he had a distinct presentiment of death. At last he fell into deep slumber.

CHAPTER FIVE

CHECK TO THE RUSSIANS

HERBERT dreamt that he heard the train which passed close to his house at home; the sound increased in volume to an unwonted extent, and the engine burst into the room; a kick roused him. "Get up; the drums are beating the Alarm," shouted a voice. It was 2.40 a.m., nearly daylight. In less than a minute the men were drawn up in the street, from every side came the sound of bugles, of words of command, the tramp of feet and the clatter of horses' hoofs. Officers ran about looking immensely important and getting in everybody's way, as though they carried the entire burden of the Ottoman Empire on their shoulders. The battalion was marched off to join two others on the Janik Bair. Herbert found the three mile march exhilarating; it was a glorious summer's morning; the sun shone brightly, the breeze blew freshly and the sky was dark blue.

Reaching the ridge the men were deployed along the banks of a ravine, and they lay down, taking advantage of the cover offered by trees, shrubs and boulders. Below them the bank shelved steeply, the opposite bank rising gently to a slope covered with bushes. As they lay waiting for the enemy to appear, the sun shone through the branches and drew a fantastic pattern of light and shade on the ground, covered with daisies and buttercups. In the branches overhead, nightingales sang and the wind whispered through the leaves. From a hole in the bank, a field mouse popped out and scampered about. At 5 a.m. the report of a gun, acting like a magician's wand, transformed this perfect idyll into the barbarous glamour of war.

In less than a minute, the Turkish and Russian batteries were banging away and Herbert could see the Russian shells whizzing overhead. A Circassian scout came galloping back,

50

and the subdued command, "Ready for fire", was passed from man to man, like a persistent echo, until it became lost in the distance. "There they are," softly whispered one of the men, and in a clearing 200 yards away, Herbert saw men in dark uniforms gliding stealthily from tree to tree, and in a few seconds the ridge opposite was swarming with Russians, hundreds of them, who seemed to have grown out of the ground. Behind them on the summit of the ridge, came dense masses of infantry, moving forward swiftly and noiselessly, and to his imagination, like cruel Fate herself, with inevitable, irresistible doom. Herbert could see mounted officers waving their swords, the burnished steel of bayonets glittering in the sun, and the air was shaken by the roll of drums. His hand tightened round the butt of his revolver. On the opposite bank, 150 yards away, a villainous bearded face, crowned by an ugly cap, rose slowly above the bushes. A bugle sounded and from the Turkish line the long drawn out clatter of rifle-fire broke the slumbering echoes of the glen, and around them arose a thick white cloud. Bullets whizzed past, like bluebottles on the wing; the man next to Herbert fell on his face and never stirred; another had part of his ear shot away. At the bottom of the ravine three Russians writhed in ghastly convulsions. Down the ridge came dark masses of men in serried ranks. The Turks broke into a rapid fire, some, Herbert noticed, jabbering like idiots; others seemingly possessed of devilish fury; others silent and no more concerned than when at target-practise. On his left, a corporal swore at the 'Infidel dogs'. Herbert's company was ordered to retreat on the main body. They were not pressed as the Russians were slow in climbing the bank of the ravine, but in another minute they would have been annihilated.

The Russian attack was launched against the Turkish positions on the Janik Bair, from north and east. On the right flank at Bukova, the Russians drove the Turks back to the outskirts of Plevna, where they were halted by a hot fire from behind hedges and from ditches. On the left flank, opposite Grivitza, the Russians captured three lines of Turkish trenches after a short struggle, but the Turkish centre held and the Russian flanks were thrown back and chased to their own lines. By 5 p.m. the fighting was over, the Russians having lost 3,000 men and the Turks 2,000.

Like William Herbert, Dr. Ryan came under fire for the first time. Making his way on to the Janik Bair, Ryan could hear the Russian shells buzzing over like hornets. In a Turkish battery, he found three artillerymen lying dead. One who had been shot in the stomach presented a terrible spectacle with his entrails all hanging out. The legs of two others had been carried away by shells. A few minutes later he saw a man killed. Ryan was lying on the summit of the hill watching the Russian gun-fire, when he saw six simultaneous puffs of smoke and six flashes of fire dart from a wood on the distant slope. One of the Turkish gunners was squinting along the sights of his gun to get the elevation of the Russian battery when the six shells started on their journey. The flashes of fire were the last things the man saw for one of the shells struck him in the face, taking his head clean off. There was a spurting of blood from the vessels in the neck, and then the headless corpse spun round in a circle, the legs moving convulsively like those of a chicken when its throat is cut. Ryan turned cold all over and was horribly sick, but, a few months later the frequent repetition of such sights had so dulled the sensitiveness of his nerves that he could look upon the most shocking casualties without the least physical inconvenience.

When Ryan reported to the hospital to which he had been ordered, he found that it consisted of two large rooms in a Bulgarian school. Now it was filled with wounded men, and the laughter of the children had been replaced by groans of agony. Already the courtyard was full and, looking up the road, he saw a long string of Bulgarian arabas, each drawn by two white oxen, bringing the wounded down from the battlefield. Hundreds of others were dragging themselves along on foot. The long line of arabas, each bearing its load of suffering men, stretched as far as the eye could reach, each cart being driven by its Bulgarian owner escorted by a Turkish soldier to see that the Bulgarian did not dispatch the unhappy victims before their time. The entrance to the hospital was blocked by the jostling drivers all anxious to get rid of their loads, and by the wounded staggering in on foot. Inside, the hospital was quickly assuming the appearance of a slaughter-house, as the dead and dying were pulled from the arabas, matted together and clotted with blood.

All day Ryan and six other surgeons worked in the hospital, one of several established in the town, and all day the arabas kept arriving with fresh loads, until there was no place left in which to lay the sufferers. In all his surgical experience, Ryan declares, and he lived to become chief medical officer to the Australian forces in Europe in the First World War, he never knew men to exhibit such fortitude under intense agony as did the Turks at Plevna, nor did he meet patients who recovered from such terrible injuries in the remarkable way that these men did. The Turks, he found, were magnificent material for a surgeon to work on, men of splendid physique, unimpaired by intemperance or any excess. He never, he says, saw a private soldier under the influence of liquor, and many lives might have been saved if he could have persuaded some of the wounded to take stimulants, but it was impossible, he found, to get any of them to touch alcohol, even as a medicine. The humble Turk would rather die than violate the precepts of his religion.

Of those wounded by rifle-fire Ryan noticed that, while the Berdan bullet drilled a clean hole through a man, thus simplifying the surgical treatment, the older Krenck rifle, with which the majority of the Russians were armed, inflicted a much larger wound, and not infrequently left the bullet embedded in the body. Amongst those who were brought to him was a young Turk who had been shot through the head; the Berdan conical bullet had pierced the left side of his skull, about an inch and a half below the crown, and passed out in a straight line through the other side, leaving two holes, one at each side of the fez which the man was wearing. The bullet had bored a clean hole through the upper portion of the brain but the sufferer, though he was weak from loss of blood, was perfectly rational. Ryan syringed and dressed the wound and after six weeks the man was discharged cured.

Most of the men shot in the chest died for in most cases the surgeons could not readily locate the bullet, and they could not waste time searching for it. Several men who recovered were sent back to their regiments with an ounce of Russian lead hidden somewhere in their bodies. Occasionally, Ryan found, a bullet would take a most erratic course. In one case a bullet entered the back of a man's neck and came out at his wrist.

As Ryan moved about the hospital, followed by an attendant carrying his box of instruments, a basin of water and a supply of bandages, he heard on all sides the piteous moan, "Verbana su, hakim bashi"—"Give me a drink of water, Doctor." All cases requiring serious operations were put aside for the following day and, if a case was hopeless, and the man sure to die, the surgeons made him as comfortable as possible on the floor and left him there. All day the carts brought more wounded and Ryan never stopped whipping out bullets, cleaning and sewing up wounds and putting fractured limbs into splints. At 3 p.m. he was sent to take over a private house to which wounded had been taken, and he found about a hundred men, many of whom had been there since early morning without medical attention. Ryan worked by the light of four candles stuck on bayonets until eleven o'clock at night, when he dragged himself off to bed.

Lieutenant Herbert did not come under fire again that day, and about 1 p.m. he and his company were sent back to their old position on the ravine, now littered with thirty Russian corpses. The Turks were too exhausted by their long march to pursue the fleeing Russians, and towards evening the army was marched back to Plevna, Herbert finding the ground strewn with Russian corpses, many in the most grotesque postures. One had his fists doubled up in front of him, like a boxer ready to spar; another was sucking his fingers; another was spread out in the shape of a cross. They passed, too, many cartloads of dead, the poor fellows, Herbert noticed, piled one on top of the other like so much human rubbish, friend and foe sleeping in peaceful embrace.

Back in their quarters, the men after a meal and a few hours rest sat talking and singing round a bonfire, while, outside, a scratch band marched up and down the street, pouring out barbarous music with much beating of drums, clashing of cymbals and jingling of bells carried to the number of fifteen to twenty on a gaily decorated pole with a half moon on the top. From a nearby mosque came the wailing cry of the muezzin, calling the faithful to prayer.

As soon as his men were rested, Osman set them to make Plevna impregnable with earthen redoubts and trenches, for he knew that the Russians would soon be back in greater numbers. The wounded were sent to Sofia, and reinforcements were brought up, strengthening his garrison to 20,000 men.

Working in relays, the troops dug day and night, by the light of fires, and two great redoubts were built on the eastern end of the Janik Bair, named by the Turks the Bash Tabiya and the Kanli Tabiya, which became known to the Russians as 'Grivitza I and II'. A long line of trenches and gun emplacements were built along the summit of the ridge, making a stronghold three and a half miles long. The two great redoubts, the walls of which were twenty feet thick and high, were protected by a deep and wide ditch on three sides, and flanked by trenches four feet deep running at an obtuse angle from which the attacking Russians could be raked by flank fire as they tried to assault the redoubts. In each redoubt embrasures were made for guns and a banquette ran round the top for the riflemen. Sleeping chambers, store-rooms, and stables were hollowed out of the walls, and an ammunition magazine was dug deep beneath the floor. To provide for their comfort the Turks borrowed furniture from the abandoned houses of the Bulgarians, and in one redoubt a magnificent mahogany wardrobe served as a sleeping chamber for six soldiers, lying in tiers. Sanitary arrangements were generally lacking, and William Herbert who made makeshift arrangements for his men, was laughed at by his superiors with good-natured contempt.

Life in Plevna quickly returned to normal. When the army first marched in the Bulgarian shopkeepers quickly shut up shop, but Osman Pasha was a strict disciplinarian, and he promised them that any attempt at looting would be promptly and severely punished and that, and the sight of five executed Bashi-Bazouks who had been caught red-handed plundering corpses, induced the shopkeepers to take down their shutters. Osman could not stop the ghoulish plundering of the Circassians and the Plevna bazaar was filled with Russian uniforms, boots, great-coats, silver and bronze crosses, photographs of sweethearts and the other personal effects of the dead. The Plevna Jews reaped a rich harvest buying up Russian roubles for a few piastres. From one of them Dr. Ryan purchased a heavy signet ring with a large red stone, carved with the figure of Aesculapius, easily recognizable from the traditional accessories of the snakes and the cock.

On Osman's orders, no one was allowed to leave or enter the town. A party of Bulgarians who were trying to sneak out with all their goods and chattels, including a cat, a canary and a squalling baby, were turned back, and a crowd of Rumanian Jews, with long curls, in grey gaberdines and shaggy top-hats, with a stock of second-hand clothing, buttons, thread and indecent photographs, were turned away, lamenting their lost bargains.

Lovtcha was recaptured on the 26th by a detachment sent out by Osman, and the next few days were spent in a fever-heat of preparation, for the Circassian scouts brought news that the Russian army was massing on the east of Plevna. The two great redoubts were completed on the 29th, and a series of trenches were built on the south-eastern ridge, opposite Radishevo, and on the south of Plevna.

In ten days, the town had been turned into a strongpoint of considerable strength, but its earthen fortifications were as yet nothing to what they were to become in a few months time.

CHAPTER SIX

THE FIRST ASSAULT

TOWARDS the end of July, Forbes and Villiers were advised by General Ignatieff, the Russian diplomat, that they might find something worth seeing in the direction of Plevna, and they were given a letter of introduction to General Shakofsky. Leaving Russian headquarters on the afternoon of the 27th, they reached Pavlo the same night, and bivouacked in a Bulgarian farmyard. From there onwards they plunged into a *terra incognita* with only the map for a guide and in Bulgaria, as Forbes found, even the best maps are bad. They were blind guides and the Bulgarian peasants little better, as Forbes relates: "They reckon by hours, and with most irritating looseness. 'How far to Akcair?' 'Two hours, sir.' 'What direction?' A wave of the hand to the right and an indescribable howl, is the answer. 'How far to Akcair?' 'Three hours.' 'What direction?' A wild, indefinite wave of the hand to the left front, and a howl as indescribable as the previous one, is the reply of this exponent of local geography."

Forbes turned to the map on which was depicted a main highway running from east to west; once on it there could be no doubt as to the route for it led straight to Plevna. But where was it? "We searched for it first in Burunti," he says. "It was not there. Nobody had ever heard of it. The map made it running through the village of Akcair, but the only roads about Akcair were mere cart tracks. At Studeni, although according to the maps that village stood on it, all declared it to be a myth. In despair, I made a sort of cast, as a huntsman might whose hounds are at fault, and quite casually, in the middle of a plain, I found the road. It had been wonderfully well made for a Turkish road—a ditch cut on either side, metalling laid down on its surface, and nothing was wanting to constitute it a highway but the traffic upon it. But tall grass grew through the stones upon it, and grass obscured the profile of the ditches. I do not believe that a wheeled vehicle had ever passed along it. It is a road which to all appearances has no *raison d'être*, carefully avoids the villages, and accommodates nothing and nobody. My idea is that the Turks, in some sudden spurt of ardour for keeping up with the times in matters military, had been

F. VILLIERS
Artist of *The Graphic*, with the Russians

advised that a great military road athwart Bulgaria, from Widdin to Shumla would be a valuable work, and that accordingly the section of it between Plevna and Jantra was taken in hand. Made, it has never been used."

But the road, once found, led them to the village of Karajac Bugarski, where they found Prince Shakofsky. He was at dinner and Forbes and Villiers had had none; according to the canons of Russian hospitality, whether that of a general or private soldier, they expected to be invited to join in, but the general's words were chilling, "Well, gentlemen," he said, "it is lucky for you to have brought this note for I have no alternative but to allow you to remain; otherwise I should have requested you to quit the camp at once. Good evening." Forbes and Villiers were forced to set up their tents in pouring rain and go to bed supperless, but when Villiers woke at dawn he found Forbes, the old campaigner, standing at his side with a dozen new-laid eggs he had procured from somewhere.

Villiers continues: "When the reveille sounded, as it had ceased raining, I lifted the fly of my tent to look at the morning, and I saw a quaint figure standing out against the sky. It was a tall, eccentric looking man, in pink silk pyjamas, with a monocle in his left eye, who was slowly stirring a steaming glass of tea with a silver spoon. He was gingerly standing with bare feet on a small mat of wet straw which his servant had collected from the stubble around, to prevent his master from soiling his feet with the thick clayey mud which oozed about him. He continued stirring his tea until his monocled eye glanced on me, when he good-naturedly handed me the cup.

" ' Well,' said my newly-made acquaintance, stretching himself and yawning, and turning his eye-glass to the quagmire around him, 'this is beastly. Why did I ever leave Paris to come to this infernal hole?' As I gazed at him in some surprise he lit a cigarette and continued: 'You see, my dear sir, though I am a Russian I am almost a Frenchman. Lived in Paris nearly all my life, and this sort of thing,' looking over the cheerless fields and waving his hand, 'is beastly—absolument! Why did I leave France? you would say. Well, you see, patriotism was the prime incentive. I left the army when I was only a sous-Lieutenant, and having resided in the gay capital ever since, I felt bound to do something for my country when in distress, and here I am attached as an extra nothing in particular to Shakofsky's staff, and find that all my friends of my early military career are either dead or full blown Generals, and the latter when I see them no doubt think I am very much in the way. For I have no special duty, and, in fact, why I am here, God only knows.' He then dropped his eye-glass, gave a deep sigh, and swallowed his tea."

No forward move was made that day but, "in the dead of night," as Forbes relates, "that extraordinary fellow General

Skobeleff the younger turned up in Prince Shakofsky's head-quarters. He is the stormy petrel of the Russian army. If I were riding along a road in a given direction in expectation of seeing a fight, and I chanced to meet young Skobeleff riding in the opposite direction, without any enquiry or any hesitation I would wheel my horse and ride in Skobeleff's tracks, in the full assurance that I was doing the best thing for myself and my readers. He is in the thick of everything. He is, I sometimes think, a little mad, but a man of real value in a kind of warfare such as this. It would be em-barrassing if every General was a Skobeleff: but a few Skobeleffs scattered up and down through a great army have their uses. They generally end by getting shot, and earn a short memoir and a good many decorations. But I hope it will be a long time before Skobeleff meets his inevitable doom, for he is a right good fellow, and a staunch comrade."

On the morning of the 29th Prince Shakofsky and his headquarters staff, to which Forbes and Villiers had attached themselves, moved up in the direction of Plevna, Forbes marvelling "to find ourselves faithfully followed at a very short interval by the whole of the headquarters baggage train. Now, the headquarters baggage train of a Russian General commanding an army Corps is no light thing. With the Russian Army, it is not only that every general officer has his carriage—most have more than one—but the larger proportion of field officers have vehicles too. On this staff there is a baggage waggon between every two officers, and a surprising number of miscellaneous vehicles besides. The chief of the artillery has a travelling chariot drawn by four horses, driven after the manner of a four-in-hand with us. Servants swarm, and every servant contrives to find a place in or on a vehicle of some kind or other. The staff train is half a mile long if it is a yard, to say nothing of escort, marketenders (the Army sutlers) and the priest who rides in a vehicle of his own. Order is not its strong point, and that it is badly superintended, or not superintended at all, is obvious from the manner in which it wandered after us through the forepost line. It was countermarched with some precipitation when the chief turned his horse's head and rode backward."

In the afternoon there was a regular council of war, from which Krudener went away gloomily, predicting defeat. He had, Forbes learned, remonstrated against the assault on the Turkish entrenchments with an inadequate force, but he had received peremptory orders from the Grand Duke Nicholas to carry on with the attack. For Forbes it was a fine opportunity to observe the diverse types of Russian officers. Of these, he says, "there are several schools: roughly, the old ignorant school, the young ignorant school, the old refined school, the young cultured and scientific school, and the young dashing, reckless, refined school, fluent in languages, knowing not much of the art military, but fine gallant soldiers. The representatives of the first two schools are rather boorish, give one a general impression of having been sergeants, and with few exceptions are hearty fellows with a pronounced liking for vodka, and not very particular about knives and forks. The officers of the old refined school, are simply charming, full of a spontaneous courteous bon-homie which at once puts a man on his ease: fair linguists, men who have travelled, and mostly know Courts, and who are full of consideration and kindliness. I am not sure that modern soldiering is their strong point. The gentlemen of the young cultured and scientific school, with the Military Academy badge on their breasts, are very much of the type of our Engineers: a little priggish in their way, slightly mysterious over trifles, which they choose to regard as secrets, dry in manner for the most part, but when you come to know them downright good fellows, whose friend-ship is a privilege. It is in holiday time, or about the fag-end of an adverse battle, that I should like best to meet a batch of youngsters belonging to the fifth school I have roughly designated. They rather interfere with assiduous letter writing, but they are dear boys, and if one wishes them further sometimes, one cannot help loving them."

All these types came to and from the headquarters tent as Forbes watched; "the grey-bearded, hard-faced old Major who, without 'protection' had fought his sturdy way through the grades with long delays, much hard service, and many wounds. He was an ensign in the Crimea, and afterwards

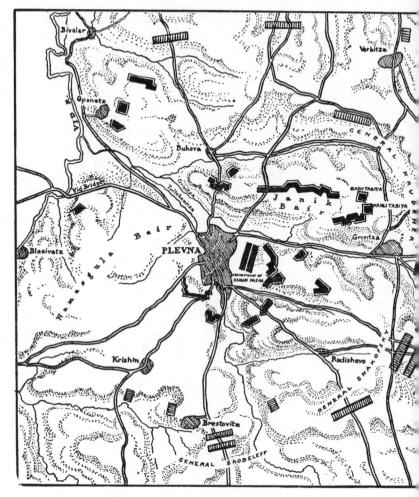

PLEVNA, 30 July, 1877. The First Assault

was forgotten for Heaven knows how many years in some
odd corner in the Caucasus. He is only a Major, but he has
half a dozen decorations, and, please God, he will gain
another tomorrow, if he has the luck to stand up. He is as
hard as nails, and would as lief live on biscuit and junk as
on champagne and French cookery. There is little in common
between him and the tall, stately, grizzled General, an

aide-de-camp of the Emperor, a man of the Court, yet who has never forsworn the camp, a man who will discuss the relative merits of Patti and Lucca, who has yachted in the Solent and shot grouse in the Highlands: who wears his decorations, too, some of them earned in the forefront of the battle. He can gallop, can this young hussar in the blue and red, he can cut the sword exercise, he can sing French songs of a somewhat improper character; he can pick up a bottle of champagne between his teeth, and holding it there let the contents run down his throat: he would give his last cigarette either to a comrade or to a stranger like myself: he has the portraits of his mother and of a French lionne of the demi-monde in his bosom, and in his secret heart he has vowed to earn the St. George tomorrow."

The council of war over, Forbes learned that the Turks were reported to be standing fast and their positions were known to be strong, but the order was to succeed, cost what it may. Tomorrow's sun, thought Forbes as he turned away from the headquarters tent, will set on smoke and fire and all the lurid grandeur of the battlefield. All night long, in incessant rain, Forbes and Villiers lay on the grass with their tents struck and their horses saddled waiting for the *alerte*. Around them in the darkness slept the two great armies of Generals Krudener and Shakofsky, 35,000 men in all, with 170 guns on the heights above waiting to pulverize the Turkish positions as a prelude to the two assaults, one under General Krudener on the Grivitza redoubts on the north-east, and the other under Prince Shakofsky from the south-east, based on the village of Radishevo.

From their fitful slumber, Forbes and Villiers were awakened at dawn by the boom of the Russian guns, throbbing through the fog like muffled drums. About them the Russian infantry were moving up into position. As they mounted and joined Prince Shakofsky's staff, Villiers' Russian friend joined them. "Ha, *mon cher* Villiers," said he. "Listen! Now ze ball is about to open—listen!"

Within the Turkish lines all was ready. Each infantryman was issued with 500 cartridges, eighty to be carried in the pouch and the rest stored near at hand. Their bread bags were filled with biscuit and their flasks with coffee. Tubs of drinking water were placed in each redoubt and ample food was made ready. Carts stood by to carry the wounded to the rear and horses were harnessed and saddled to drag the precious guns to safety should the redoubt be taken. Swords and bayonets were sharpened, and the surgeons laid out their knives and saws. Each of the two Grivitza redoubts was garrisoned by 1,000 men; the remainder of Osman's force being distributed in the trenches or organized into a general reserve in the valleys immediately east of the town. As dawn broke, the men stood to the *alerte* along the parapets and trenches gazing into the impenetrable white mists. As nothing appeared to be happening they were stood down and given breakfast of boiled rice and fresh bread. At 8.30 a.m. the first Russian shells came whizzing over but still nothing could be seen.

Forbes and Villiers moved up to the Radishevo ridge to watch the attack from the south-east. About 11 o'clock the mist began to lift and Plevna was revealed to their view, lying in the hollow of a valley, the ground in between forming three great waves, with their faces set edgeways to the valley of Plevna and end on to the Russians. Astride all three waves were the Turks, their redoubts and trenches making ugly, menacing gashes in the soil and their camps, with tents standing, as Forbes thought, making it clear that they did not intend to move if they could help it. On their right was the Grivitza ridge on the highest point of which stood two great redoubts. Below this ridge and crossing the valley of the Grivitza stream, were a series of strong earth-works extending leftwards to the Tultchenitza brook and the Lovtcha road, and crowning the country rolling towards the town of Plevna, the red roofs and white minarets of which could now be seen sparkling in the sun. Immediately in front of them Forbes and Villiers saw a series of short valleys, red with an early harvest of Indian corn, and wet with the recent rain, the maize sheafs gleaming like stacks of gold against the purple of the hills. Further away to the left they could see the Green Hills, on the west of the Tultchenitza and a further line of trenches protecting Plevna from the south.

The Bashi-Bazouks at bay

The July assault from the southeast. Sketche

Szatchmáry, Painter to the Rumanian Court

Death of Colonel Rosenbaum of the Archangel Regiment (July assault, as observed by Forbes and Villiers)

Osman Pasha, the defender of Plevna

General Michael Skobeleff of the Russian Army

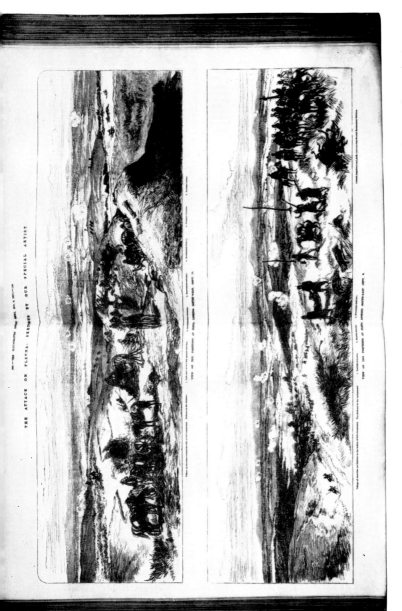

The Great Assault. *Top:* The Russian attack from the southwest (MacGahan's viewpoint)
Bottom: The Russian attack from the southeast (Forbes' viewpoint)

Attack on a redoubt

A Turkish family in Plevna

On the ridge between Radishevo and Plevna, Forbes and Villiers found themselves among the Russian guns, the long row of cannon reminding Forbes of the German batteries on the crest of the ridge of Verneville on the day of Gravelotte. Looking down into the village of Radishevo, which had been captured that morning, they saw bewildered groups of peasants standing in front of their houses, the children playing unconcernedly about the dust heaps, oblivious to danger, as the Turkish shells crashed into the village. Yet, as Forbes learned later, not a single villager was killed by the hundreds of shells that fell there.

From his place of vantage on the heights Forbes could look right down into the Turkish positions on the central ridge, and he noted that they were well placed for searching with their fire the valleys by which they must be approached. Beyond were more and yet more earthworks right up to the edge of the broad valley where the roofs and church towers of Plevna sparkled in the sunshine from a circle of verdure. It had an aspect of serenity strangely contrasting with the turmoil of the cannon fire raging in front of it, and it seemed so near that a short ride would have brought him there to breakfast yet, ere they could reach it, many men must die, thought Forbes sombrely.

It was now 1 p.m. and the Russian infantry, advancing slowly under cover of the guns to reach their assault positions, were not yet engaged. Looking to the right Forbes could see that Krudener's men were lagging far behind Shakofsky's. The close co-operation essential to success between the generals—the one too slow and the other too rash—was lacking and the two assault forces, both too weak for what they had to do, were moving independently when it was essential that they should strike the Turks simultaneously if they were not to be destroyed piecemeal.

While Forbes was observing Krudener's slow advance on the Grivitza redoubts, Villiers had been keeping watch on the left front where Skobeleff had last been seen making for the Lovtcha road with his mixed force of Cossacks to test the Turkish defences on the south of Plevna. Now, suddenly catching Forbes by the arm, Villiers drew his attention to a wild looking band of horsemen galloping in the direction of Krishnin. It was Skobeleff, they learned later, returning from his dash almost into the streets of Plevna which, if it had been supported, might have taken the town.

Later in the day, Skobeleff made a manœuvre which saved Shakofsky's force from annihilation, and showed his military genius. In his reconnaissance he had seen that the Turks had an immense camp of reserves hidden in a valley, and that, if they were moved on to the Green Hills, on the Lovtcha road, they could enfilade the whole of Shakofsky's line and take him in reverse as he advanced. Shakofsky would be able to do nothing against them as this position was separated from his own by the rocky Tulchenitza ravine. It was of vital importance to keep the Turks away from this hill, so Skobeleff determined to launch an attack with his little detachment. He moved forward and kept the Turks from the Green Hills until sundown. When he finally retreated he had lost fifty per cent of his force.

But, to return to Forbes and Villiers on the Radishevo ridge.

Suddenly over the whole battlefield a strange silence fell; the cannon on both sides held their breath, and even Krudener's artillery, semi-circling the great Grivitza redoubt, hushed their distant howling. For a moment there was a pause in the bloody artillery duel, and the battle hung breathlessly, waiting. On to the ridge came General Shakofsky and his staff, being forced to dismount as a hurricane of shells were directed by the Turkish gunners on the prominent group of officers. After a long and anxious inspection General Shakofsky despatched an officer galloping down the slope to the infantry, and soon the hillside was alive with bristling bayonets as the men sprang up to the cry of "Forward", and advanced over the stubbled fields, spreading out as they went till their lines stretched out at right angles across the valley, and up the steep slope beyond. General Shakofsky, Forbes saw, had launched a mere 10,000 men against commanding entrenched positions held by an immensely superior force, and no whit crushed by the preliminary bombardment, and he had left no general reserves to either back them up or to support them if they were repulsed.

As the Russian lines breasted the slope, the anxious watchers could see puffs of smoke leap from the Turkish works, and in a second the trenches were enveloped in one long orange flame which, though they redoubled their fire, the Russian artillery men were unable to quench. In Forbes' imagination, the still unbroken yellow flame played like sunshine on the ocean's ripple along the earthen parapets. Soon the valley became a haze of smoke and Forbes could tell only by the bright flashes from thousands of moving rifles how the advance was going.

As the grey and white masses of Russian infantrymen neared the Turkish positions, the trenches burst into flaming volleys of rifle-fire but the now jagged line of moving men sprang onwards, nearer and nearer to the Turkish works. The roll of rifle-fire is incessant yet, to the watchers on the ridge, it is dominated by the fiercer and louder turmoil of the artillery above them. From behind, the ammunition wagons gallop up with fresh fuel for the fire and the guns redouble their cannonade. In front, the crackle of the rifle-fire rises into a sharp continuous peal, and the clamour of the hurrahs of the fighting men are wafted back on the breeze making the spectators' blood tingle with the excitement of the fray. The full fury of the battle has entered on its maddest paroxysm. A quick order from Shakofsky and supports are thrown forward up the hill.

From out of the stifling smoke of battle, nearer now to the Turkish trenches, come .limping men with torn and bloody clothes, many without caps and not a few without their rifles. Some drop fainting by the way, others struggle unsteadily back up the Radishevo slope. Here and there come little groups of men carrying maimed comrades. To where Forbes and Villiers stand comes one of these groups: two soldiers, slightly hurt, are carrying a less fortunate comrade who lies groaning on a blanket fixed stretcher-wise across their rifles. A dark liquid slowly drops from the saturated blanket, and marks a bloody trail down to the village below the ridge where the doctors wait with their ambulances, and the bloody trail grows wider and ruddier as it is followed by other bearers and a muddy path is made across the valley. On the stubble fields and amongst the maize the dead and more seriously wounded are left to lie as the battle moves on.

Wave after wave of Russians steadily feed the straggling front, sowing the field with heaps of dead and dying as they break under the terrible hail from the Turkish trenches, but the living wave of fighting men pour on over the black and white dots of their dead and wounded comrades, splitting into groups as they hover like angry hornets uncertain where to place their sting. As Forbes and Villiers watch from their shell-swept ridge, they see blue flashes of light gleaming for a moment as the officers wave their swords urging their men on to close. The Turkish fire begins to waver, and more supports stream into the Russian line. The officers signal for a concentration. A small number of the most reckless rush the first work, led by a colonel. The Turks in the shelter-trench hold their ground and fire with terrible effect into the faces of the Russians. The colonel's horse goes down, but the colonel is on his feet again in a second, waving his sword and leading his men on foot. But only for a few paces. He staggers and falls. From his men rises a tempest-gust of wrath, half howl, half yell, as they rush on to avenge him. "It is the bloodiest battle of the century," declares Forbes to Villiers who glances up and down again to his drawing block as he hurriedly sketches the scene.

From the pall of smoke rises a chaos of noise, the sharp crackle of the rifle fire, the whine and ping of the bullets, the crash of exploding shells and the shouts of reckless men bent on victory or death. The Russians are over the parapet and shelter-trench and in among the Turks like an avalanche. The watchers see the flash of bayonets and hear the roar of triumph, sharpened by the clash of steel on steel. The outer-edge of the Turkish position is won. The battle rages in all its splendour and horror as the Russians mass again to rush the earthworks beyond. With one final volley the Turks abandon the work and retreat to the shelter of the batteries behind them.

"We're in, we're in," cries Forbes. "Yes, certainly," announces Villiers' Russian staff friend who is standing by them, supplementing his monocle with a binocular. "We shall sup in Plevna tonight," says he. "Look at that, *mon cher* Villiers. See how our brave fellows use ze steel: we are very good, we Russians, at ze bayonet." He hands his glasses to Villiers. "Ah, that lens reminds me of the last time I looked through it at *ze Grande Opéra de Paris*." Bang! A shell splinters into fragments a few yards away. The Russian continues undisturbed, "Surely you remember ze *saison* of 1876 and ze *belle première danseuse*, eh?" Crash came another shell. "I mean ze *petite brunette* wiz ze *nez retroussée*." Another shell ploughs the ridge and a clod of earth strikes the Russian, bringing him to his knees. As he regains his feet he quickly readjusts his eye-glass and, shaking the muddy soil from his clothes, he alternatively rubs the place where he has been hit and angrily shakes his fist towards the Turkish guns. "*Mon cher* Villiers," he cries, "these Turkish *canaille* are so barbarous; they have not ze sympathy. Such is war—so *vulgaire!*"

The battle in front reaches its height: from the advancing infantry burst flaming volleys of rifle fire. As the crackle of fire swells into a sharp continuous peal, the blood of the spectators on the ridge tingles with excitement. The full fury of the attack has reached its maddest moment. An almost irresistible craving comes to Forbes and Villiers to throw themselves into the fray, and the excitement of the moment surges through their brains like strong drink, such is the convulsion of their emotion.

The fate of Plevna seems certain. A battery of guns has followed the infantry into the captured works. The Turks are retiring. Villiers, watching General Shakofsky, sees a smile of satisfaction spread on his face. The coveted goal is within his grasp; the Grand Cross of St. George dangles before his eyes, tempting him to rashness. The word is again 'Forward', but Forbes is not so sure. Krudener, on the right, he can see is clearly jammed. The Turks in the Grivitza redoubts are fighting furiously and Shakofsky, he thinks, would be wiser to strengthen the position he has won and wait until Krudener has carried the redoubts and come up in line with him. Forbes, who had stood on the ridge at Gravelotte and seen most of the battles of the Franco-Prussian war, is a keener observer and he knows that Shakofsky's success at the first position was child's play to the grim starkness of the second Turkish position. The Russian infantry, he can see, are blown; in the fresh advance they hung a good deal, exposing themselves recklessly and falling fast, and they were not progressing with much speed. It was a job, Forbes knew, for fresh men, but where were they?

Shakofsky, with his finger on the throbbing pulse of the battle, sees the hesitation, and in the nick of time throws in half his reserve brigade; the new blood tells at once and the advance goes forward but the Turks too have hurried up reinforcements, and Forbes sees a swarm of men flying across the green stretch of vineyard.

A bugle sounds the 'Charge' and with bayonets lowered a huge mass of Turks comes hurtling down the hill with ever increasing momentum. "Feel each other's elbows," flies from mouth to mouth as they come nearer and nearer to the Russians. "Hurrah, Hurrah," comes from the Russian ranks, "Allah, Allah," from the Turks, as the two masses meet like colliding railway trains. In the surging mass of humanity there is a chaos of stabbing, clubbing, hacking, clutching, shouting, cursing, screaming men in knots of two and three clinging to each other on the ground in their death agonies; above, a surging mass of heads, the butt ends of rifles rising and falling, mounted men sweeping down their swords on the heads beneath, colours flying, horses charging, rolling over, burying men already mutilated beneath them, frantic faces streaming with blood; a madhouse; a seething cauldron of human animals; a legion of demons gone riot; hell let loose. Utterly fatigued the Russians die where they stand, and the mass dissolves as the Russians break and flee, leaving thousands of black and white dots in the furrows and ruts of the heavy soil, and a weird silence falls over the field. Away to the right the rattle of Krudener's fire is faintly heard like the pulse of a dying man, fitful and weak.

Amongst the dead and dying a Turkish colonel, shot

through the thigh, sees a Russian officer lying wounded. The urge to kill comes to his mind as he crawls over to him. The Russian points to his wounds, the Turk to his. He draws his long Kurdish knife and severs the Russian's head, the windpipe gurgling and bubbling as the knife cuts it. "He was a fine man," the Turk tells the English doctor who finds him still clutching the Russian's head. "I shall never forget his face. You are horrified. I was not a man then. I was a wild beast. I killed him as he lay there because he was in my power. If I had been in the same position he would have killed me. It was destiny."

From the costly won trenches a horseman comes galloping. As he passes Forbes and Villiers, they see his forehead scarred by a passing bullet, his face pale and covered with beads of perspiration, the blood from his wound mingling with the sweat that trickles down his cheek. Breathless and quivering with excitement, he was an ominous messenger. General Shakofsky impatiently listens to his story. Then, stamping his foot and clenching his hands in a delirium of passion, he addresses his officers. "Look at the general," exclaims Villiers. "There is something up. Some serious news. Look at that."

From the captured earthworks the Russian batteries are coming back. The horses, clearing the curtains at a bound, dash down into the trenches and struggle up again with guns intact as the drivers lash furiously at their straining flanks and they come careering madly across the valley. "By Jove, you're right, Villiers," exclaims Forbes. "There is something up. The whole game's up!" As the Russians fled down the slope there was not a man to cover their retreat. All depended on the position being held and now, as the sun sank in lurid glory behind the smoke-mantled field, the Russian defeat was dire. As dusk fell the Turks swarmed down the hill in pursuit, emptying their rifles into the mass of fugitives.

Within the Turkish lines, and from every side converging on Plevna, comes a long procession of carts and wagons, drawn by oxen, horses, mules, donkeys and dogs, and a decrepit wheelbarrow in which a soldier pushes his maimed

comrade, carrying the wounded to the hospitals manned by
Turkish and European volunteer surgeons with sleeves rolled
up and bloody hands, striving to stem the tide of death.
Groups of less seriously wounded stagger along supporting
each other, or are carried by their friends on improvised
stretchers made from pieces of furniture. Solitary men crawl
by themselves, leaving trails of blood behind. On the ground,
unnoticed, lies a young Russian lieutenant, awaiting death
in awful loneliness. All over the battlefield companies search
for their officers, and officers for their men, amidst piles of
corpses, broken gun-carriages, riderless horses, torn shell
holes, shattered swords and discarded rifles. No attempt can
be made to turn the Russian rout into the annihilation of
their army as the Turks, with few cavalry, are too exhausted
to pursue. Content with their victory, they give thanks to
Allah and lie down to sleep where they have fought.

The Russian rout was complete. Generals Krudener and
Shakofsky had lost 23 per cent of their force. One hundred
and sixty-eight officers and 7,167 men lay dead and dying
in front of the Turkish earthworks. As darkness fell, the
dreaded Bashi-Bazouks spread over the battlefield to smite
and spare not. Lingering on the ridge Forbes could hear the
entreaties for mercy and their bloodthirsty fanatical yells of
triumph, and he began to wonder if there were any of the
troops who had so nobly advanced left to return. A great
battle, one of the bloodiest battles of the century as Forbes
was to call it, had come to an end. It was time to go. Villiers
had gone down into the village to help with the wounded,
and soon Forbes became fearful of his fate.

Forbes stood with Prince Shakofsky and his staff on the
summit of the ridge; from the valley below arose the screams
of agony of the wounded and the firing from little knots of
Russian infantrymen as they slowly retreated, holding off
the Turks. On the ridge there was no conversation for "our
hearts", as Forbes says, "were too heavy for talk". "We sat
about on the knoll gazing down into the pandemonium
below. The general, alone and apart, paced up and down
a little open space in the oak copse, gloom settled on his face.
All around us the air was heavy with the low moaning of the

wounded, who, having limped or been aided thus far out
of the fight, had cast themselves down to gain a little relief
from the agony of motion."

When did he admire the simple Russian soldier most?
Forbes asked himself. When he is plodding along without a
murmur, verst after verst, under a burden just double what
the British soldier carries, cheering the way as he tramps
with a lusty chorus? Or when, with cheers that ring with
sincerity and with an alacrity which is genuine, he presses
forward into battle? Or when he is standing stubbornly
confronting his enemy, conscious of being outmatched, yet
never dreaming of running away? Or when he is lying
wounded but uncomplaining, helping his neighbour in the
same plight with some trifling act of tender kindness, and
waiting for what God and the Czar shall send him, with a
patient, unwavering calm that is surely true heroism?

As the moon rose on the battlefield, Forbes could see
dark forms moving over the corpse-strewn ground, and from
the valley came shrieks for mercy and yells of barbarous
triumph. Warm as was the summer night, Forbes shivered,
wondering where Villiers could have got to.

Once again the ridge on which Forbes and the staff stood
came under fire. "Through the darkness," he was to write in
a few hours time, "we could see the flashes of the cannon
shots: a second more and nearer and nearer came the whistle
of the shells, with a swiftly gradual crescendo into a scream
as they sped over us and crashed down in the village in the
valley behind us: and yet nearer there was the flashing of the
musketry fire in the darkness: one could watch the streaks of
flame foreshortened down in the valley there, and nerves
tried by a long day of foodlessness, excitement, fatigue, and
exposure to the sun and the chances of the battlefield,
quivered under the prolonged tension of endurance, as the
throbbing hum of the bullet sped through or over the
straggling group. No man dared to say to that stern lowering
chief, eating his heart out in the bitterness of his disappoint-
ment, that it was a bootless tempting of fortune to linger
longer on this exposed spot, nor did any man care to quit
for the sake of greater safety the companionship which had

endured throughout the day. So we lingered on till our senses became dulled, until some dropped off into slumber, regardless of the scream of shells and the hum of bullets."

Then, Shakofsky awoke to the situation. "Gentlemen," he said to his staff, "we and the escort must keep the front; these poor wounded must not be abandoned." At the general's order a bugler persistently sounded the assembly, and before long stragglers from a dozen different regiments had collected to keep the Turkish irregulars at bay, while the wounded were loaded into ambulances and on to bullock wagons. When all were accounted for Forbes, who, although he makes no mention of it, worked hard with the rest helping the wounded, and the staff turned the heads of their jaded horses and rode away. The general had lost an army, and the army had lost its general, and Forbes had lost his friend Villiers.

After a fruitless search in the village of Radishevo, Forbes, fearing that Villiers must have fallen a victim to the Turkish prowlers, set out to ride through the ruck of the army on his way to Bucharest, the nearest point at which he could put his story of the Russian defeat on the wire to London. All night long as he rode there were alarms that the Turks were surrounding and cutting off the Russian retreat. At one point he and the party riding with him were fired upon by the Russians under the impression that they were the dreaded Bashi-Bazouks; at 3 a.m. whilst giving his horse a rest in a field of barley, he and a number of wounded were woken from a fitful slumber by the firing of a party of Turks who luckily passed by without finding them. His fears for Villiers were not allayed by hearing that after the battle the Bashi-Bazouks had worked round to the left flank and butchered all the wounded that Villiers had gone to succour. As Forbes rode on in the morning he could not help thinking of Villiers' mother who, at her quiet house in a London suburb, had told him that she let her boy go to the war with an easy heart because she knew he would be with him.

From the battlefield of Plevna to Bucharest was a long ride and Forbes killed his horse making it, arriving there on the morning of 2 August. As he approached the office of the Russian censor, the thought assailed him: would the Russians pass his story of the defeat and rout of their army? Fearing that it would be too grim for them to stomach, he decided to ride the eighty miles into neutral Hungary. He had prepared for just such an eventuality, and on the suggestion of his American colleagues he had established a 'pony express' with horses standing by at every ten-mile stage across the Carpathians to Kronstadt. Forbes' story of the Russian failure at Plevna, wired from Kronstadt, was read in London and New York the following day and cost £400 in telegraph charges alone. He told his readers, "The entire campaign is altered. The truth is, Plevna must be taken," for it was quite impossible, he said, "for the Russian advance to continue with such a formidable force of Turks left unaccounted for on their line of communication."

Back in Bucharest, Forbes, who had not slept for three days, hearing no news of Villiers, discussed with his friends, Colonel Wellesley, the British Military Attaché, and Colonel Mansfield, the British Minister to the Rumanian Court, whether he should telegraph Villiers' mother with the news of his loss, or wait another day. Colonel Wellesley who was leaving by train for England offered to carry the message for Forbes. That evening Forbes was dining in the garden of Broffts Hotel with the English Consul and Beatty Kingston of the *Daily Telegraph*, when he heard a familiar voice call out, "Waiter, quick, dinner: I'm beastly hungry!" It was Villiers, equally relieved to find Forbes whom he had given up for dead. A hurried telegram to Colonel Wellesley, which reached him at Strasburg, relieved him of his mission.

Villiers on leaving Forbes on the ridge above Radishevo had gone down into the village with the intention of helping with the wounded but, his pony becoming uncontrollable, he was caught in the retreat and swept along with the Russian fugitives, and pursued by the Turkish irregulars following on the heels of the retreat. For hours he rode along the road crowded with panic-stricken soldiers, ambulance carts brimming over with wounded, and ox wagons to which those able to walk clung on. Towards midnight the Bashi-Bazouks, glutted with blood, slunk back to their lines, and Villiers came upon General Shakofsky, looking terribly dejected, and his friend of the eye-glass, silent for once and with nothing to say. Caught with the remnant of the army, Villiers found it impossible to get through the choked roads, and after spending the next night on the floor of the court-yard of an inn, with the bridle of his horse secured to his wrist, he managed to cross the Danube and catch a train to Bucharest. From there, when he had recovered, he was able to post a bundle of his sketches to the *Weekly Graphic*, in the faded copies of which may still be seen those eye-witness drawings of the young artist who was to send them hundreds of sketches from the battlefields of the world during the next twenty-five years.

Forbes' fears that Russian headquarters would find his report of the failure at Plevna unpalatable were unfounded, and by the Grand Duke Nicholas himself he was told that telegraphic instructions had been given for the Russian news-papers to print his despatch in full, as substantially accurate as regarded details and results.

Into Plevna a long line of carts, their wooden wheels creaking over the cobble-stones, brought the seriously wounded and, as the hospitals became full, they were directed to the houses of Moslems, the Christians refusing to take them although at least a thousand were wounded Russian prisoners. Dr. Charles Ryan who had been out in the trenches all day, returned to his hospital, a mosque, to find a hideous sight. Its square floor was covered with dead and dying men. There were about eighty all together and his first task was to separate the living from the dead, not an easy one as the dead were lying across the living and the living across the dead. One man he found half suffocated by his own blood and the weight of a dead comrade lying across him. The walls of the mosque were plentifully bespattered with blood. In the less seriously wounded, Ryan found a determination to avoid the amputation of a limb, for the Moslems believed its loss would prevent their entry into Paradise, which would be ensured by death from a wound received in battle against the infidel. Many preferred to die with the certainty of reaching Paradise than risk expulsion.

Next day, the burial parties buried 1,000 Turks and 3,000 Russians on the south-eastern battle ground, and Dr. Ryan walking beyond the Grivitza redoubt counted the bodies of 1,500 Russians, lying in heaps as they had been mowed down by the Turkish magazine rifles. Those that had died instantly, he noted, were serene in face or expressed the tumultuous passions of the fight. Most of the dead had been stripped by the Bashi-Bazouks and their loot was put on sale in Plevna market, Ryan securing a little painting of the Virgin and Child of great antiquity on a piece of wood, a family heirloom given, perhaps, by some Russian mother to her son as a talisman. Those Bashi-Bazouks who were caught red-handed looting or mutilating corpses were hanged at once, on Osman Pasha's orders.

On the day following the battle, the Turkish wounded and Russian prisoners were sent to Sofia, and the returning convoy brought an aide-de-camp from the Sultan who, in the presence of the whole garrison, presented Osman Pasha with the Order of Osmanli, the highest Turkish military decoration, and read out a despatch in which the Sultan congratulated Osman on his great victory. Osman was presented with a diamond-studded sword, and his second-in-command, Ardil Pasha, with a brace of magnificently-mounted pistols. Osman then addressed the troops saying that although the Sultan had decorated him personally, the credit of the great victory did not belong so much to him as to his brave officers and troops, who, he felt certain, were eager and ready to try conclusions with the enemy. He reminded them that the battle they had fought was not the end of the campaign. They were fighting for their hearths and homes, for wives and children, and though the fighting still in store for them would probably be even more severe than that which they had already gone through, he placed the fullest confidence in their bravery and their patriotism.

Work was immediately commenced to make the fortifications of Plevna even stronger and by 31 August there were twice as many redoubts and trenches as there were on the 31 July.

CHAPTER SEVEN

RUSSIAN INTERLUDE

THE great Russian offensive, the triumphal march to the Bosporus, was halted. The Russians had fallen on the 'sick man of Europe' in his death agonies, as they thought, and at Plevna they had been violently kicked in the stomach. The despised moribund Turk had given the most unmistakable proof of the strongest possible vitality. For twenty-four hours the Russians were in hopeless panic; Osman Pasha was believed to be in hot pursuit. At Sistova, the cry was raised, "The Turks are coming", and the Bulgarians, the Jews, the brandy sellers, the receivers of pillaged goods, hosts of camp-followers, and numerous drunken Cossacks, stampeded across the bridge into Rumania where the panic spread to Bucharest. The evacuation of Tirnova by the Russian head-quarters-staff led to the wildest rumours, and the roads already congested by the fleeing Russians were choked with Bulgarians seeking to escape the revenge of the terrible Turk. When a begrimed and exhausted dispatch rider rode into the Imperial headquarters with the news of General Krudener's defeat, the Grand Duke Nicholas telegraphed Prince Charles of Rumania: "Come quickly to our aid. The Turks are annihilating us. The Christian cause is lost."

If the Turks sought to capitalize the advantage they had gained, the Russians were in a perilous position. Their army south of the Danube was strung out on an immense arc with a circumference of 180 miles. There was now no chance of dealing the enemy a decisive blow, and there was even talk of retreating north of the Danube. But that would mean abandoning the Christian population of Bulgaria to the savage revenge of the Turks, a fearful loss of prestige which the Russian leaders dared not face. But, when Osman did not pursue the routed armies of Krudener and Shakofsky, Russian spirits began to revive. Plevna was only a check. The Russian failure to capture it was annoying, because it held up the advance, but it was only a matter of time before Osman was swept from their path.

Forbes had no illusions about the Russian position and the vast change that had been brought about by Osman's victory. A week before, how bright had seemed the Russian military future; Gourko stretching out his arm almost within clutching distance of Adrianople; the Czarewitch waiting but the word to cast a girdle of stalwart soldiers round the fortress of Rustchuk; Krudener and Shakofsky in full expectation of wiping out the slur of Schilder-Schuldner's failure. One bad day, or rather six hours hard but disastrous fighting, and all was changed, the sunshine eclipsed by black clouds, and the advantages of the Russians had crumbled like burnt out tinder. Beaten and disorganized, there was no certainty that the Russians could withstand a Turkish attack. "There is not a single Russian battalion," wrote Forbes, "to prevent Osman and the Army of the Quadrilateral shaking hands at Tirnova." As long as Osman was undefeated, Plevna would remain a standing threat to the Russian security. The capture of Plevna was, Forbes declared, the absolute *sine qua non* of the continued stay of the Russians south of the Danube.

Leaving Bucharest, Forbes paid a visit to the Imperial headquarters at Gorni Studen, where the Czar, and the Grand Duke, with their staffs and innumerable ducal and princely advisers, lived in barbaric splendour and insanitary squalor. The little village of mud-walled houses, straggling on either side of a smelly creek, had blossomed forth with Kurdish tents of felt, white pavilions, bright uniforms, staff officers gay with aigrettes on prancing steeds and with sword scabbards glistening in the sunshine, the Cossacks of the Guard in blue and gold, hussars in blue and brown and red and green, strange visaged Asiatic servants, carriages and *calèches*, coachmen in plumes of peacock feathers, noble chargers of high mettle led by English grooms, valets, cooks, grand dukes and statesmen, and the Cherkess escort,

brilliant splashes of colour in their red silk tunics. A place,
Forbes thought to himself as he rode in, where every soldier
thinks himself braver, and every general considers himself
more talented, than any other in the world, the only doubter
being the Czar himself, Alexander II, already a victim of
melancholia, the curse of the Romanoffs. In this camp of
grand dukes, princes and generals, every table is spread
with gleaming silver and the whitest damask, and there is
not a lavatory in the place. The burnished boots of the
staff squelch through filth and offal, and carcasses of dead
animals are left to lie where they had fallen.

Amidst all this splendour and filth, the Czar lives, in
startling simplicity, in a dismantled Bulgarian house, his
bedroom a tiny chamber with walls and floor of mud. He
is seldom seen except at meal-times when 200 officers breakfast and dine in a large marquee erected in his garden. The
Czar is the fount of military honour. In theory no act of
bravery escapes his eye. From the youngest to the oldest
every eye is turned on him as he enters the tent. Behind
him an aide-de-camp carries a cushion with crosses on it, and
perhaps half a dozen sword knots of honour—the riband
of St. George, orange and black—to be worn attached to
the sword hilt. Instantly expectation is at its height. The
Czar's voice calls the chosen name, all make room for
the envied man to pass: he comes blushing and flushed,
receives the prize, bends low to kiss the Imperial hand, and
retires bowing at every step, a made man for life, the admired
and courted of all beholders. He is embraced and kissed on
both cheeks by his friends, and he is so overcome with this
mark of distinction that he walks about weeping, with the
prized decoration in his hand, half dazed.

Gaunt, worn and haggard by the anxieties of the
campaign, a man of noble presence and kingly mien, Forbes
declares, Alexander II spent many hours visiting hospitals
and refugee camps, talking to the wounded and to the
Turkish prisoners. On one occasion, visiting a camp of
Turkish prisoners, he took out his case and offered cigarettes
to the unfortunate inmates. The Imperial staff felt bound
to follow the royal example, and as there were fully two

hundred officers in the Czar's entourage, the Turks benefited to the extent of some two thousand cigarettes.

Amongst the Russian officers Forbes found a sense of paralysis, no move could be made against Plevna until reinforcements came from Russia. An Imperial Ukase had been issued calling up 188,000 men of the militia, and nothing could be done until some of them reached Bulgaria. Amongst his officer friends Forbes found a great sense of disillusionment. The war had lost its character of a crusade. Many of them found that they had laboured under the most profound misconception as to the condition of the Bulgarian Christians. They had gone to war believing them oppressed, impoverished, impeded in the exercise of their religion, and not sure for an hour of their lives, the honour of their women or of their property. In this belief they had embarked with enthusiasm on a war of liberation. But, what did they find? The Bulgarians live in the most perfect comfort; the Russian peasants cannot compare with them in prosperity (nor could the English peasantry, observes Forbes). Their grain crops stretched far and wide; every village has teeming herds of cattle, horses, goats and sheep. Their houses were palaces compared with the Russian hovels. For every mosque there were half a dozen churches.

But, though no longer a crusade, the war had to be won and Plevna taken. From the towns and villages of holy Russia, the recruits and reinforcements set out on their long journey to Bulgaria. In the town of Simibirsk, a small boy, the son of an Inspector of Primary Schools, watched the men marching to war. It was his seventh birthday, the 22 August, and his name was Vladimir Ilyich Ulyanov. We know him better by the name of Lenin.

During this period of inactivity, Forbes hung around the Imperial headquarters, a welcome guest in the tents and lodgings of his Russian friends of all ranks and classes. Amongst the Russian diplomats and Imperial officials, for Gorni Studen was the centre not only of Russian military life but of all the affairs of government as well, Forbes was welcome as the representative of a great British national newspaper which, if not pro-Russian, was certainly anti-Turk, and one of whose reporters had exposed the atrocities which had given the Russians an excuse for a war of aggression. But Forbes was welcome for himself for he was a shrewd observer of war and, if some of his observations were unpalatable, his experiences with the Germans in 1870 provided a never-ending fund of conversation. It was in the tent of a staff officer that he heard the story of a poor old general at Plevna who, the commander of a division, had

LIEUT.-COL. BRACKENBURY
The Times, with the Russians

been so overcome with panic that he had fled from the field of battle. He had been dealt with in typical Russian fashion. After the battle he had been sent for by the Grand Duke, who observed that he was ill, and there was no chance of a return to health unless he returned to Russia. "But, your Imperial Highness," stammered the old general, "I am not ill at all. I never felt better in my life." "Allow me, please, to know better," replied the Grand Duke, "I can see you are ailing seriously, and I must recommend you to recover your health in the bosom of your family."

One day MacGahan appeared from Bucharest where he had been to dispatch a batch of reports of his experiences in the Shipka Pass. The Russians holding the vital pass, were, he told Forbes, fatally weak. If the Turks advanced in force, they would have difficulty in holding the door into Turkey which they had so bravely won. With him from Bucharest, MacGahan brought a batch of letters for Forbes and his inseparable companion Villiers. Mr. Robinson, the general manager of the *Daily News* wrote to praise Forbes for his brilliant dispatches from Plevna, but he was concerned for his correspondent's safety. "Keep off those shell-swept slopes," he urged.

When Forbes appeared at the Imperial headquarters on the morning of 21 August he saw at once that something was wrong. On all sides he was met with gloomy faces and with the news that Suleiman was attacking the Shipka Pass, the 'lock of the door' to Constantinople which General Gourko had so recently 'burst open', with a vast army of experienced troops. Gourko had gone back to St. Petersburg to bring the Imperial Guard to Bulgaria, and only a small force had been left to guard the vital pass. With their habitual shiftlessness the Russian High Command had failed to support the Shipka Garrison. No one at headquarters seemed to think that the Shipka Pass could be held, and Forbes could see the Czar in the little garden at the back of his quarters walking up and down, his head drooping on his breast, his shoulders bent, his attitude eloquent of discouragement. General Ignatieff was, for him, curt of speech when he outlined the position to Forbes. The situation was grave. If Suleiman burst through the mountain barrier, the Russians would be caught between three fires. Forbes decided to act on the advice given by Prince Frederick Charles to his officers to 'ride in the direction of the cannon thunder', and he and Villiers set off at once to the Shipka.

As they rode from Tirnova to Gabrova, they found the country one vast melancholy encampment, and the road one continuous mournful procession of fugitives from south of the Balkans, fleeing in terror from the rapine and murder of the Turks, as the ruthless Bashi-Bazouks surged up through the fringes of the Balkans. At Gabrova they met long convoys of ambulance wagons laden with wounded men and above them they could hear the booming of cannon on the Shipka.

Through the townsfolk, as they clustered in the pale moon-light, ran a visible shudder, as they listened to the ominous roar of the cannon. Between them and massacre stood but a few Russian bayonets. As Forbes and Villiers rode on the roar of the cannon high above them, seemingly in the very clouds, swelled louder and louder in volume, and the tally of wounded increased from a trickle to a flood. Beside them marched the belated reinforcements, sent to hold the Pass, which Forbes knew might be lost before they could arrive. On the road-side scared women huddled under the trees, praying that the good God would strengthen the arms of the soldiers hurrying by. When Forbes and Villiers came out on the pass which, he was to explain to his readers, is not a 'pass' at all, no gorge, no defile, no Thermopylae where 300 men could hold up 10,000, but a saddle or ridge flanked by shallow hollows and cavernous gorges providing excellent cover for an attacking force, Forbes could see that the situation was desperate.

The Russians held the saddle but the Turks were masters of the parallel ridges on either flank and were trying to encircle the Russians and cut them off from Gabrova. As Forbes lay on the ridge, the target of a dozen rifles, taking in the situation, he could see that the claws of the Turkish crab were about to close and outflank the Russians. It was a dramatic moment, one of crisis on which the whole campaign might turn. The grimed, sun-blistered defenders were worn out with heat, fatigue, hunger and thirst. No food had been cooked for three days, there was no water and the ammuni-tion was running out. The bare ridge was swept by Turkish fire, and from the cliffs and valleys rose the triumphant shout of "Allah il Allah". At any moment the final rush might come, and the Russians would be overwhelmed.

Besides Forbes, the two Russian generals, Derozinski and Stoletoff, were anxiously scanning the steep road leading up from Gabrova, for Forbes had told them that General Radetsky's men were labouring up the steep defiles and narrow paths in the rear. Suddenly Stoletoff cries aloud in excitement and, clutching Derozinski's arm, points down the pass where the head of a long black column is plainly visible against the reddish brown of the road. Both generals leap up and wave their caps as the wearied troops decry the long black serpent coiling up the road, and they break into a cheer which drowns the Turkish war cries and rings a welcome to the comrades sent to succour them.

As the senior officer present, General Radetsky, takes over the command of the Shipka garrison. He sees at once that the Turkish positions on the right flank must be carried and he sends his men to take them at the bayonet point. As Forbes scribbles in his notebook and Villiers hurriedly sketches the scene, the mad clamour of the battle surges round them. Wounded men come staggering back and, beside them, General Dragomiroff is struck in the knee and is borne away on a stretcher, crying good fortune to the arms of the Czar. The crisis of the battle has come. The Turks and Russians are lost in a wood, and the fight is in the balance. One more heave and the Turks will be driven out. Radetsky, realizing that fortune sometimes needs a little wooing, throws himself into the fray at the head of the reserve, and fortune yields. A tremendous volley of Russian "Hurrahs" tells Forbes that the Turkish ridge is cleared and the position won.

General Radetsky comes back to the ridge and leans panting on a rock with a quiet smile on his face. "It seems to me, General, you will be able to hold on, now?" says Forbes. "With God's help, I will," Radetsky replies, and as Forbes rises he asks, "So you are going, are you? Well, you can tell them what you have seen; and you will find me here when you come back, dead or alive."

Forbes believed that the Turkish onslaught on the Shipka was held. Such a moment, he knew, was the crisis of fate in a war correspondent's career. If he believed that the Shipka was safe, he should ride to the nearest telegraph wire to announce the victory. But what if it were not won? he asked himself. He had drawn his conclusion and should back it, he reassured himself. Experience had taught him to read a battlefield through the blurred fog of slaughter, confusion and chaos. "Yes, I'll back myself," he muttered as he tightened the girths of his horse and set out to ride the 180 miles to Bucharest. As he plunged down the steep track, he could hear behind him the fury of the Turkish counter-attack, the fresh assault which might brand him as a false prophet and as an unsagacious observer.

Changing horses at Gabrova, Forbes set his course for Gorni Studen, ninety miles away, where another horse waited to carry him across the Danube. A maddening delay occurred when a drunken Russian corporal thought him a spy and would not be satisfied by Forbes' 'papers', which he was unable to read, but in the end a couple of roubles set Forbes free and he was able to get out of the town, having eaten only a morsel of cheese and a crust of black bread.

Steadily through the soft, beautiful night, Forbes rode, listening to the cool splash of water over the mill wheels and breathing the scent of the balsam and the thyme from the cottage gardens. The sun rose long before he reached Tirnova, and it was not until noon was past that, dead tired, faint from want of food, and with the knowledge that he was behind the schedule he had set himself, he rode into Imperial headquarters.

As he pulled up in the village square, General Ignatieff came out of his tent. "Ha, Mr. Forbes, where from now, you great galloper?" was the general's jovial greeting, for Forbes had gained some little reputation among the Russian headquarters people for riding hard when news had to be carried fast. "From the Shipka," was his reply. "I saw a battle there all day yesterday, and left Radetsky at eight last night." "The deuce you did!" returned Ignatieff bluntly. "Why, we have no tidings so late. You have beaten all our orderlies. Come into my tent and tell me the story."

It meant delay, Forbes knew, and of all things then delay was what he could least afford, and he grudged every moment that kept him from the telegraph wire. But he had been obliged to the general for many kindnesses, and it would be ungrateful and unseemly for him to excuse himself. Forbes dismounted and joined General Ignatieff in his tent.

"And you think," was the general's comment when Forbes concluded his narrative, which he had made as short as he decently could, "you think that Radetsky can hold on, that the Shipka is safe?" "For what my conviction be worth," was Forbes' response, "I prove it in the fact that I am here, I shall commit myself to it in the telegram, to dispatch which I am hurrying to Bucharest." "Well, your belief is dead in the face of all our opinion here," replied Ignatieff, "but you know your business best. Pray heaven you may be right, and all our experts wrong."

Forbes went across the street to eat while his fresh horse was being got ready. The meal, the first real food he had tasted for nearly two days, was about to be served when he heard General Ignatieff calling him; "Hi, hi, Mr. Forbes. Where are you? I want you at once. Come along, make no delay. I have told the Emperor what you have said, and he has commanded me to find you and make you his compliments and express his desire that you come and relieve his anxiety by telling him all you know."

The summons to the Czar's presence was, Forbes knew, no doubt complimentary, but it was embarrassing. He was in a great hurry for the readers of the *Daily News* were more important to him than all the Emperors of the habitable globe, and, besides, his longed for meal was being placed on the table. With a sigh Forbes rose from the table and joined Ignatieff in the street. What a state he was in, he noticed. He had not washed for three days, and his clothes were smeared with the blood of a wounded officer. But Ignatieff would take no excuses; he had ventured to rouse his Imperial master from sleep and Forbes must not let him down.

Ushered into the dismantled house, Forbes found the Czar, even more shrunken and stooped than when he had seen him last, pacing to and fro. It was the worst period of ill-fortune to the Russian armies and anxiety was plainly visible on the Czar's face. Shaking Forbes' hand, the Czar complimented him on the speed with which he had travelled, and urged him to repeat the story he had told General Ignatieff. Forbes outlined the position, and drew a rough sketch to illustrate the relative positions of the Russians and the Turks. The Czar asked innumerable questions, and he expressed the same hesitation to accept Forbes' view of the situation, but, so exact were Forbes' details and so confident was his appraisal of the situation, that the Czar asked him, speaking in English, "Mr. Forbes, you have been a soldier?" "Yes, Your Majesty," Forbes replied. "An officer in the artillery or engineers, doubtless?" the Czar asked, to which Forbes could only reply, "No, Your Majesty, I was a trooper in the dragoons." "General Radetsky will hold the Skipka," Forbes assured the Czar, and before he left, the Czar, saying that he had heard of the example Forbes had shown in helping the wounded at Plevna, invested him with the Order of St. Stanislaus, with the crossed swords, a decoration given only for personal bravery under fire.

But Forbes was not allowed to leave yet. The Grand Duke had to hear his story, and he insisted that Forbes continue his journey in a carriage he placed at his disposal. When he finally reached Bucharest Forbes had been three days and nights in the saddle and under fire in the Shipka trenches, without food or sleep. He was dead tired, but his dispatch had to be written; he had news of the battle on which the fortune of half Europe depended, but it was as much as he could do to keep his eyes open. Ordering the waiter at his inn to bring him a pint of champagne, he put the neck of the bottle to his mouth, drank it down, and and wrote four columns for his paper.

Returning to Gorni Studen, Forbes learned that the news from the Shipka was ominous: the position was nearly lost and General Ignatieff was far from cordial and the Grand Duke cut him dead, but six days after leaving the pass, Forbes was back there to find Radetsky victorious. He had been right in his conclusion: the Russians had held the pass.

While Forbes covered the Shipka engagement, Mac-Gahan attached himself to General Skobeleff who, under the command of Prince Imeretinsky, had been placed in charge of an operation dear to his heart, the capture of Lovtcha, the Turkish stronghold twenty miles to the south which threatened the rear of any force attacking Plevna from that direction. Skobeleff reconnoitred Lovtcha soon after the defeat at Plevna. MacGahan watched him, dressed as usual in white and riding a white horse, gallop towards the

Turkish lines, assailed by a tempest of fire. His escort were
killed and his horse wounded. MacGahan saw him mount
another horse and shouting and gesticulating to the Russian
skirmishers; again MacGahan saw him go down. 'He has
got it this time,' he thought. 'It's the fourth horse he has
had shot under him in ten days. It is impossible for him to
go on in this way without getting killed. It will be a miracle
if he comes back alive.' As MacGahan watched, Skobeleff
became lost to view in a cloud of smoke and dust. Two
minutes later he emerged and MacGahan saw him trotting
up the road on another horse, looking as fresh as ever. He
had not received a scratch.

Skobeleff's assault on Lovtcha was launched on 1 September. By his strategy, losses were reduced to a minimum, and
every soldier went into battle with a clear understanding of
what he had to do. "I direct the soldiers to the fact that
in a bold attack the losses are minimized and that a retreat,
especially a disordered retreat, results in considerable losses
and disgrace," Skobeleff declared in his Order of the Day.
In his report, Prince Imeretinsky did Skobeleff full justice:
"The reputation which this brilliant General has acquired
by his military talents and bravery is," he wrote, "known
by the whole army, and it is sufficient for me to say that it
is principally to him that I owe the success that has been
obtained at Lovtcha."

The Czar took the much needed hint and at a dinner
party at Imperial headquarters he hailed Skobeleff as the
'hero of Lovtcha.' Forbes had the pleasure of informing
General Skobeleff Senior of the latest prowess of his gallant
son. The old man, moved to tears, solemnly descended from
his saddle and threw his arms round Forbes and kissed him
on both cheeks. Forbes never forgot the incident because the
diamond ring on the old general's finger scratched his neck
while he hugged him with fervour and emotion.

On the day following the capture of Lovtcha, a Grand
Council of War met at Poradim, in front of Plevna, to plan
the Great Assault. Prince Charles of Rumania was nominated
commander-in-chief of the allied army of attack, and the
Russian General Zotoff, his chief of staff.

CHAPTER EIGHT

TURKISH INTERLUDE

IN Constantinople the news of Osman's resounding victory, coming as it did soon after the gloomy news of General Gourko's almost bloodless capture of the Balkan passes, put new life into the Turks. The Turks had proved that they could fight and that they could beat the Russians. Abdul Hamid, hopeful that the European Powers would intervene to prevent the Russians reaching Constantinople, needed to gain time and Osman, by his defence of Plevna, was buying valuable time for the Russians could not move as long as Plevna held. After the disclosure of the Bulgarian atrocities, Turkey had been faced with an enraged Europe; now, the victory of Osman's gallant little army was sweeping public opinion in their favour.

A week before Osman's victory, the collapse of the Ottoman Empire seemed imminent, resistance appeared hopeless. Abdul Hamid's supreme desire was to preserve his Empire, and he threw himself into the task with an energy which was foreign to the Turk. No sultan had ever worked like he did. Brought up in the seclusion of the harem, he had been suddenly and unexpectedly enthroned as the earthly ruler of 35,000,000 people of widely different races, and of two opposed religious beliefs, and as the Kalif of Islam the spiritual leader of hundreds of millions.

He knew nothing and he was surrounded by advisers and officials whose only object was to strengthen their own position and line their own pockets. The whole system of public administration and of government had broken down. Turkey was bankrupt and relied solely on foreign loans. As an Oriental people, the Turks were inheritors of the ancient fatalism of the East, inclined to accept the inevitable and disinclined to do today what could be put off until the morrow. Abdul Hamid roused them in the only way they could be roused; he appealed to their religious fanaticism, and he produced a national reawakening and a new wave of Moslem fervour. The Sultan, the Mullahs declared, girt with the Sword of the Prophet, would sally forth against the Infidel and rout the enemies of God, which sounded well though Abdul had no intention of leaving the security of his palace. The most timid of men, he so feared assassi-nation that he had built himself a new palace composed of tiny rooms, apparently disconnected but linked by under-ground passages, down which he could disappear at any sign of danger.

Scarcely a year after his accession to the throne, Abdul found himself honoured as no sultan had been for genera-tions; he was now the champion of the East against the West, the hope of Islam against the hated Christians. Inspired by their ruler, the Turks marched to a Holy War, and Constantinople became the gathering place for the soldiers pouring in from every corner of the Empire on their way to the Balkan front. They marched in, warriors of the ancient past clutching heavy shields and inlaid muskets, in bare feet and flowing robes, in strange helmets and visors of hanging steel-net, with the light of lawless vigour in their eyes; they had left their burning deserts and mountain eyries with empty pockets they expected to fill with plunder, and they cared little if they could not be paid. In a few weeks they were formed into regiments, equipped with modern rifles, and sent off to the front fully prepared to live on a crust of bread and a jug of water, and to kill until they were killed. Hardy tribesmen, they had been reared with a rifle in their hands, and inured to privation and hardship, and at Plevna they were to prove themselves the greatest fighting men in the world.

The Moslem fugitives streaming into Constantinople from the Balkans proved an unexpected aid to Abdul and his green and white-turbaned religious agitators who stood at street corners proclaiming the Holy War. They told terrible tales of the atrocities committed by the Bulgarians and Cossacks; of women raped, children speared and the aged bayoneted. Easily inflamed, the soldiers of Mohammed set out to avenge their co-religionists and to slaughter the invading Russians, who had brought all this misery, without mercy and without remorse. As the refugees streamed in they were shipped to the interior where their tales of the atrocities of the Christians brought a fresh wave of volunteers to the Turkish armies. From ten thousand minarets, ten thousand white-robed priests called the faithful to battle.

In Plevna, Osman knew that he had won a respite only. The Russians would soon be back in greater numbers, and Plevna would be subjected to an assault which would make the July affair look like child's play. For the July battle, Osman had had time only to build two redoubts on the north-east and to throw up a few earthworks elsewhere. Now, these lines of trenches and redoubts must be built into a comprehensive defence system. On the northern front, five redoubts were constructed between Opanetz and Bukova and these were connected by rifle trenches and covered ways with the two great redoubts already built on the Janik Bair. On the south-east, between the Bulgareni and Lovtcha roads, six great redoubts named by the Turks the Atouf, the Araba, the Ibrahim, the Chorum, the Omer and the Tahir Tabiyas, were built, each a marvel of intricate construction, with store rooms and sleeping places, with walls 20 feet thick and 7 feet high on the outside, and surrounded with moats 15 feet wide and 10 feet deep. One redoubt covered an area of 10,700 square yards and each was protected by deep and narrow rifle trenches in front and on the sides. Inside massive traverse walls protected the defenders from attack from side or rear.

On the southern margin of Plevna, in the direction of Krishnin, where in July there had been a few entrenchments, there now arose six great redoubts, the Kavanlik, Issa and Baghlarbashi Tabiyas close to Plevna and the Milas Talahat and Yunuz Tabiyas near Krishnin. Another redoubt was built on the west, facing the Vid bridge.

The Grivitza redoubts were the key to the position on the north, and the Krishnin redoubts on the south, for both these works were on points commanding the country around for a range of 3,000 yards on all sides. The middle group of redoubts, opposite Radishevo, were on a lower level and they were commanded by the redoubts on the north and south. These redoubts could only be reached by climbing steep bare slopes, swept by withering fire.

In Plevna itself life soon returned to normal. The Bulgarians, as long as they behaved themselves, were allowed to keep their shops open and attend to their farming and they were not molested. Wandering round the bazaars, Dr. Ryan added to his collection of souvenirs of Plevna, which he was to take back to Melbourne. For a few francs, he bought a Russian officer's sword and two beautifully mounted revolvers, and from the garden of his quarters he gathered seeds from the asters, zinnias and balsams which flowered there, and forty years later their lineal descendants were still gracing his Australian garden. The weather was glorious, food plentiful and the only shortage was tobacco, a serious matter for the Turks. There was no fighting and one night Dr. Ryan, "tossing about feverishly in bed, suffering agonies from the domestic insects which in Bulgaria attain to stupendous proportions", was surprised to hear a tremendous volley of firing. Believing that a night attack was developing, he leaped out of bed but in a few minutes the firing died down. Next day he learned that there had been an eclipse of the moon and the Turks, acting in accordance with ancient superstition, were trying to scare away the monstrous animal which was endeavouring to devour the Silver Queen of the night. Plevna was not invested and communication was open with the west and south, but towards the end of August the Russians began to gather in a vast semi-circle round the north, east and south.

Soon after the July defeat, the Russians commenced to throw up strong defensive works around Plevna, and these were growing stronger each day. Osman decided to make a sortie against the Russian lines at Pelishat, south-east of Plevna beyond Radishevo, on 31 August. The operation was well directed by Osman and gallantly pursued by his men, but it came too late. If Osman's attack had been made at the time when the Russians were hard pressed in the

Shipka, and the Turkish army of the Quadrilateral had moved in synchronization, the Russians might have been given a terrible jolt. Osman moved out of Plevna at daybreak with 20,000 men and, due to the lie of the ground, took the Russians by surprise.

Most of the newspaper correspondents had left the Russian lines in despair of anything happening and MacGahan was saddling his horse to follow their example when

WENTWORTH HUYSHE
New York Herald, with the Turks.

his ear caught a dull, scarcely audible thumping that sounded more like a horse stamping at flies than the booming of artillery. But artillery it proved to be, and in a few minutes it grew louder and louder. Looking towards a line of low hills in the direction of Plevna, some four miles distant, MacGahan saw columns of white smoke rising behind them, showing where the artillery was already hard at work. MacGahan set off in the direction of the cannon thunder.

As he rode towards Pelishat, he met great crowds of Bulgarian refugees flying from the Turkish advance. The whole population had put all their movable effects into wagons and carts, with the women and children, and were driving their livestock before them. Crossing the level plain between Poradim and Pelishat, MacGahan met the ambulance wagons coming back with the wounded and above the hills in front of him he could see clouds of white flecked balls of smoke, and he heard the sharp savage roar of small-arms mingled with the deep thunder of the artillery.

Alongside him was a Russian battery which appeared to be throwing its shells right over the hills into a Russian redoubt MacGahan knew lay there. This could mean only that the Turks had captured the redoubt and that the Russian line was in danger of being turned. Full of anxiety MacGahan galloped to the top of the hill. He could see at once that the position was serious. The redoubt, he learned, had been taken by the Turks, retaken by the Russians and taken again by the Turks. He had not been at his standpoint more than five minutes when the crest of the hill, a mile in front, suddenly grew black as with a line of ink drawn across the sky. What was it? Looking through his field glasses he saw that the Turks, who had just crowned the hill, were advancing on the Russian centre to drive the Russians out of Pelishat. The position MacGahan had taken up was becoming hazardous, but what should he do? he asked himself. If he fell back he would see nothing, and if he remained there was a strong possibility he might be cut off from the main army. As he watched the Turks began to descend the hill in his direction and they came about half way, the Russian shells tearing up the groups among them in the most savage manner.

Just as MacGahan was beginning to think it expedient to clear out, there came a change. The Russian infantry fire began to roll heavily along the hill-crest, and the Turks dropped rapidly, and changed the direction of their attack towards the Russian trenches. For a time the Turks were lost to MacGahan's view in a hollow but he could see the Russian trenches flaming and smoking as they poured a storm of fire into the advancing Turks. This went on for fifteen to twenty minutes and then the Turks began to withdraw. But they had not had enough, MacGahan could see, for they re-formed and went at the Russian trenches again. They dived down into the Valley of Death and there followed a death struggle of giants between men of equal bravery. After the battle he found the bodies of many Turks lying within ten feet of the Russian trenches and the little slope on the crest of which the trenches were placed was literally covered with dead.

The Turks were again repulsed and again they retreated up the hill. To MacGahan it was barely believable that they would attack again, but they did. To him it seemed madness for the Russian fire never slackened for an instant and the Russian lines never wavered. The scene of carnage was repeated but it lasted only for a moment for the Turks, completely broken, withdrew, sullenly firing and taking time to carry off their wounded and many of their dead. But they still held the redoubt, and now the Russians went at it like a whirlwind.

Hearing the firing in the distance, Dr. Ryan rode out to see the fun, and he soon found his services in demand. Within three hours he had taken nineteen bullets from wounded men brought back by their comrades. Continuing on, he galloped towards the sound of the guns, passing on the way two captured Russian guns which were being taken back to Plevna as trophies. The Russians, who had been left behind when their comrades fell back from the first Turkish onslaught, had been given, as Dr. Ryan could see, short shrift by the Turkish irregulars. He saw a Circassian with a most diabolical expression on his face, stooping down to pluck something out of the long grass, on which he proceeded to wipe his sword. Dr. Ryan rode up to see what he was doing and found that he had cut the head off a wounded Russian, and he was holding his horrid trophy in the air. Reaching the Russian position captured by the Turks early in the day, Ryan saw that the first company of Turkish attackers had died to a man, every man having five or six bullets through him. The Russian redoubt was full of dead and Ryan could see the Russians massing 500 yards away to recapture the position. Osman Pasha and his Lieutenant Tewfik Bey were in the thick of it, and Ryan heard that Osman had had three horses killed under him.

When the order was given to retire, all the Turkish wounded were got away, except two. Knowing what their fate would be, Ryan decided to make an effort to save them. One had been shot through the neck and was bleeding profusely, and the other had been struck in the left thigh by a fragment of shell which had shattered the bone. Ryan managed to get both men on to his horse and he set out to join the retreating Turks who were now half a mile away. As he left the

W. KINGSTON
Daily Telegraph, with the Turks

redoubt with the two wounded men on his horse the Russians were only about 400 yards away and were coming up fast.

The Russians were firing at the retreating Turks and they were firing back, so Ryan was caught between two fires. His pace was necessarily slow, for he had to walk the horse all the way and hold the wounded men on. About half way back to the Turkish lines, one of the men fell off dead, and after a period which seemed like a lifetime he reached the Turkish lines without receiving a scratch, and joined the retreat to Plevna.

Ryan got his wounded man back into Plevna, and three days later on 3 September, he was ordered to join a column going to the relief of Lovtcha, which had been assailed by

Skobeleff. On the outskirts of Plevna there were many
Turkish beggars who pestered the troops for money, and
as it was considered lucky to give something to charity
before going into action, the beggars reaped a rich harvest
of piastres.

En route, Osman was informed that Lovtcha had fallen,
but he decided to push on. Reaching the top of a hill the
Turks looked down on to the vast amphitheatre in which
the town lay. Below, Ryan saw a green plain intersected by
the silver thread of the river Osma and in the distance
Lovtcha nestled at the foot of the hills. Osman called a
council of war at which it was debated whether to try to
recapture the town or not. Much against his will, Osman
decided it would be madness to attack such a strong position
defended by an immensely superior force, and he ordered
a return to Plevna.

Scouting around with the Circassian cavalry, Ryan came
across ghastly evidence of the ferocity of the Cossacks. Four
hundred Turks, who had evidently tried to escape from
Lovtcha, were lying dead together, cut down while making
a last stand. Every corpse was fearfully disfigured and
horribly mutilated, and the faces had been slashed with
sabres, as Ryan could see, after death. The Circassians
rode away vowing vengeance on any Russians who might
fall into their hands alive.

In order to avoid the Russians, Osman decided to make
a detour and approach Plevna from the west. Passing through
a Bulgarian village, Ryan was a witness to a demonstration
of the severity with which Osman punished any infraction
of his orders against looting. A Turkish sergeant, pining for
a cigarette, could not resist the temptation offered by a
small field of tobacco, and he climbed in and proceeded to
fill his pockets with the dry leaves. Observing the incident
Osman Pasha, putting his horse at the fence, seized the
sergeant and tore the stripes from his shoulder, degrading
him for his insubordination.

Riding into Plevna, Ryan was surprised to see a man,
who though dressed in a nondescript get-up, including a
little forage cap, patent leather boots, and an enormous

cavalry sword, could only be an Englishman. Introducing himself he found that the stranger was Drew Gay, the correspondent of the *Daily Telegraph*.

In Constantinople, Drew Gay was most anxious to get into Plevna, but he knew that Osman allowed no newspaper men in his camp. He decided to appeal to the Sultan by whom, as the representative of a pro-Turkish paper he had been granted an audience on several occasions. Gay found Abdul Hamid just as eager as he was to get information from Plevna, and he was given a letter from the Sultan himself to Osman on the strength of which the latter could hardly refuse him entry.

Travelling by train to Sofia, Gay set out on horseback for Plevna, intending to travel via Lovtcha which, though he did not know it, was being attacked by the Russians. Riding out of Orkhanie, Gay found the road from the north choked with the fleeing Turkish peasants. As far as the eye could reach, for a distance of several miles, the road was covered with refugees toiling their weary way along the burning road, terror-stricken, footsore, starving and hopeless. Thousands of bullock wagons, bearing pots, pans, babies, women, wooden tools, bowls, benches, sacks and faggots, were huddled and heaped together in one apparently inextricable mass, each guided by either the father of the family or by the wife in her heavy woollen yashmak. Alongside the carts trudged thousands of men, women and children, old women of sixty years and more struggling along under the burden of pots and pans, all they had to save from the Russians, crying and sobbing with fatigue and grief, mothers with babies on their backs and others at their side, each infant carrying something from the abandoned home or helping to drive, perhaps, a calf or a goat or a sheep. Then would come a young girl, holding her yashmak to her face as she passed the stranger, driving two or three bullocks; a widow with her young family all helping to urge a troop of donkeys and goats to move along; old men hobbling along helping equally old women. In one place, Gay saw an old fellow of sixty-five or more, carrying on his back an ancient shrivelled dame, presumably his wife. Thousands upon thousands, 40,000 Gay estimated the throng, all fleeing from the ruthless Cossacks, fearing that at any moment a Cossack whip would be plied upon their backs or a Cossack lance plunged into their babies.

Reaching Plevna, Gay learned that Osman had gone to the relief of Lovtcha, and fears were expressed for his safety, but next morning he heard that Osman was back and he found him in capital spirits, and ready to accept him on the Sultan's instructions.

In Plevna, all was bustle and excitement for it was evident that the Russian assault would be launched at any moment. Each man in the redoubts and trenches was issued with 600 cartridges, and boxes of a thousand were placed to hand, eight days biscuit, a quantity of maize for porridge and bread, rice and fruit. One hundred shells were issued for each gun and a few head of cattle were housed in every redoubt for food. Behind each redoubt ox carts, wagons and pack-horses were lined up, ready to save the guns and precious shells. Each redoubt was linked with headquarters by telegraph and behind Osman's tent a group of Circassian dispatch riders stood ready to carry his messages to any point in the line.

On the slopes and hills around Plevna, 150,000 Turks and Russians stand ready to fight the battle that will decide the fate of the campaign.

CHAPTER NINE

THE BOMBARDMENT

"Plevna must be taken," commands the Great White Father, the 'Divine Figure from the North', as the newspaper correspondents irreverently call him. Now it is to be carried by storm, at the point of the bayonet, despite the lessons learned in July. Where, then, 20,000 men assaulted the Turkish ramparts, now 100,000 lie encamped, ready to strew those shell-swept slopes with their corpses. Four hundred and forty-four guns are in position to pound the Turkish earthen defences into submission. All the power of the Colossus of the North is concentrated around Plevna. The great assault is to be watched by the Czar himself, seated on high like Xerxes at Salamis. Russian prestige is at stake, her credit shaky. All Europe has its eyes on Plevna. It must be captured before a single step can be taken in the direction of Constantinople, the longed for goal. To sweep it from the Russian path the Imperial Guard has been brought from St. Petersburg and the despised Rumanians have been called in as allies.

As the Russian and Rumanian armies move up to their positions on the north, east, and south of Plevna, the newspaper correspondents follow. At Gorni Studen they stock up with food from the Jewish army sutlers, quantities of pork and garlic sausage, dried fish, bread and vodka to make a change from the eternal 'soup' or meat stew of the army rations. Then they hurry to the front. Villiers, eager to secure a sketch of the Turkish positions, gallops out beyond the Russian forepost line; a party of Bashi-Bazouks on reconnaissance chase him back; he is arrested by the Russians as one of the Englishmen known to be fighting with the Turks; he shows his credentials as a war-artist but he is lugged off to headquarters; nearby are sitting three

American colleagues who grin at his discomfiture; "Never seen him before," they say, "dangerous looking chap, don't like the look of him." By the Russians Villiers is shown a rifle taken from the Turks, an 'English rifle' they say: Villiers examines it. "This is not an English rifle. The mark is 'Springfield, Massachusetts,' " he points out, and, with a wave of his hand, "made by the countrymen of your American friends here." Discomfiture of the Americans.

In the correspondents' camp Villiers finds his friends Forbes, MacGahan, Millet, Frederick Boyle of the *Standard*, and Dobson of *The Times* supping with Skobeleff who has joined them, followed by two stately Circassians carrying a bucket of soup, the general's contribution, a marvellous compound of meat, cabbage, pumpkin, onions and maize. After supper there is a sing-song round the camp-fire led by MacGahan whose ditties no one can number, declares Boyle, but Skobeleff says he has learnt none since his Khiva ride.

The Russian plan has been explained to the correspondents. They know that the preliminary bombardment will continue for some days, and that under its protection the assault troops will move up into position. At 6 a.m. tomorrow 6 September, the guns will start to throw their shells in to Plevna. Awakened in the morning by the booming of the guns, Forbes rides out to see what is happening. Everywhere troops are moving up, he finds. The scene is singularly impressive. A long column of cavalry, gay with dancing pennons and prancing steeds, winds up the gentle slope of the downs; a regiment stands in a dense black square waiting for the command to march; another sweeps briskly forward, with bayonets flashing in the sunshine, cheering their general as they pass him; battery after battery of guns gallop by, the rattle of their wheels muffled by the grassy carpet; six great siege-guns and their ammunition, drawn by labouring teams of straining oxen, lumber forward; hospital wagons pass by the score; dispatch-riders dash past; an officer rattles by in his carriage; a little group of Bulgarian peasants stop for a moment to watch, then they bend to work again for it is harvest time.

Forbes moves on. There is no one point from which it will be possible to see the whole of the approaching battle, he knows, and he wishes to spy out the land well in advance to pick the most advantageous spot at which to station himself. The morning is cold and fine; his ride a pleasant one. There is a weird impressiveness in this period of waiting, he finds, watching the east for the light which will herald the fell game of battle. There has been a sharp frost overnight and he rides through patches of fog, hanging in sheltered places waiting to be dispelled by the sun's rays. He turns his horse's head towards Radishevo, and reaches the 'shell-swept ridge' of July memory. From it now, field-guns and a battery of giant siege-guns are firing towards Plevna, the siege-guns lobbing their shells into the Grivitza redoubt on the right. The guns in the redoubt reply spasmodically. A shell whizzes overhead and into the village behind the ridge. Down the Lovtcha road to the left comes Skobeleff galloping at the head of a *sotnia* of Cossacks with whom he has been on reconnaissance towards Plevna. As Forbes watches more shells come crashing on to the ridge. Away in the distance lies Plevna, its white towers and sparkling roofs smiling serenely in the sunshine, still far from being taken, Forbes thinks. The Russians are taking a third bite at the cherry. Will they do it in three? he wonders. Behind him the village of Radishevo is blazing. Forbes rides back to camp.

The heavy pounding of the Russian guns starts again at dawn, and Forbes is out again to watch. Gazing through his binoculars he can see that the parapets of the Grivitza redoubts, jagged and torn the night before by Russian shells, have been repaired and look as strong as ever. On the right the Russian guns have been moved up overnight, and he sees their shells bursting on the redoubt and in it; there is a pause in the Turkish reply to repair damages, but the firing soon takes up again. Forbes thinks that the Russians are dispersing their fire too widely: it would be better to throw the whole weight of the bombardment on one set of redoubts and render them untenable by a hailstorm of shells. Through his field-glasses he takes in a wide sweep of the positions in front of him:

Behind every swell, in the hollow of every depression, lying down behind the screen of Indian corn, are soldiers, some far away out beyond the batteries, and the Russian shells and Turkish shells whistle over their heads without disturbing them. Others are snugly stowed to the left and right of the batteries, lying on the reverse slopes so as to be clear of the hostile shells. All round the edge of the horizon, from the River Vid on the north, to the Lovtcha-Plevna

HERR WINTER
Vienna *Tagblatt*, with the Turks

road on the south, the white smoke of cannon fire rises up against the pale blue sky. The Turkish horseshoe is girdled by a circle of cannon fire and armed men; but the Turk gives back shell for shell, as in the impending fight, Forbes knows, he will return cheer for cheer, rifle shot for rifle shot, and bayonet stab for bayonet stab.

It is a curious, lazy moment for a correspondent, observes Forbes. There is little to record. A regiment rises out of one hollow and marches through the tall Indian corn to another hollow, which is thought a better place. The villagers of Grivitza down there in the hollow between the batteries, with shells interminably whistling over their heads, are actually engaging in treading out the barley on the primitive threshing floor of hardened mud, the men shaking the straw, the women driving the ponies in the endless round. Stoicism, or fatalism, or indifference, or despair, which are we to call it? he asks himself.

Seeing General Krudener, Forbes goes to join him in rear of a battery of twelve siege-guns, each throwing an 84 lb. shell into the Grivitza redoubt. Some of the spectators say that Osman has evacuated the redoubt; Forbes will not agree for he can see masses of Turks lying in the hollows of the hill. They have been sent out of the redoubts to lie scattered in safety while the Russians pulverize empty earthworks which can be rebuilt overnight. In front he watches the Archangel and Uglaskosky regiments advancing through the maize fields, driving in the Turkish outposts. Returning to the Radishevo ridge he finds that everywhere the Russian cannon are drawing closer round the Turkish positions. Down below him on the right comes the Czar with the Grand Duke Nicholas, visiting the battlefield he has not yet seen.

The Turkish positions, Forbes can see, are far stronger than they were in July. There are twice as many redoubts on the north-east where in July only the two Grivitza redoubts stood, and these have been greatly strengthened. On the centre swell, assailed by Prince Shakofsky in July, there are now eight separate redoubts, all protected by rows of shelter trenches. On the left the hills through which the road from Lovtcha winds, are studded with redoubts and gun emplacements. The longer Forbes gazes upon these massive and well-sited earthworks, the more he comes to realize the toughness of the job the Russians have taken in hand. Earthen forts are comparatively new in war, he knows: his American colleagues have told him of the terrible effects of magazine rifles protected by earthworks in the War of Secession, and he recalls the Russian rout in July. Four times as many men will assault those earthen defences now as in July but the Turkish defences are far far stronger, and the Turkish defenders double in number. Forbes with all his experience in war, begins to wonder if the Russian hopes will not again be broken on those terrible slopes and glacis.

MacGahan, too, is out to observe and assess the scene. Riding by a siege-gun battery, he notices a contraption of ladders, seventy-five feet high sustained by ropes, on the summit of which stands a soldier with field-glasses watching the results of the shell fire. It occurs to MacGahan that the position of this man, when a shell comes along as it does now and then, threatening to cut the ladder in two and bring him down with a rush, must be very disagreeable.

Hearing that General Zotoff has ordered Skobeleff to advance his positions on the south of Plevna, MacGahan moves in that direction and seats himself under the shade of a tree to eat his lunch and watch the attack. From the hills around Plevna rise columns of white smoke and although the sun is hot, a white pall of smoke hangs in the valleys. Looking to the left he sees the Russians moving up the Lovtcha road, accompanied by the sharp whip-like cracks of the field-pieces mingling with the dull heavy boom of the siege-guns. To get a better view MacGahan climbs a tree. On the hills through which the road to Plevna winds, the Russians are advancing in loose order, led by Skobeleff whom even at that distance he can recognize in his white uniform and on his white horse. Reaching a clump of trees the Russians are fired on by Turkish outposts and for some twenty minutes the fight is lost to MacGahan's view. A thin blue smoke wafts through the trees and there comes the rattle of small-arms. The Russians drive the Turks through the trees and back to their redoubt. Emerging into the open the Russians come under a hail of fire. From the redoubt streams a steady wave of flame, and the scene is hidden from MacGahan in a heavy fog of smoke. When it clears he sees that the Russians have withdrawn to the shelter of the trees and are digging in there, and sheltering behind trees, banks, boulders, anything for cover from the withering Turkish fire. Behind the hill the sun is setting against a mass of clouds, its fiery blood-shot eye tinged by smoke to the colour of blood. As darkness settles on the scene, thousands and thousands of jets of flame flit like fireflies across the hill. The Russians lie in a perilous position not a quarter of a mile from the Turkish redoubts. If they can hold it until the assault, Skobeleff will have an ideal position from which to launch his attack.

MacGahan is back next morning to see how his friend Skobeleff is getting on. The Russians, he sees, have withdrawn to the west of a low woody knoll, and are throwing shells into the redoubts below them. From one of the redoubts rises an immense pyramid of flame rending the sky to its zenith. It is followed by a mushroom of smoke, white as snow against the thunder-cloud approaching in the distance, and there comes the roar of an explosion. A Russian shell has hit a Turkish magazine. From the hilltop comes a great shout of triumph. The Turks ply their guns and in a moment the crest of the ridge vomits smoke and flame. Balls of flame flash and disappear, leaving small round fleeces of white smoke. The burst of the shrapnel over the heads of the Russians is deafening, silencing for a moment the 'boom, boom' of the siege-guns firing along the twelve mile semi-circle of bombardment.

To the defences of Plevna the great Russian bombardment did little harm. There were few casualties and the damage done to earthen parapets was quickly repaired. Throughout the four days of the Russian bombardment, Osman Pasha sat at his headquarters receiving messages by telegraph from all sectors of the defence. Never for a moment was his composure disturbed. Calmly and coolly he assessed each report and gave the necessary orders, to evacuate a redoubt temporarily, to strengthen another, or to reallocate his forces to positions shown up by the Russian bombardment as likely places of assault. One fact Osman does not know: the date and hour of the assault and how long the bombardment will continue. All his forces are kept at the *alerte* for the guns may stop and the greyclad Russians come storming up the slopes at any moment.

When the Russian guns first opened fire at 6 a.m. on 7 September, the Turkish drummers beat the alarm, and in less than a minute each redoubt and every trench was manned, and the guns replied. All day long for four days Russian shells smashed into the parapets or exploded inside the redoubts. Each night the damage was repaired and the wounded sent back to the Plevna hospitals. During the second afternoon Rumanian infantry came towards the Grivitza redoubts, but they were swept away by rifle fire. Skobeleff, or 'Ak Pasha', the White General, as they called him, the Turks knew had established himself on the Green Hills, south of the town, and made himself a sally-port from which to launch the attack they knew would come from that sector, at least.

In four days, 30,000 shells had been thrown against the Turkish defences. Five hundred Turks had been killed and wounded, 50 per cent of whom died at the explosion of the magazine in the Krishnin redoubt, but no redoubt had been rendered untenable and in maintaining their fire for four days at extreme range, many Russian guns had been put out of service.

About 5 p.m. on the evening of the 10th, heavy rain set in and the Russian bombardment died away. As night fell, wet and misty, the Turks knew that the great assault could not be long delayed.

CHAPTER TEN

THE GREAT ASSAULT

TUESDAY, 11 September, dawned with drizzling rain and a white mist which shrouded the field of the impending battle from friend and foe alike. From their entrenchments and redoubts the Turks gazed out into the impenetrable fog wondering if, under its protective cover, their enemies were creeping up on them. On and off during the morning the Russian cannonade continued its intermittent bombardment, the heavy moisture laden air deadening the sound of the guns. For minutes at a time the long lines of men, lying but a few hundred yards apart in places, were cloaked in an eerie stillness, more frightening, perhaps, than the continuous boom and crash of fire. The ground was a swamp, each slope a slithering trap, the face of each redoubt a sheet of mud. The Russian infantry lying out in the open were soaked to the skin, their Turkish foes warm and comfortable in their redoubts. On a twelve mile semi-circle 150,000 men faced each other, few knowing that this was the day of the Great Assault, chosen because it was the name-day of the Czar, who would be there to watch his men storm into Plevna.

The Russian sappers had built a platform on a little eminence between Grivitza and Radishevo, out of the line of fire, from which the Czar, the Grand Duke Nicholas and their staffs could watch the battle. Floored with wood and surrounded by a railing, the enclosure was provided with a marquee in which a table was spread with the choicest wines and foods, which reminded Forbes of an English country race meeting. Of the food and wine, he noticed, the staff partook with gusto but the Czar neither ate or drank. All day he sat gazing out with haggard straining eyes at the efforts of his troops to storm the Turkish lines. Forbes watched the pale strained face quivering and wincing as the men struggled up the treacherous slopes, made more slippery with blood, to be swept away in a maelstrom of fire lashing out from those grim and terrible redoubts and trenches.

To the gaze of the Czar, and of the newspaper correspondents, the Turkish lines took the form of a giant reaping-hook (MacGahan's phrase), the point of which faced towards Bukova on the north, the middle curve facing towards Grivitza on the east, and the end of the handle pointing at Krishnin on the south, and the junction of handle and blade lying on the Lovtcha-Plevna road. From Plevna, three great ridges extended outwards to the north-east, the Janik Bair protected by a line of earthworks and by the two great Grivitza redoubts, to the south-east in the direction of Radishevo on which were placed the middle group of redoubts, named by the Turks the Tahir Tabiya, the Omer Tabiya, the Atouf Tabiya, the Ibrahim Tabiya, etc. and to the south or south-west where six great redoubts between Krishnin and Plevna protected the town from attack along the three roads converging from that direction. The west of the town was naturally protected by a great hill, the Namasgula Bair, and by the River Vid. All three ridges were strongly fortified and to take the town one at least had to be carried by assault. The villages of Grivitza, Radishevo and Krishnin are each approximately three miles from the centre of Plevna.

The Russian plan of attack was an ambitious extension of the plan of July, but now four times as many men would be thrown at the Turkish works. According to the military text-books, a certain number of men were required to carry a fixed position. X number of men would be killed covering Y many yards of ground, leaving Z number of men to reach the entrenchment and carry it at the point of the bayonet. The loss was proportionate to the risk; to storm an entrenched position was merely a matter of starting with enough men. This theory may have operated successfully in the old days of the muzzle-loading musket and defenders drawn up in lines and squares, but magazine rifles and entrenched positions had rendered it as obsolete as the armoured Knight

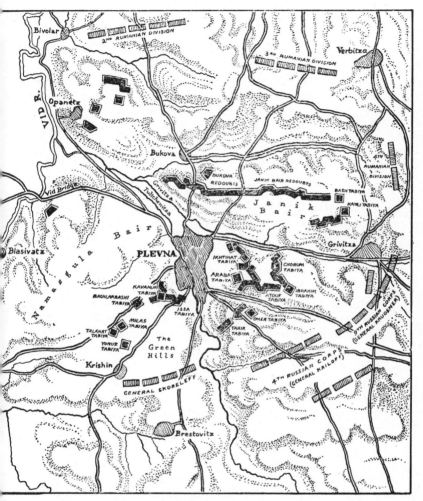

PLEVNA, 11 September, 1877
The Great Assault

at Agincourt. The Russian High Command had learned
nothing from the failure in July, and they knew nothing of
what had been learned in the American Civil War where
the combination of rapid fire and earthworks had proved its
impregnability. Determined to belittle their adversary, the

Russian generals ignored the already proven fact that the Turks were masters of applying field fortifications to battle tactics, and that the Turk by nature was superbly adapted to bulldog defence.

The three Russian assaults, planned to operate simultaneously, were as follows: on the north-east, the Grivitza redoubts would be attacked by the Rumanians from the North and from the south-east by half General Krudener's IX Army Corps, based on the village of Grivitza. On the south-eastern sector, based on Radishevo, General Kriloff's IV Army Corps would attack the middle group of redoubts (the Tahir Tabiya, the Omer Tabiya, and others of that group). From the south, based on Brestovitz, under the nominal command of Prince Imeretinsky, General Skobeleff would assault the 'Krishnin' and 'Plevna' redoubts (according to the Turks the 'Yunuz Tabiya', 'Talaat Tabiya', 'Milas Tabiya', 'Baghlarbashi Tabiya', and the 'Kavanlik Tabiya'), which guarded the three roads to Plevna from the south and south-west (the 'Lovtcha road', the 'Krishnin road', and the 'Tepina' road). The 2nd Rumanian Division and five forces of cavalry were stationed round the north and west of Plevna.

The Grand Assault was timed to start at 3 p.m. and the guns were ordered to fire intermittently all morning to keep the Turks guessing. They were to start firing again at 2.30 p.m. to mask the assault.

Forbes we shall find in his old position on the Radishevo ridge from where he had watched Prince Shakofsky's failure in July. MacGahan, as usual, would be with his friend Skobeleff but, as it turned out, he was in a better position than Forbes to see General Kriloff's attack on the centre. Neither witnessed the Rumanian-Russian attacks on the Grivitza redoubts.

The combined Rumanian-Russian attack on the two Grivitza redoubts suffered from the fatal defect of divided command, and the final meeting of the Rumanians and Russians in Grivitza I was more by accident than design. When the 3rd Rumanian Division moved up to assault Grivitza I at 3 p.m. they were quite unaware that Grivitza II lay behind it, and enfilading it, for the contours of the ground

hid it from their view, and no one on the Russian headquarters staff had realized that the Division, which had
recently come up, would be ignorant of that all important
fact. The two Grivitza redoubts were so placed that to take
one would be useless without taking the other; and the
original plan called for a simultaneous Rumanian assault
on one and a Russian assault on the other. When the
Rumanians, who showed great bravery in their baptism of
fire as a nation, reached Grivitza I, the Russians of General
Krudener, who again proved himself slow getting off
the mark, had not set out to attack Grivitza II, and the
Rumanians were thrown back. By 5.30 p.m. the Russian 5th
Division had passed Grivitza I, and, on being repulsed,
attacked Grivitza I in the rear as the Rumanians came up
again in front. The redoubt was in their undisputed possession by 7 p.m. having cost the Rumanians 58 officers and
2,511 men, and the Russians 19 officers and 1,019 men.
To the Turks the loss of the redoubt was of minor importance
as long as the redoubt behind remained in their hands,
and no attempt was made to retake it. Some time before
the redoubt was taken, Osman Pasha, heavily engaged on
the south by Skobeleff, had transferred two battalions
from the Janik Bair to the south.

After an early breakfast Forbes and Villiers took up their
positions on their old 'grandstand' on the Radishevo ridge
where they were joined by Colonel Wellesley, the British
Military Attaché, and General Grant, an American reporting
for *The Times*. Beside them, the Russian siege-gun battery
threw an occasional shell, which went over with the sound
of a railway train, into the Turkish positions, almost invisible
in the teeming rain, and the desultory firing continued until
about 10 a.m. when a total silence fell on the battle-front,
the calm before the storm thought Forbes. So unnatural was
the silence after the thunder of the last four days that everyone spoke in whispers, and then the fog came down again
veiling friend and foe alike from their gaze. It was impossible
to see twenty yards. From the valleys to the south a roll of
hidden rifle fire rings out. Skobeleff must be at work but
they can see nothing, hardly each other as they lie on the

crest of the ridge. The rifle fire swells in volume: to the anxious listeners it is a mysterious, weird situation, intensely torturing to hear but not to see the battle. Forbes complains to Villiers that the battle for Plevna will be fought in a fog as thick as that of Inkermann, and they will see nothing. Suddenly the air above them is torn by the whistle of bullets and the scream of shells as the Turks, feeling themselves assailed by invisible foes, fire aimlessly into the fog in which they fear an attack may be developing, where they do not know. As the thick waves of fog swathe the landscape in a dingy pall, Forbes and Villiers chafe for the merest glimpse of action and the Russian artillery general beside them is almost mad with irritation at his inability to see anything.

At 11 a.m. the fog lifts as dramatically as it fell, and although the rain continues, the whole battlefield is laid bare to their gaze. On a vast semi-circle the roll of Russian fire swells up but as yet no assault has developed. Colonel Wellesley and the newspaper correspondents retire to the shelter of a mulberry tree and Forbes improvises an awning with his overcoat to keep the rain from his note book. Below and in front of them the Ughtz and Jaroslav regiments, under the command of General Schnitnikoff, mistaking the fire of Skobeleff's men for the start of the assault, leap up with a cheer and charge forward up the slippery slopes. For a time the Turks hold their fire, but then flaming volley after flaming volley lashes out at the Russians. For five minutes the fight hangs in the balance. Then, tortured by fire, the Russians fall back, slowly at first and presently at a run, pursued by the volleys of the jubilant defenders. Though deprived of half his force by this unfortunate mistake, General Schnitnikoff, with General Kriloff's agreement, decides to adhere to the original plan and advance at the appointed time with the Kazan and Shirja regiments, holding the Kostaff and Woronesh regiments in reserve.

When General Kriloff's assault was launched at 3 p.m. MacGahan, who had stationed himself on the ridge more to the westward than Forbes, was in a better position to see it.

"It has been said," writes MacGahan "that nobody ever saw a battle. The soldier is much too excited with the passions of the fight as well as enveloped in smoke to see far around him. The General is too far away from the actual conflict, too much busied with the news arriving from different parts of the field, and with giving orders, to see the battle, although he knows it better than anyone. It is only the correspondent who is daring enough to take and hold a good position who really sees a battle." On that terrible September morning before Plevna, MacGahan enveloped in dense fog, thought that here was a battle he would not see, but as the fog cleared he was able to watch, through the thunder of the artillery and the crash of musketry, the assaults of General Kriloff on his right and of Skobeleff on his left.

General Kriloff's attack developed first.

On the ridge above and behind him, MacGahan could see the Russian gunners, appearing like giants, magnified by the fog, and the guns themselves enlarged and distorted and looking like uncouth monsters, vomiting forth globes of flame, red and lurid, as they poured their shells into the Turkish defences. "The uproar of battle," says MacGahan, "rose and swelled until it became fearful to hear—like the continuous roar of an angry sea beating on a rock-bound coast, combined with that of a thunderstorm, and with the strange unearthly sounds heard on board a ship when labouring in a gale." For two hours the terrible storm of battle continued without ceasing. Under cover of the artillery fire, the Russian columns cautiously advance to get into position for their final rush. Suddenly a mass of Russians rise up and push forward with a shout, and as it dies away, a stream of fire flashes, swaying backward and forward, along the parapet of the redoubt over which the smoke rises in a heavy white cloud. One continuous crash fills the air with bullets from which, to MacGahan, it did not seem possible that even a rabbit could escape.

"Into this storm of bullets," MacGahan telegraphed next day, "plunged the Russians with a shout as though of joy." They disappeared into a hollow and for a moment were lost to his view. Then they emerged again, disappeared into the low ground at the foot of the glacis, and rushed onwards as though the bullets were but paper pellets; but alas! sadly diminished in number. "Would it be possible for them to reach the parapet?" MacGahan asked himself, "Was it possible for flesh and blood to break that circle of fire?" "To me," he says, "it seemed utterly out of the question. Did but one bullet in ten find its billet, not one of those gallant fellows would return through that cornfield. While waiting to see them emerge from this little hollow, my excitement was so great, my hand trembled so that I could not hold the field-glasses to my eyes, and for a moment I was obliged to trust to my naked vision." As they emerged near the redoubt "a rush might do it", MacGahan told himself. Victory was within grasp, but they needed help, a fresh impetus to carry them over the parapet. MacGahan looked to see if reinforcements were coming up, but there were none. The general was doing nothing to help the gallant fellows struggling against that circle of fire.

On the ridge stand Generals Kriloff and Zotoff: breathless officers come riding up, all with bad news. The generals peer forward, holding lorgnettes to their eyes, as their gallant men rush into that throbbing furnace. "This is nothing to Sebastopol," they exclaim.

As MacGahan looked in vain for reinforcements, his heart sank beneath him for he saw that all this bravery, all this loss of life, would be useless. When victory was trembling in the balance, and these men were throwing away their lives madly fighting in desperate struggle, not a man was sent to help them. "They were left to die," says MacGahan, "overwhelmed, broken, vanquished. It was sublime, and it was pitiful. I see a few of them struggle up the glacis, one by one. They drop, and they come back, a confused mass of human beings rushing madly across the cornfield, less than half of those who went forward." As this disorderly remnant comes streaming back, their general sends two more battalions to rally them and carry them back to the assault. 'Two more battalions,' thinks MacGahan, 'they might as well have sent a corporal and two more men.' Two more regiments were required to carry that hesitating mass into the redoubt. "Instead of this," declares MacGahan, "General

Kriloff sent two battalions, and that was when it was too late. The poor fellows went over the hill singing gaily, and disappeared into the fog and smoke. I could have cried for pity for I knew that most of them went uselessly to simple slaughter. Those two battalions, like the rest, were doomed to almost certain destruction."

MacGahan, one of the most humane of men, could watch no more. The second attack was repulsed more easily than the first. Failure was inevitable and he foresaw it from the first: too few men were sent to assault entrenched positions, defended by magazine rifles. Pursued by flaming volleys, the Russians were thrown back, and by dusk the Russian defeat was complete. A hundred and ten officers and 5,200 men were killed in the two assaults from Radishevo, MacGahan heard later.

With the failure of the Russian assault from Radishevo, MacGahan turned his eyes on the attack from the south, commanded by Generals Imeretinsky and Skobeleff where, as MacGahan saw, the assault was being conducted in a very different manner.

While Skobeleff had been moving men on to the knoll he had taken on the 9th for assault on the redoubts and trenches system around Krishnin, the Turks had launched three counter-attacks which had been repulsed by Skobeleff's manner of defence. He ordered his troops to reserve their fire until the Turks came within a hundred yards, then to open upon them a sudden and withering fusillade against which no troops could stand.

It was four o'clock, and, at the moment of Kriloff's second repulse, Skobeleff had not yet made his assault. Now, with his men far forward, Skobeleff, risking his artillery, brought up his guns to no more than 1,000 yards from the Turkish redoubts, to make a desperate effort to capture the three 'Krishnin' redoubts in front of him, one a double redoubt in the bend of the Lovtcha road (the Turkish redoubts Yunuz Tabiya, Talahat Tabiya, Milas Tabiya). His force consisted of four regiments of the line, and four battalions of sharpshooters, 12,000 men in all.

Under the umbrella of the murderous fire of his advance

batteries, Skobeleff formed two regiments in the little hollow at the foot of the low hill on which was built the double redoubt he sought to take. Then he placed himself in a position where he could feel the pulse of the battle, and ordered the advance, the two regiments marching forward with their rifles on their shoulders, with music playing and banners flying. Soon the advancing column could only be seen indistinctly, a dark mass in the fog and smoke. Feeling, as it were, every throb of battle, Skobeleff sees the line waver and hesitate, instantly throwing in another regiment in support. Borne forward by this fresh impetus the momentum carries the mass nearer, but the Turkish redoubt, flame and smoke pouring forth, sends such a torrent of bullets that again the line is shaken. Skobeleff himself sits on his white horse in a hail of fire untouched, but all his escort are struck.

Skobeleff sees the line waver. Riding over to a regiment fresh on the field and waiting for orders, he calls to them, "Well, my men, go and finish the work. All Russia is watching us. A regiment has retreated from the redoubts. You are not of that sort, are you? You are picked men. What handsome fellows you are! Where are you from?" he asks a snub-nosed yokel. "From the Vitibsk Government, your Excellency." "Why, the very sight of you alone is enough to make the Turks run." "It is your Excellency." "Now, look out. Don't let me see you without the St. George on the day after tomorrow. Do you hear? Use your eyes, men: don't shoot blindly. March straight up to the redoubt without wasting powder. These fellows must be got at with the bayonet. Do you hear? And you, old Knight, are you from Sebastopol?" he said, turning to another. "What did you get the St. George for?"

"I got it at the Malakoff, your Excellency." Skobeleff took off his cap to him. "Then show these young fellows how a Russian soldier fights and dies. Captain, present this old man to me after the battle if he is still alive: I will recommend him for a commission." And then to the regiment he called, "Ah, my fine fellows, you have smelt fire already: you know how to fight. Good-bye, comrades, we shall meet at the redoubt."

Skobeleff has thrown in his last regiment. He watches the dark mass of men climbing the rising ground towards the redoubts, picking up stragglers as they go. The men run fast and the distance to the yellow earthworks decreases. As they scale the hill a cheer resounds, followed by a roll of drums. The men are straggling now and dropping in hundreds. Clouds of smoke cover the redoubt and the hill seems to tremble and rumble with the uproar. Volley after volley is poured into the advancing men. An officer on horseback gallops to the top of the hill: rider and horse roll back down the slope. The dark figures reach the scarp and swarm up the ramparts. Flaming volley follows flaming volley. Bayonets bristle. To the soldiers the redoubt seems like a live monster vomiting fire and baring its fangs. The wave of men is broken; it starts to recede and the hill is covered with flying figures and black with bodies.

To Skobeleff it was the moment of crisis. Not a moment must be lost if the redoubt is to be taken. He has only two battalions of sharpshooters left. Putting himself at their head, he gallops forward calling to MacGahan as he flashes by, "Good-bye, MacGahan. Wish me luck, old friend," and MacGahan hears him shout to his men, "Follow me, I will show you how to thrash the Turks," and his voice is drowned by the roll of drums as the men rush forward, their hard faces lit with rage, their teeth clenched.

MacGahan sees the men ascend the slope. In front rides Skobeleff on his white horse, conspicuous in his white uniform. He picked up the stragglers: he reached the wavering, fluctuating mass, and gave it the inspiration of his own courage. He picked the whole mass up and carried it forward with a rush and a cheer. The whole redoubt was a mass of flame and smoke, from which screams, shouts, and cries of agony and defiance arose, with the deep-mouthed bellowing of the cannon, and above all the steady, awful crash of that deadly rifle-fire. Skobeleff's sword was cut in two in the middle. Then a moment later, when just on the point of leaping the ditch, horse and man rolled together on the ground, the horse dead or wounded, the rider untouched. Skobeleff sprang to his feet with a shout, then with a savage yell the whole mass of men streamed over the ditch, over the scarp and counter-scarp, over the parapet, and swept into the redoubt like a hurricane. Their bayonets made short work of the Turks still remaining. Then a joyous cheer told that the redoubt was captured, and that at last one of the defences of Plevna was in the hands of the Russians.

MacGahan could see the charge only at a distance. One of Skobeleff's officers, Captain Nemirovitch-Dantchenko, as he followed the general, saw the Turks pouring out of their redoubt, and running down the scarp littered with the remnants of the previous attack. "Comrades, see what they are doing to our men," shouts Skobeleff. A groan passes through the advancing ranks. "See how those brutes are torturing our wounded," he cries, and the men redouble the energy of their charge. The Turks stoop down to the wounded Russians and the cold air is pierced with screams. Some of the wounded try to escape: their tormentors allow them to crawl or stagger away until they are overpowered by loss of blood and fatigue: the Turks overtake them: one wounded man rises to his knees and fires at an approaching tormentor. The Turk leaps aside and throws himself on the Russian, and a fearful scream is wafted back to his hurrying comrades. "Forward," cries Skobeleff, "Charge these brutes. Let us save those who have been spared and punish the infamous."

The hill trembles under the sound of the maddening fire. The distant ramparts seem to be falling to pieces; the sound like shattering granite. The fog of smoke hides the redoubt from view; it can no longer be seen, only heard. In the soldiers' imagination it was as though evil spirits had torn themselves loose from the chains of hell and were revelling in the depths of fog; it was as though the Prince of Darkness himself was holding holiday amidst the rage and tumult of the storm: as though the planets had dashed together, and had fallen in a thousand pieces. In the din mingled the crash of rifle-fire and the clash of steel. Clouds of bullets and bunches of grape-shot pour into the advancing Russian lines. Grenades hit the ground and burst into splinters; above their heads, shrapnel explodes with a sound like the snapping of gigantic cords by invisible hands. Men lie dying in pools of blood, the screams of their death agonies drowned by the roar of the tempest of fire. Into the whirlwind rode Skobeleff, his nostrils dilated, his eyes on fire. "Follow me, my lads," he shouts, and from the fierce, maddened throats rise a cheer that for a moment drowns the turmoil of the guns. "Remember your tortured comrades," Skobeleff shouts back and his words fall like a spark on gunpowder and the men fly on. On the ground a wounded man, green in face, shot in the chest, cries "Hurrah", and spits blood as his comrades pass him. "Get into the redoubt on your comrades shoulders," cries Skobeleff. Beside him a soldier brings the butt end of his gun down on the head of a Turk, squashing his head like a melon.

Skobeleff's words are lost in the thunder of the volleys pouring from the redoubt. His men lose formation. Thousands have poured over the ridge, hundreds have fallen but thousands are rushing at the redoubt. Skobeleff rallies his men, like a huntsman calling his hounds, and they rush the yellow ramparts. "On, on, on," shout the men in the rear. Wounded men crawl forward on their hands and knees: the dying raise themselves and with their last breath cheer on their comrades. The soldiers' bayonets are red with blood; blood is on their hands; blood on their faces, blood is all over them. Friend can hardly distinguish foe. To the older men, visions of Balaclava and the Malakoff arise.

"Allah, Allah," resounds from the ramparts. An old Turk, in a green turban, leaps on to the parapet, and crying, "Allah", is bayonetted as Skobeleff's horse rolls over. In a moment, covered with mud, Skobeleff is up, leading the hand to hand encounter: a bayonet is thrust at his breast: the 'fine fellow with the turned-up nose' smashes his rifle on to the Turk's head, but the general is over the top, not even knowing to whom he owes his life, scarcely realizing the danger that had menaced him. The wild beast has awakened in the charging multitudes that followed him into the redoubt, and the wild beast shows no mercy. All the Turks that have not fled are slaughtered.

Skobeleff had done what MacGahan thought was beyond flesh and blood to do. He had broken the Turkish defence line and pushed a wedge into Plevna, but at what a sacrifice. In that short rush up the glacis he had lost 3,000 men, one-fourth of his whole force. Skobeleff, MacGahan knew, looked upon infantry attacks on such entrenched positions and against such fire-power as almost criminal. He had been ordered to make such an attack. He disapproved of it but he believed that if such an attack is to be made it must be carried out by a continuous rush in which wave follows wave, not, as was the practice of other Russian generals, to allow a wave to expend itself before sending the next wave in. Skobeleff's theory was that it is better that the loss be incurred and victory won, than to incur half the loss with certainty of defeat. MacGahan and Skobeleff in their long friendship, dating from the Russian campaign in Khiva, had spent many hours discussing the lessons of the American Civil War and Skobeleff had been impressed by MacGahan's account of how the American generals on both sides had always followed up the assaulting columns with fresh troops without waiting for the first column to be repulsed.

Skobeleff had the redoubt which commanded the Green Hills, the gateway to Plevna. Down below him, on the outskirts of the town, stood Drew Gay, the *Daily Telegraph* correspondent, who had got into Plevna just before the Russian assault, and he describes the flight of the Turks.

"The Bashi-Bazouks came fleeing down the side of the hill, the Russians running in amongst the trees and firing upon their retreating foes, knocking them over like pheasants fluttering out of a reserve. The road at the foot of the hill, crowded with hundreds of terrified irregulars, was thronged with women and children flying from the outrage and death which they believed awaited them: hundreds of men were trying to remove their household goods and their families, all struggling, shouting, crying, running to escape the foe who was now on the hillside: even some of the regular troops who had forsaken the redoubt got mingled with the terror-stricken mass, and were running, head down, rifle held very loosely ready to be thrown away at a moment's notice, anything to save dear life."

During the afternoon Charles Ryan who had been in the Grivitza redoubt all day, decided that he could be of more help on the south from where the roar of battle told him that something fearful was happening. As Ryan crossed the Lovtcha road, he saw the Turks fleeing from the redoubt Skobeleff had captured. One of the fugitives came running past him, and as he tried to climb a fence he was struck by a bullet and fell back with his back broken. Ryan tried to rally the fugitives, and two old Turkish civilians, who were standing by, called him a noble fellow. All round him troops were flying pell-mell into Plevna, and shells were exploding at the rate of twenty or thirty a minute. The roar of the artillery, the rattle of rifle-fire, the explosion of shells, the cheers of the Russians and the cries of the wounded sounded to him like the cries of hell. In the streets of Plevna there was a regular panic. Fugitives were running like sheep before a brush fire, and civilians old and young were crying: "The Russians are coming. The Russians are coming." Wounded men, old, bedridden, half-naked women, and screaming children were all crowded together, watched by surly Bulgarians who thought at last the hour of their deliverance had come.

As he hurried in the direction of the Krishnin redoubts, Ryan came across three isolated rifle pits in which a dozen ancient Turks, civilians, armed with antiquated rifles, were busily firing upon the Russians. Showing nothing but a pair of gleaming eyes and the long brown barrels of their rifles above the level of the ground, they were knocking over their men at long range. As Ryan reined-to, the old men cursed him and ordered him away, lest he should draw the Russian fire on them, and as he left they were still diligently potting the unconscious enemy.

CHAPTER ELEVEN

THE COUNTER-ATTACK

SKOBELEFF held the key to Plevna: could he turn the key in the lock and burst open the door? Could he keep the key in his possession? The double-redoubt he had taken was dominated by the great Krishnin redoubt on the left, and it was exposed to Turkish fire on the right. Its back, now Skobeleff's 'front', was solid rock, on which it was impossible to build a parapet. The position was untenable unless he could capture the other redoubts too. His battalions had shrivelled and shrunk and many of his officers were dead. While he sent urgent demands for help back to headquarters, Skobeleff exhorted his men with hopes of victory: help would soon come, he told them, Plevna would be taken, the decisive blow struck for their country. But the afternoon wore on and no reinforcements came.

In the captured redoubt the exhausted men stood or lay in pools of blood. Even the slow falling rain seemed saturated with blood. There was no room to move; the place was choked with corpses and slippery with blood; at the front and rear of the redoubt they lay in piles, and from each pile came groans and shrieks. Into one corner the Turks had fled like a herd of cattle, screaming for mercy as the Russians beat them down with the butt ends of their rifles. Those who cried for mercy had shown no mercy, and they were butchered where they stood. Now the victors sat silently viewing their handiwork. One young Russian, a novice in war, stood staring down at a gigantic Turk lying stretched out in a pool of blood, looking at him as if to ask: "Why have you and I, the one from the frozen north and the other from the warmth of the south, met here in a Bulgarian town to fight and kill?" But the Turk, lying with his arms spread out, and his eyes staring with lifeless rigidity, had no answer to the age-old question of the fighting man.

Skobeleff moved about the redoubt: "Thank you, my men, for your service," he said gently. "You have fought like eagles, like lions. I am proud of you. Are you tired?" "Yes, we are tired," they replied. "Then rest, you have done half your work: thank you, my men, once more. Look, the sun is coming through. Put the flags on the ramparts." A slight breeze began to blow and the flags, lighted by the sun, opened out and flapped in the wind.

"Major Gortaloff," Skobeleff called. "You will remain here in charge of the redoubt. Can I depend on you? You must remain in this position at any price." "Remain or die, your Excellency." "Give me your word that you will not leave the redoubt. This is the key to the enemy's position. Over there"—pointing in the direction of headquarters— "in the rear they do not see this yet. I am going to convince them. Give me your word that you will not leave the redoubt." Raising his hand as if pledging an oath, Gortaloff assured him, "I will not leave here alive." Skobeleff embraced him. "God help you. Remember there may be no reinforcements. Count only on yourselves. Farewell, my heroes."

As dusk fell, Skobeleff galloped away. On the crest of the hill, he turned to look back. On the redoubt the flags fluttered in the gathering gloom. "Consecrated to death," he muttered as he turned his horse's head and galloped off for help.

On the Green Hills, the battle raged. Everywhere else it was finished, the Russians defeated. The Czar sat in his eyrie staring out on the corpse-strewn slopes until 9 o'clock when he was persuaded to return to his headquarters where a conference had been called to decide whether to renew the assault next day, or to abandon it.

On the outskirts of Plevna, Osman Pasha stands scanning the Green Hills in front through his telescope. In the magnified circle of vision he can see the Russian eagle fluttering on the captured redoubt in ominous threat to Plevna; beside him waits an orderly; behind him stand thirty Circassian dispatch-riders on their wiry ponies; from a rough shed run three lines of wires, the telegraph station which keeps him

in touch with each sector of the defences. From the streets
of Plevna come marching the three battalions he has ordered
up from the north. Osman has no illusions: Skobeleff is
within his lines; from the captured 'Krishnin' redoubt he
can thrust on to the nearer 'Plevna' redoubts. If they fall,
Plevna falls. By the mercy of Allah, the Yunuz Tabiya
still holds; at all cost it must be held. "Shoot down any
man who tries to leave the ranks," Osman telegraphs to its
commander, before the wire is cut.

In the reinforcements from the north marches William
Herbert. For four days he has been under shell-fire in the
Grivitza redoubts. Now he and his men are thrown into
the Baghlarbashi redoubt on the south. In it the confusion
is terrible; six battalions are mixed together, an indescribable
medley of Turks, Circassians, Arabs, Syrians and Asiatic
mongrels, screaming and shouting in a babel of tongues.
As dusk falls, Circassian scouts come in to report that the
Russians are advancing through the vineyards. Crashing
volleys of fire flame across the hillside. In the back of the
redoubt the surgeons are trying to cope with hundreds of
wounded men. The mutilations of one, too ghastly for words,
make a German surgeon exclaim, "Such a sight one ought
to show to the Kings and Emperors." Water grows short
and the men lie on the earth lapping from the muddy-bloody
pools of rain. All night long the rain pours down. Frequent
roll-calls keep the men awake. To Herbert it seems ludicrous
to hear one young fellow singing sentimentally of the
nightingale's love for the rose, and of moonbeams kissing
open the lily's closed chalice amidst all the misery and
death.

The men have no food, no water and no hope of victory
and they are soaked to the skin. Out beyond hundreds are
dying, the wounded moaning mournfully. A party goes out
to fetch water from a brook: they meet a Russian party
similarly engaged. An armistice is arranged by signs and
both sides fill their casks. At midnight a huge flare-up
illuminates the battlefield; a store of forage has been set
alight by the Bulgarians to indicate a Turkish magazine
to the Russians. Dawn comes, grey and cold; the heavy rain,

which has been falling now for twenty-four hours, has turned the ground into a morass.

Dr. Ryan, who had taken refuge overnight in a hovel on the outskirts of the town, awakes at dawn: rifle bullets patter ceaselessly on the roofs of the houses, and as he looks out two shells explode in his garden. A bullet comes zinging through the door and buries itself in the wall above his head. In the square outside lie 1,500 wounded men. Setting his Circassian servant on the roof to watch for the Russians, he gets to work. A Turkish soldier crawls away from him, stopping every minute to rest and holding some object in his hand. He had been shot in the abdomen and two feet of the small intestine are hanging out. He refuses help and Ryan heard afterwards that he lived for fifteen days in that condition.

Osman Pasha spent the night, the fourth he had been without sleep, organizing the counter-attack. The first streaks of dawn reveal that the Russians have dug in all over the Green Hills. Thousands of the enemy are within his lines. Osman determines to carry the captured redoubt by direct assault, sending out two columns, one to attack the Russians in front, the other in the rear. It is a desperate hour and Osman sends in twenty battalions, all he has to spare, for he knows not whether the Russian assaults on the other sectors will be renewed. By 6 a.m. his troops are in motion. As they march past he cries out "The Prophet protect you", and he waves the stub of pencil he habitually carries behind his ear.

In the captured redoubts the Russians have spent a miserable night in the rain. On the exposed rear of the redoubt they have built a parapet of corpses. All night long volleys of Turkish fire have swept around them. Behind them the Yunuz Tabiya is still in Turkish hands, a standing threat to their security. On the second and third 'knolls' the Russian guns are battering the Turkish positions, and from the rear Skobeleff's officers have gathered a thousand men to protect the guns. Ammunition carts are brought up to the redoubt, but the differences in armaments amongst the various regiments causes difficulty, for some are equipped with the Krenck, others with the Berdan rifle, of different calibre. No ammunition has been brought for the Berdans and they cannot be fired until a Cossack sergeant and twenty men gallop up with a consignment of cartridges in their horses' nose-bags. Without help the Russians know their situation is untenable, and anxious glances are thrown in the direction of the Lovtcha road for the hoped for reinforcements.

Back at his headquarters in Brestovitz, Skobeleff has sent an urgent request to General Zotoff for help, to hold the position he had won and with which to assault the remaining Turkish works south of Plevna. At fearful cost he has driven a wedge into the Turkish defences; he has the key to Plevna; it is now or never, if there is not be a 'third Plevna' he urges. To Colonel Orloff who has come from headquarters to inform himself of the state of affairs, Skobeleff declares that without reinforcements he will be too weak to maintain his position. His plea made, Skobeleff lay down to catch a few hours of sleep. He is awakened at dawn; an aide-de-camp has ridden in from the Imperial headquarters. Tearing open the copy of the order addressed to Prince Imeretinsky, he reads, "By direction of the Commander-in-chief, I order you and General Skobeleff to entrench and maintain yourselves in the positions captured today. We cannot send reinforcements, because we have none," and it was signed: "Zotoff, Lieutenant General."

"We are quite deserted," groaned Skobeleff. "They will give us nobody and nothing to help us; and this when everything has been done." "There is nobody to send," replied the aide-de-camp. For thirty hours Skobeleff has been fighting. He has seen his finest regiments destroyed in front of his eyes, his best friends killed, the change of fortune from defeat to victory, and now from victory to defeat. The overwrought nerves of this man of iron snap, his face twitches and he breaks into tears. "Nothing?" he cries. "Not even a single brigade! Why we hold the key to Plevna. If we can establish ourselves, Osman is lost." "Not a single regiment can be spared, not a man can be sent," was all the aide-de-camp could say.

All morning the Turks attack. Slowly, gradually, the battalions creep up the steep slopes of the hill, coming under heavy fire from the Russians. Below, the roofs of Plevna are crowded with Turkish civilians anxiously watching the course of the battle. The Turks take the first entrenchment with a rush, an hour later the second trench and three-quarters of an hour later the next line. From his head-quarters on the south of Plevna, Osman can see that his men are ready to storm the Russian redoubt. As he watches, the bugles sound 'Storm' and 5,000 yelling men hurl themselves at the blazing parapets. Torn and shattered by the volleys of the defenders, the impetus of the charge expends itself and the Turks fall back, leaving 500 of their number dead on the ground. Impassively, Osman orders two fresh battalions forward.

Skobeleff has come to the redoubt: his chief of staff, Captain Kuropatkin who was to survive to become commander of the Russian armies in Manchuria in 1904, has been knocked unconscious by the explosion of a gun; another officer was blown to pieces. General Dobrovolsky commander of the Rifle regiments, has been killed. Verastchagrine, the brother of the great Russian artist, has been wounded. The redoubt is choked with dead and dying. "Help will soon arrive," Skobeleff tells his men, "Plevna will be taken," victory will crown their efforts. Before coming up to the redoubt, Skobeleff has again informed the commander-in-chief that his situation is desperate. Again he has pleaded for reinforcements. The battle elsewhere, he knows, is at a standstill: on his front only has an advantage been gained. He has appealed also to General Kriloff who, on his own authority, sends him the remnant of the Shouysky regiment—a thousand men. Now from headquarters comes Zotoff's final reply. "If you cannot hold the captured positions," Skobeleff reads, "you are to fall back. The attack is not to be continued and we are to fall back slowly."

Skobeleff calls his officers to him. "Gentlemen," he says, "we will retreat: we will return the Turks what we have taken. Today is a day of triumph for our enemies: it is also a glorious day for us. We will not blush when we remember the 11th September." The Shouysky regiment will be brought up to cover the retreat, he tells them, meanwhile they must hold on. In a moment, his horse has leaped the parapet and he gallops back, a lone figure raked by Turkish fire, to bring up the supports.

In the great redoubt the last scene of the tragedy is enacted. Five times the Turks have sought to take it by storm; five times they have been thrown back with fearful loss but, with each assault repelled, the numbers of the defenders are less. Two of the Russian guns have been knocked out; two others are without gunners or teams. Fresh guns have been sent up but one of their ammunition wagons has been blown up by a shell, killing and wounding many including Major-General Trebjanik. Water parties sent to the brook have been shot down, fiendish shouts of Turkish glee greeting the fall of each man. The Turks mass front and rear. Knowing that this will be the final rush, the defenders prepare to die with honour and sell their lives as dearly as they can.

At 4.30 p.m. the Turkish bugles sound the 'Advance'. Five thousand Turks, crying "Allah, Allah", come sweeping towards the redoubt: the Russians are too few to hold them back by rifle-fire alone: from front and rear they come pouring in, fighting hand to hand with the defenders, dying only to be replaced by fresh hordes who in turn have others waiting to take their place. Enemies, throwing away rifles and bayonets in the crush, strangle each other, gouge each other's eyes out and tear each other's mouths. A dying Russian fallen with his foe, fastens his teeth in his flesh and can only be made to let go by a rifle butt brought crashing down on his skull. An officer fences with five Turkish soldiers, each stabbing him with his bayonet. The 'snub-nosed yokel', his face cut to ribbons and blinded with blood, stands swinging his rifle butt with deadly effect. The old soldier who earned the St. George at the Malakoff lies dying, around him four dead Turks. In the centre of the redoubt stands Major Gortaloff with his arms crossed, the ship's captain awaiting the death he has promised to accept rather than retreat. About him hundreds of Russians and Turks die together, their blood mingling to enrich the soil for future generations of peaceful farmers.

A young officer, Lieutenant Karaboff, comes to Gortaloff and shouts above the din, "Listen, Major, where are those shots coming from? Look, it's Skobeleff clearing the way for our escape." On one side the Turks have fallen back, the way is open; under the raking fire of the Shouysky regiment, the Turkish attack is faltering. Gortaloff gathers the few hundreds of men about him. "Comrades," he orders, "make a way for yourselves with your bayonets. The redoubt can be held no longer. Captain Abayeef, you will lead them. God bless you, my children. Farewell." Baring his head, Gortaloff makes the sign of the cross over his men. "And now, in God's name, go," he commands. "And you?" they ask. "I, I will remain with these," pointing to the dead and dying. "Tell the general I have kept my word. I have not left the redoubt. Tell him I am here, dead."

As they climb out of the redoubt the soldiers turn. Gortaloff stands alone. For a moment the soldiers pause; they raise their hands in farewell and, carrying their colours, they stumble down the slope. Alone Gortaloff faces the storm, his arms folded on his breast. As his men glance back they see a crowd of Turks leaping around him: he is lifted on their bayonets; he struggles on the cold, sharp steel and disappears beneath a dark wave of men.

From the redoubt rises the triumph of the victors and the groans and shrieks of the wounded: in a moment the banner of the Crescent waves again where for a moment of time the Russian eagle had looked down into the streets of Plevna. The Turks have proved their courage in attack as they have already shown it in defence. In the redoubt the triumphant victors sing and shout and dance like maniacs. Everywhere the Russians are in retreat. The Great Assault has failed. To the redoubt comes Osman. Assailed from three sides he has refused to be beaten: it is his hour of triumph. He staked his last man against Skobeleff and he has won. As they see him enter, his men kneel to give thanks to the Prophet for their deliverance. "Allah is merciful," declares Osman, and he orders the end of the slaughter.

The Russian survivors are pursued by a hail of fire but they cannot hurry for they are encumbered by wounded men, carried on crossed rifles or painfully dragging themselves along. When they hear the screams of those left in the redoubt they are tempted to turn back to avenge them, but they are too few.

The Shouysky regiment stands firmly covering the retreat as the remnant of those who had gone out so strong come marching back, their heads erect. Eagerly Skobeleff counts their ranks and as the dark mass comes nearer he sees that it is terribly small; behind them as they march on, the wounded left on the hillside turn their faces to the ground so as not to see the fate that awaits them when their comrades are gone.

"How few, how few," exclaims Skobeleff. "What a dreadful day. But see how they retreat. No confusion. No disorder. These are men." To a staff officer he calls, "Send me a Cossack." A dried-up Cossack on a dried-up horse rides up. "Do you know where General Kriloff is stationed? I think I have sent you there before. You will go there immediately. Tell him we have been beaten out of the redoubt. We are retreating in order covered by his Shouysky Regiment, and thank him for me." "If General Kriloff had obeyed orders," Skobeleff tells the survivors from the redoubt "and refused to send any assistance, none of you would have escaped alive."

The battle is over; the night is silent; on those terrible slopes in front of Plevna, lie fifteen thousand Russian and Rumanian dead. There is blood on the fields of Plevna and the ravens, screaming joyously, are unbidden guests of the feast of blood. From afar comes the distant howling of wolves, a foretaste of the winter which will soon close down upon besiegers and besieged.

That night MacGahan met Skobeleff in a fearful state of excitement and fury. His uniform was covered with mud and filth; his Cross of St. George twisted round his neck; his face black with powder and smoke; his eyes haggard and bloodshot, his voice gone. He spoke in a hoarse whisper of the battle he had won and lost. An hour later, MacGahan found him in his tent, quite calm and collected: "I have done my best," he said, "I could do no more. My detachment is destroyed: my regiments no longer exist: I have no officers left: they sent me no reinforcements and I have lost three guns." "Why did they refuse you help?" MacGahan asked, "Who was to blame?" "I blame nobody," replies Skobeleff. "It is the will of God."

Skobeleff lay down to sleep, but not to sleep. As he gazed into the dying embers of the fire, the recollections of that day surged before him. Why had he not been killed? Why was he left to bury his finest regiments and mourn his friends? How his men had fought, and for what? They had gone to their deaths because of their faith in him; because he had ordered them to go. Was their death due to some mistake of his? Bitterly he cursed those for whom the sacrifices had been made in vain, for the bloodshed which would have been compensated by the crown of victory, so nearly won, which could have been won. What purpose had the deaths of these men served? To prove over again that thousands of men, however gallant, cannot be thrown against earthworks defended by magazine rifles.

CHAPTER TWELVE

INQUEST OF DEATH

THE Great Assault on Plevna has failed. In two days the Russians and Rumanians had lost 300 officers and 15,000 men, some 20 per cent of those actually engaged. One hundred and twenty-six officers and 5,332 men had died, or been seriously wounded, in the capture and defence of the Green Hills, Skobeleff's sector. Shocked by the slaughter and despairing of success, the Czar has ordered that the assault be abandoned and Plevna be starved into submission.

Forbes left the scene of carnage to wire from Bucharest the results of the two days' fighting which he found himself, with the din of battle ringing through his ears, unable to estimate dispassionately. Another newspaper correspondent, Boyle of the *Standard* had left before him, to telegraph, after Skobeleff's success at the Krishnin redoubt, that Plevna was doomed and victory was in sight, to find that, while he galloped along with his apparent scoop, the situation had turned topsy-turvy. Forbes, more experienced and knowledgeable, told his readers that the Russian-Rumanian army "has abandoned now even the pretence of prosecuting the attempt against Plevna". He expressed great doubts whether another attempt would be made to take Plevna by storm, and even stronger doubts whether such an attempt, if made, could be successful. "The truth is," he declared, "the Turks are better soldiers individually than the Russians and of that, after seeing not a few battles, I stand assured." The strategy of both, he said, was equally bad, but in both major and minor tactics the Turks are immensely superior. They are better armed than the Russians, and are flushed with success, the Russians depressed by failure after failure. Forbes gave his opinion that "there is no braver man alive than the Russian soldier", but a brave soldier cannot continually face more than the fair chances of war. The Russian soldier knows, said Forbes, that if he is but struck in the ankle by a bullet, when he is in the front of an unsuccessful attack, the chances are even that he will die a death of torture, humiliation and mutilation, and this must lead to some hesitation in attack. More than once he had noticed, he says, a wavering in the advance.

MacGahan, a thoughtful observer of warfare and long experienced in Russian methods and psychology, declared that the lesson to be learned from the Russian reverses at Plevna was the madness of assaulting trenches defended by breech-loaders. There were other lessons to be learned too. Artillery fire, to be effective against such positions, should be directed, not against heaps of earth, but against the men behind them. The Russian artillery bombardment did the Turks little harm. The destruction of earthern parapets was easily repaired, because the Russians failed to bring up their infantry and field-guns to prevent by their fire the Turks executing such work.

The reserves that should have been available to support Skobeleff's success on the Green Hills were frittered away elsewhere. Skobeleff had won a foothold on the perimeter of the Turkish defences. Without support his position was untenable. Who was responsible for the blunder that led to the loss of the position which had been so gallantly won? MacGahan says, "The melancholy part of it is, that the Generals who send men by thousands to perish under fire, themselves have no idea of what fire is. They have no grip of the battle, no feel of fire, and they have no way of discovering that a position is untenable, or a line of resistance too strong, except in seeing their soldiers in flight, after having performed prodigies of heroism and valour." When Skobeleff sent his urgent requests for help, he was told to wait a few hours while the headquarters staff deliberated the situation. An hour after the redoubt was lost, a regiment arrived to help Skobeleff hold it. In the twenty-four hours it was held by the Russians, its defence cost 4,000 men. To push home the advantage won, a division, not a regiment, was required.

The whole Russian plan of attack on Plevna was mis-
conceived. But, having been begun, the assault should have
been continued on the second day. The defence line had been
broken. In MacGahan's opinion, if the Russians had concentrated their strength at the Grivitza redoubt taken by
the Rumanians, or on the Green Hills, captured by Skobeleff,
they would have carried Plevna. Their loss would have been
fearful, but the way would have been open to the Bosporus.
As it was 15,000 lives had been thrown away and the
Russians were no nearer their objective.

In MacGahan's view, the 65,000 bayonets hurriedly
assembled for the great assault were not enough to do the
job: that number of actual fighting men were insufficient
to give the Russians any marked superiority over the Turks.
But numerical superiority was not vital. MacGahan says,
"An inferior force, skilfully handled, will often suffice to
beat a much superior force, and the Russians who had, when
we consider the advantages of the position held by the Turks,
an inferior force or power, should have endeavoured to make
up for this by concentration against one or two points,
making only demonstrations elsewhere at the same time.
This would have given them the required numerical
superiority on all given points." The Russians had launched
three separate assaults, when two were all they could manage.
They had dissipated their strength by a futile attack on the
south-east, and the two army-corps of Generals Krudener
and Kriloff should have been kept as a reserve to support
the two other assaults.

Success could have been achieved in one of two ways.
In the first, 120,000 actual fighting men should have been
hurled against the Turkish positions, brigade after brigade,
in the manner of Skobeleff, until by mere force of momentum,
they sweep everything before them like the waves of a
rapidly rising sea. The loss would have been fearful, some
30,000 men, but Osman Pasha's army would have been
annihilated. The other method was to advance by flying
saps, narrow shelter trenches rapidly constructed under
cover of night, or heavy gun-fire.

MacGahan's comments fell on deaf ears. After an interval

of four centuries the power of defence in warfare had revived, and the magazine rifle, and its big sister the machine-gun, were to reign supreme for the next sixty years, until Hitler's panzers came rumbling down the roads of Northern France. The lesson established, as far as Europe was concerned, at Plevna was not learned. Even greater masses of cannon fodder were thrown at entrenched positions in the First

J. ANANIAN
Artist of *The Graphic*, with the Turks

World War and the casualties were on a scale undreamed of in the wildest nightmares of the besiegers of Plevna.

MacGahan accused the Russian generals of lack of talent and capacity. All those in command, he says, were very old men trained to conduct a war forty or fifty years before. Since then, while a revolution had taken place in warfare, they had learned nothing. Their whole lives, declared MacGahan, had been passed in one occupation: their whole minds, whatever they had, concentrated on one object, and that one of the most trivial to which the human mind can descend—card-playing. They have done nothing else, thought of nothing else, for years, he alleged. Their minds have rusted until they are dull, as heavy and as incapable of receiving new impressions, as the veriest clodhopper. Called, he said, from their card-tables by the trumpet of war, they rise, rub their eyes, look around them completely bewildered, and are as thoroughly out of the current of modern war as if they had been asleep for forty years. Not even Rip van Winkle, with his rusty gun dropping to pieces after his long sleep, was more bewildered and lost than the majority of these poor old generals suddenly thrown into the campaign at the heads of brigades, divisions and corps.

Why, MacGahan asked, does not the Emperor send these old dotards back to their card-tables, and replace them by younger men and men of talent, of which the Russian army was not destitute? There was a tradition in Russia, he said, according to which no functionary must be removed or disgraced as long as it could be helped, for some absurd idea that the prestige of the Government would suffer. The Government would be acknowledging its own fallibility! The result is that the Government, instead of renouncing, assumes the responsibility for all the stupidity, of all the idiocy, all the perversity, and all the dishonesty of the functionary. Then again the Emperor cannot bear the idea of depriving an old, and as he considers a faithful, public servant of his position, and thus disgracing him, and so unconsciously prefers to sacrifice the lives of thousands of brave soldiers to this misplaced feeling of kindness.

The Times correspondent said that at Plevna "a holocaust of mangled humanity was offered up to the inefficient helplessness of the General Staff Department of the Russian Army".

When Europe heard the news of the Russian disaster at Plevna, men could hardly believe that a handful of Turks had held the mighty hordes of Russia, the bogy-man of the period, at bay. Russia's enemies rejoiced and public sympathy, long repelled by the stories of the atrocities of the unspeakable Turk, switched to a glorification of the courage and valour of the bulldog Turk, and Osman 'Ghazi', Osman 'the Victorious', as the Sultan had named him, became the man of the hour. Innumerable dogs, not a few cats, the son of an English peer, and a new type of lavatory-pan were christened 'Osman'. Thus England gave her accolade to the Defender of Plevna.

When the Czar applied to the money-lenders of Europe for credits with which to prosecute the war, he found loans hard to raise for the rouble had lost a third of its value. The Russians were now faced with a winter campaign for which they were ill prepared.

In three months' campaigning the Russians had crossed the Danube, when the Turks were asleep, taken the fortress of Nikopoli, secured the Shipka Pass, at a cost of 50,000 men, a third of their original force, and they were still a long way from Constantinople. No move southward could be made until the menace of Plevna had been removed.

CHAPTER THIRTEEN

ESCAPE OF A CORRESPONDENT

WITH the battle for Plevna over, Drew Gay, the correspondent of the *Daily Telegraph*, the only newspaper man in Plevna, decided that he must try to get out before the town was completely surrounded by the Russians. He had a story to tell and it must be put on the wire from Sofia or Constantinople as soon as possible. When he informed Osman of his intention, the Turkish commander was dubious of his chances. The country round Plevna was infested with Russian Cossacks who would take no notice of Gay's credentials. He would be tortured, killed and horribly mutilated. Of thirty Circassian dispatch-riders Osman had dispatched to Sofia, two only had got through. It was impossible for a party of men to go through the Russian lines without being caught, Osman declared. Even if he succeeded, Osman warned Gay, he would only be out of the frying-pan into the fire for, failing the Cossacks, any Bashi-Bazouks he encountered would murder him for the sake of his horse and clothing.

It was a chilling prospect, but Drew Gay was nothing daunted. "Well, if you will go do so, but it is almost certain death," Osman told him. "But since you are determined to try I will take care that the Circassians do not kill you, for I will send a couple of Zapthiehs (mounted policemen) to guard you from your friends. If you are to be murdered, the Cossacks shall have the task, not our own rascals." Gay had already promised two Circassians a reward of two thousand piastres to conduct him through the Russian lines; and the reward was now split between them and the two Zapthiehs.

The party set out at 11 o'clock at night. With Gay was a German artist named Lauiri who had accompanied him from Constantinople, and both were disguised in Russian uniforms. A small crescent moon illuminated the scene as they crossed the battlefield of the previous few days. On one side was a Turkish redoubt filled with armed men standing at their embrasures with rifle in hand to shoot first and ask questions afterwards; on the hill opposite sparkled the camp-fires of the Russians. On the ground lay thousands of unburied dead, some thickly, others alone. Many of the Russian dead had been stripped by the Bashi-Bazouks, some

MR. JOURDAN
Daily Telegraph, with the Turks

of them, as Gay could see, were beardless boys with thin faces and fair hair. Others had crept into holes to shelter from the storm of fire; hundreds lay in the fosse of the redoubt; two lay athwart the branches of a tree. There is a great deal of glorious pomp in war, Gay thought to himself, a broad gold belt and a bright uniform are admirable aids to vanity in time of peace; but that glory is somewhat dimmed when the wearer is running between two lines of fire, unable to escape; when at length, shot down, he is dying on the cold ground under the feet of flying men and horses; when hope has gone, and help has fled and death approaches.

Slowly the little party picked their way over the corpse-strewn ground: first rode the two Circassians with their Winchester rifles charged with twelve cartridges; then the Albanian Turk, Gay and Lauiri, followed by a groom with a baggage horse and the Zapthiehs with a spare horse. A Turkish colonel carrying dispatches brought up the rear.

During the first hour all went well. Unchallenged by the Turkish outposts, they approached the Russian lines, one of the Circassians going in advance to see if the coast was clear. Ahead loomed a camp-fire and Gay discerned a number of men lying on the ground. Changing his cap and other parts of his dress to conform to that of the Cossacks, the Circassian rode up to the fire and engaged the Russians in conversation in their own language while the rest of the party slipped by unnoticed. Drew Gay was reminded of his childhood days, gloating over the adventures of Fenimore Cooper's heroes in the wild west, but the realities were far from being agreeable. At every step as they slowly advanced through the Russian lines, they seemed to be treading upon bayonets and sabres. It was by the merest accident that they avoided the dreaded Cossacks. Sometimes, the party had to halt for a quarter of an hour to allow a party of stragglers going from one part of the camp to the other, pass by without noticing them. Their guides led them by winding paths in the shadows of hills and trees, or through thick fields of maize, until a whispered 'Halt' made them cower, and wait in an agony of suspense as a party of Russians went by.

Moving on again, and rounding a hill, they came upon a number of small fires and one very large one which Gay took for the headquarters camp-fire of a large detachment. Their path carried them so near it that he could hear the voices of the men who sat round the blaze, and saw their faces distinctly. Next came an open space, brilliantly lit by moonlight. It had to be crossed. In whispers it was agreed that each member of the party should cross alone, an interval of time elapsing between each essay. All got safely across, but they were only just in time for, looking back, they saw a hundred or so Cossacks entering the clearing. While they passed, Gay and his companions crouched by their horses, their rifles in hand, hardly daring to breathe. In hoarse whispers they arranged to blaze away at a minute's notice if the Cossacks came in their direction, and then to make their escape in the confusion of the moment. As the last Cossack disappeared, some two hundred yards away, Gay's stallion neighed loudly. In a second it was seized by the Circassians and tied round the mouth, but Gay heard the Cossack horses neighing in reply. Would the Cossacks turn back to investigate? After a few anxious moments, without sound of pursuit, the party stole to the top of a hill from where the Cossacks could be seen going quietly on their way.

Onward the party stealthily crept, until the clanking of Gay's sword against a rock brought the cavalcade to a precipitous halt. All around burned the camp-fires of the Russians; at any moment they might be spotted and challenged, or greeted by a wave of fire. Ahead loomed a village. The Circassians dismounted and went ahead to reconnoitre. In a quarter of an hour they were back to say that although the village was clear, it must be skirted on account of the Bulgarian dogs which would be sure to bark if they scented the horsemen.

But the detour was of little avail; as they passed the village, the dogs set up a howl which made their blood stand still, and lights moved in the village. For half an hour the party lay hid in a ditch, until the dogs ceased barking and the lights ceased to move. As they moved on again, the dogs began anew, and, throwing discretion to the winds, Gay and his companions set spurs to their horses and galloped past, and the same process was repeated at the next village. Riding on they came to a path which was so narrow and overhung with interlacing branches, that they had to cut a way with their swords. The moon had now gone down and in the darkness the riders fell into a hole that yawned beneath them, but fortunately without damage to horse or man.

At last came the first streaks of grey, heralding the dawn. "Quickly, get along quickly," ordered the Circassian guide, and for an hour the party rode at breakneck speed until, as daylight came, they galloped into a little village and took shelter in the yard of a Bulgarian farm. Gay threw himself down on a stack of straw, hoping for a quarter of an hour's rest, but the guide urged them on, saying that the Cossacks were close at hand. Onward they rode, every man singly with the baggage animal in the charge of Gay's groom, and the spare horse with the Zapthieh in the rear.

CAMILLE BARRÈRE
Manchester Guardian and *Rep. Francaise,* with the Turks

To the left, Gay saw a dark body of men, not half a mile distant. Realizing the Cossacks, as they proved to be, had seen them, the escape party spurred on outdistancing the pursuers, but the baggage horse, which carried all Gay's clothes, and the spare animal, had to be abandoned, Gay hoping that it would become the property of some Russian general who would be put to shame, and perhaps in danger, by its vicious habit of throwing itself down and rolling over in the face of fire.

They soon lost sight of the pursuers, but they didn't slacken their pace until another village was reached where a hospitable Bulgarian gave them some bread and a little piece of meat. He shook hands with Gay five or six times, and wished him all kinds of success, as far as Gay could perceive, for neither could speak a word of the other's language.

Six hours' hard riding lay ahead if they were to reach

Orkhanie that night, and the Turkish colonel bore dispatches relating to reinforcements for Plevna and a telegram to dispatch to Constantinople. As they rode, Gay saw thousands of miserable refugees, helpless, starving, Turkish peasants, without homes and without hope, the objects of Christian hate and vengeance, toiling miserably along, they knew not where. At 11 o'clock at night, after twenty-nine hours of hard riding they reached Orkhanie, the Plevna supply point and half-way house to Sofia.

After three hours' sleep, Gay continued on to Sofia in an araba travelling all day, seeing the same awful spectacles of human misery, and long columns of troops, ammunition-wagons and supplies moving up to Orkhanie for the relief of Osman Pasha's beleaguered army. Arriving at Sofia, Gay urged the pasha in command to hurry the hoped for reinforcements and provisions to Plevna, but all he could get out of him was that 'Please God' he would.

Five days after leaving Plevna, Drew Gay reached Constantinople where he reported immediately to the Sultan. He was received at once, placed in a chair, given a cigarette, and asked innumerable questions about the gallant Turkish soldiers and their gallant leader. For hour after hour the Sultan plied him with questions about every engagement, the condition of the troops, their courage, their clothes, their position. Maps were produced and Gay showed the Sultan the course of each Russian assault, and how it was defeated. Abdul Hamid ascribed every Turkish success to the Almighty. He had, he said, told Lord Salisbury, when he came to Constantinople before the war started, that the Turks had reason and right to hope in the intervention of the Great Ruler of the World. Events had shown that he was not mistaken. God had helped the Turks to victory. It was midnight before Gay was allowed to go, and a few days later the Sultan pinned on his chest the silver medal of Plevna.

CHAPTER FOURTEEN

THE GRIP TIGHTENS

LITTLE Plevna had withstood three assaults, and the Russians were now hopelessly bogged down, their advance halted, their safety in jeopardy and their morale at a low ebb. From the English Press arose a chorus of exaltation at their discomfiture; the Colossus of the North had shown himself to have feet of clay. The fighting qualities of the Turk were extolled and the pro-Turkish English newspapers executed war dances in print. The Daily 'Turkophil' as the *Telegraph* was christened, was jubilant and the *Pall Mall Gazette* gloated over the humiliation of the English advocates of a religious crusade against the Turks, for having urged Russia to a Holy War, whereas now, it seemed that Providence was on the side of the Infidel. So great was public interest in the fate of Plevna that the *Daily News* during the week of the assault, brought out an extra 'War Edition' each evening, and maps of Bulgaria and plans of Plevna were on sale at every bookstall and news-stand. Returning war correspondents were booked for lectures up and down the country, and to have been at Plevna was a passport to fame. Strangers of military mien in railway carriages assured their spellbound listeners that they had been under Osman's command at Plevna, and the manager of the Canterbury Theatre of Varieties in London, who had staged a scene depicting 'The Gallant Defence of Plevna', was congratulated on his realism by eleven excited spectators, each of whom had been, they told him, the only Englishman in Plevna. When, eventually Dr. Charles Ryan visited the show, and told the same story, he was met with polite scepticism. At Madame Tussaud's, the wax figure of Osman Pasha was added to the Chamber of Historic Personages.

Throughout the Ottoman Empire the Moslems rejoiced

146

as they had not done since the capture of Constantinople four centuries before. Patriotic songs with the Victorious Osman for their hero and 'Plevna shall never fall' for their theme, were sung in cafés and in the streets and bazaars of a thousand towns by enthusiastic multitudes. People could talk of nothing but Osman and Plevna, and children played 'at Plevna' in the gutters. Mosques were thronged with worshippers praying for the gallant defenders, and the last reservists were called up for the war which seemed at last to be turning in Turkey's favour.

In Plevna, Osman or Osman 'Ghazi', the Victorious, as he was now created by the Sultan's command, knew that his task was done, his mission accomplished. He had drawn upon himself an army twice as numerous as his own, he had brought the Russian offensive to a standstill and he had forced them into a winter campaign. Knowing that he must eventually be starved into submission, he telegraphed the Sultan for permission to evacuate Plevna and withdraw southwards to Orkhanie where he could link up with the army of the south, and keep his own army, which had proved itself to be the best fighting force in the Turkish ranks, mobile. No further purpose could be served by holding Plevna, he declared. In reply, the Sultan informed him that Plevna had acquired too much prestige to be abandoned and the town must be held at all costs. A great army would be gathered, Osman was told, to come to his succour. Osman set about organizing a supply line to Sofia.

Meanwhile there was much to do in Plevna. In the first place, it was the month of the feast and fast of Ramadan: from the moment the dawn coloured the eastern sky until the Ramadan gun boomed out in the evening air not a morsel of food could pass the lips of the gallant defenders, nor a drop of water, nor could a cigarette be lit. As the wailing cry of the Muezzin rises each morning above the murmur of the camp, the soldiers hurry eagerly to prayer, and unhappy is the man on duty who cannot join the serried ranks of worshippers who, sometimes in battalion and some- times in companies, face towards Mecca and follow the orisons and genuflexions of the blue-robed, white-turbaned

Inaum who stands before them. Each man takes his place in the ranks, his hands hanging close by his sides. Then he lifts them to his ears, as if to shut out all worldly sounds. Then he lays them on his knees, and bowing his head forward seems lost in contemplation. After a few seconds he sinks to his knees, and leans back upon his heels, and then bowing with his forehead to the earth, chants "Allah Akhbar" (God is Great). Three times he bows and chants, and then standing up and bowing forward he chants three times, "Ia Allah il Allah" (there is no God but God). Each soldier is standing barefoot and has provided himself with some makeshift praying-carpet, as is demanded by religious custom. One man has brought a ragged sheepskin, another a goat hide, a third the saddle cloth of his horse, a fourth, his jacket, and seeing them gather at the place of prayer suggests to the observer so many persons eager to dispose of superfluous garments, and taking advantage of the fortuitous arrival of an old-clothes man.

Then, there was the question of the unburied dead, the thousands of corpses lying on the slopes and beneath the Turkish redoubts and trenches, now, several days after the battle, giving forth an all-pervading and terrible stench. Riding out on the hills, Dr. Ryan met Tewfik 'Pasha', as he had now been promoted, Osman's chief of staff who had led the counter-attack against Skobeleff, who told him that the Russians had sent in a *parlementaire* to invite the Turks to send an officer to discuss the matter. Tewfik asked Ryan to accompany him, and they rode through the lines with a small escort. About a mile and a half from Plevna they were met by two Russian officers who, after an elaborate exchange of courtesies, broached the question of the burial. Many hundreds of dead lay between the two Grivitza redoubts the one in the hands of the Turks, the other in possession of the Rumanians. The stench, the Russians pointed out, was a serious handicap to the defenders of both redoubts, and they politely offered to send a party to bury the bodies if the Turks would restrain from potting them as they performed their melancholy task.

But the matter was not so simple as it appeared, Ryan

found. It was with the most profound regret, Tewfik explained, that he was obliged to deny himself the pleasure
of accepting the generous offer of the Russians. Certainly
the odour of the ill-fated corpses, both of the Turks and of
their so gallant and courageous opponents, was decidedly
offensive, but he could not allow the Russians to incur the
whole of the annoyance which would attach to the burial
of so many patriots who had fallen on the field of honour.
Alternatively, he proposed that each side should bury the
corpses within ninety yards of their lines. Thus the labour
would be equally divided.

The real purpose of the Russians, Tewfik well knew, was
to advance 120 yards from their redoubt and, under the
pretext of burying the corpses, secure from the crest of the
slope an uninterrupted view of the Turkish defences. The
Russian officers found themselves unable to accept Tewfik's
generous proposal and the meeting broke up with nothing
arranged. As a result the Turks were forced to change the
garrison, numbering 4,000 men, of the redoubt every forty-
eight hours lest the men contract some sickness from the
decomposing corpses.

Food, in Plevna, though not yet scarce, was plain in
fare and Ryan found himself eyeing with envy, in the yard
of a Bulgarian neighbour, a fine flock of geese, but nothing
would persuade their owner to sell one. Sitting down that
night to a dish of boiled beans, Ryan happened to mention
the matter of the geese to his two Circassian servants and,
next morning, he was awakened by the hissing of geese
and, looking out, found a dozen fine birds in his yard. The
geese could not explain why they had preferred a change
of scene, and neither of Ryan's servants could give any
explanation of the phenomena, so Ryan ate them with
the aid of some of his brother surgeons, sending a couple
of Turkish liras to assuage the feelings of the owner who had
lost them. Ryan and his servants were luckier than some
other 'plunderers', for Lieutenant Herbert saw a Circassian
subjected to the dreaded bastinado for assaulting a Bulgarian
family whose house he had entered. Punishment was meted
out equally between Bulgarians and Turks and on one

occasion he saw a Bulgarian who had kicked a wounded Turk taken out and flogged with zest and zeal, a punishment which laid him up for a month.

Riding out on outpost duty one night, Lieutenant Herbert was warned by a sentry that he had heard strange noises and seen flashes of light some quarter of a mile away. He swore he had heard the braying of asses, which convinced Herbert that it must be a party of marauders for neither the Russians or Rumanians used donkeys. Moving forward to investigate he could see flashes of light about two hundred yards away. They were coming in his direction so he placed his men in ambush and waited. When the carts came up they jumped out on the party which consisted of ten men and three women of the most brutal and debased countenances Herbert had ever seen. In the carts were the spoils of the battlefield; bloodstained undergarments, many of fine quality taken from the bodies of officers, formed half the loot: in the pillagers' ragged and filthy clothes were rings, watches, chains, jewellery, money, pocket-books and personal documents. Most of the gang were gipsies; others were Rumanian Jews, Hungarians, one a Turk and another a Bulgarian. When they were told they would be hanged in the morning they howled, whined and screeched, the noise they made bringing to the scene a colonel who ordered that they should be strung up immediately.

About a week after the Great Assault, Herbert heard a curious rumour in the camp: England had declared war against Russia, and two British divisions were already on the road from Constantinople for the relief of Plevna. There was great excitement amongst the garrison before the Turks were undeceived.

The Russians, meanwhile, had withdrawn within their own lines spread around Plevna, and were awaiting the arrival of General Todleben, the famous defender of Sebastopol, who had been summoned from his retirement to conduct the siege of Plevna. Several other changes had been made in the Russian command. The army of the west which had twice failed to take Plevna by storm, remained under the nominal control of Prince Charles of Rumania, but General

Toldeben was nominated as his assistant and placed in command of all the troops assembled before Plevna. Prince Imeretinsky was made chief of staff, and General Zotoff returned to command the IV Corps. General Gourko who had arrived at Plevna with the Imperial Guard was appointed commander of the cavalry and General Kriloff of a cavalry group west of the Vid. Prince Shakofsky was removed from command and Skobeleff, now a lieutenant-general, was made general of a division.

MELTON PRIOR
Artist for *Illustrated News,* with the Turks

Back from Bucharest, where he had been to consult with Forbes as to the arrangements for reporting the coming investment of Plevna, MacGahan called in at the Imperial Headquarters at Gorni Studen to gather the opinions of his friends amongst the general staff as to the situation following upon the great reverse. He found the feeling there not as gloomy as he had expected. While the Russians acknowledged that they had been beaten, as much by their own errors as by the bravery of the Turks, there was no sign of hesitation or weakening of the determination to fight it out. The idea of peace was not entertained. Everyone to whom MacGahan spoke felt that they were engaged in a death

struggle in which either Turkey or Russia must go to the
ground irretrievably, and the final result was not doubted
for an instant. In the end Russia must crush her adversary
by brute force, if not by science, skill and generalship.
In more caustic comment of the present age it might be
said that the Russian High Command was prepared to
fight to the last moujik. Extensive preparations were being
made for a winter campaign, MacGahan learned. A military
railway was to be constructed to Simnitza and ice breakers
had been ordered to keep the Danube open.

Skobeleff, worn out by the assaults on the Krishnin
redoubts, went on leave to Bucharest, where he was joined
by Forbes on his way to England. Exhausted by his long
rides and the anxieties and strains of battle, Forbes did not
return to Bulgaria, leaving the reporting of the siege of
Plevna to his two younger colleagues, MacGahan and Frank
Millet.

Calling at Imperial Headquarters on his way, Forbes
joined a deputation of newspaper correspondents who had
been invited to discuss their difficulties and problems with
the Grand Duke, a man who, Forbes knew, was easily
embarrassed by reporters and who did not like having his
words taken down as he spoke. Going in to the Grand Duke's
house, Forbes found himself next to a reporter of a Scottish
newspaper whom he knew had never seen a shot fired in
anger, and he was disturbed to see the man produce a large
notebook and start writing in it as the Grand Duke opened
the conference. "Do put that away," Forbes urged the man.
"Can't you carry what you want in your head?" "I have
just thought," replied the hardy Scotsman, "that I paid
five francs yesterday for dinner which I didn't put down."
The chief subject of debate, Forbes learned, was the question
of Frederick Boyle, the correspondent of the *Standard* who
had been expelled for publishing information dealing with
troop movements which the Russians considered was a
breach of his undertaking not to write anything which might
assist the enemy. Boyle's infraction of the rule had, Forbes
knew, been committed in a letter, not a telegram, to his
paper, which meant that the Turks could not have read it

until the information was hopelessly stale, but, the Russians smarting under the castigations of Boyle's paper, refused to withdraw their order and he was forced to return to London.

How forceful, and repugnant to the Russians, were some of these newspaper comments is related by Colonel Wellesley, the British Military Attaché. Finding the long evenings after dinner dull, the Czar devised the idea of a nightly gathering of his staff and the various military attachés at headquarters, at which the Minister of the Household, Count Adlerberg, read out the reports of the newspapers of Europe on the failure of the Russians to take Plevna. When the Count came to the English newspapers Colonel Wellesley found his position most embarrassing. He quotes five extracts which were read from different newspapers:

"It is too late to flaunt the impudent and hypocritical pretext that the sufferings of Christians anywhere have alone moved Holy Russia to set half a million men in motion to a career of massacre, rapine and devastation. If the improvement of Christians in the abstract had been her aim, she should have commenced by ameliorating the lot of Poland."

"Why is all that awful carnage at Plevna being wrought in the presence of the Czar, the Grand Duke, and the Rumanian Prince? We are assured that these eminent personages were gathered together on the field of action on Friday last when the conflict began, and there was especially prepared for the Divine Figure from the North a platform, or royal box, from which to survey the opening strife, wherein two hundred thousand human beings were to mangle and slay each other to the utmost extent possible, in the name of religion and philanthrophy."

"The Czar and his Counsellors have waded so deep in the river of blood, that it is now more promising to push on through the crimson stream than to turn back for the forsaken shores of peace and justice."

"There is nothing more shocking in all the horrors of the 'Crusade' than that at the present moment fresh butcheries are being prepared—not to gain territory, for it is too late, nor to evangelize Bulgaria, for that pretence is exploded, but to soothe the august susceptibilities of the 'divine figure' and shed upon his return to the North even one solitary gleam of success from the fire of battle."

"Tuesday was the fête-day of the Czar, and no doubt, as a delicate compliment to his patron saint it was chosen by the Christian champion as the most fitting for the wholesale slaughter and maiming of thousands of human beings. There is every reason to believe that the carnage was all that the most pious person could have desired. We trust that Saint Alexander is gratified by his protégé's zeal."

As these extracts were read, angry faces were turned to Colonel Wellesley and the staff expressed their stupefaction at such audacity. What should they do to the representative of a country whose Press had been guilty of such sacrilege? they muttered. But the Czar, who, after the reading of the reports of each national newspaper, bowed to its military representative, made the same polite acknowledgement to Colonel Wellesley, which confirmed that gentleman's oft-stated opinion that Alexander II was the most liberal-minded sovereign ever to occupy the throne of Russia.

In Bucharest, the 'Paris of the East' as it was called, Skobeleff, the hero of Plevna, was the man of the hour. Every woman wanted to meet him, and those who were not favoured by his attentions contrived to hint that their assignations with him were far too romantic to be disclosed. Even to Skobeleff, by no means a man to shun the attentions of the ladies, the feminine assault front and rear became too much, and he was continually receiving *billets-doux* from the lionesses of Bucharest, appointing a rendezvous. On receiving these he would exclaim, "One must flee these ladies—yes these *ladies*. A soldier must avoid them, or else he may get attached to one, and there is not room in any man's heart for two mistresses. War and a family are incompatible."

From one young lady, Skobeleff received a letter in which she informed him of her intention of calling upon him the next day, to pay him a personal tribute of her admiration. He threw the letter on the fire and forgot about it. The next day, a very tiresome old general who would only talk about the campaigns he had been through, the most recent of which had been the Crimea, was calling on Skobeleff when a lady was announced. "Who is she?" Skobeleff inquired. On the card handed him by the footman was inscribed the name of the lady who had written to him the day before. As he gazed at the card an idea came to him whereby he might get rid of his tedious guest and the venturesome young lady at one and the same time.

Knowing the weakness of his guest, Skobeleff turned to him and said, "Help me out of a difficulty, your Excellency. A lady wants to see me and I have no time. Will you receive her for me? She has never seen me. Tell her what you like; say, for fun, that you are Skobeleff." Immensely pleased with the idea, the old general accepted the part with alacrity. "If you don't mind, I will assume your character," he replied as he hurried from the room.

The elderly general afterwards told Skobeleff the result of the adventure. "What a little fool," he exclaimed. "A conceited thing. I have seen prettier ones than that in Hungary in 'forty-eight. Who did she think herself? There was nothing very wonderful about her." "Well, what did she do?" asked Skobeleff. "She looked at me," the general told him, "burst out laughing and went off, muttering something in her own language, but I did not understand her. A magpie." It was a good thing he didn't understand her, Skobeleff came to the conclusion when he heard the story the young lady was spreading round the Rumanian capital. "You Russians have strange ideas of youth," she said to General Tcherkessoff who replied, "What makes you think so?" "Why," went on the young lady, "Skobeleff is a young general according to you. Well, I saw him. He is an old baboon, and a baboon too who has lost his hair. A strange youth. I should like to see whom you call old."

Skobeleff came to Bucharest to forget, if he could, the terrible days and the nights before Plevna. "I drink and drink," he told his friends, "but the scene grows before my eyes. I see that breastwork of dead bodies, Gortaloff thrown into the air on the points of the Turkish bayonets. I can't sleep. The retreat from the redoubt rises in front of me, and the screams still ring in my ears. I am getting no relaxation in

Bucharest. I must return to my work and then only will I forget."

One day, walking in Bucharest, Skobeleff overtook an elderly officer, haggard, dusty and shabbily dressed, one of his veterans. "What are you doing here?" he asked. "I've come to dine. I have got quite starved at headquarters," replied the man. "Where are you going to dine?" asked Skobeleff. "I don't know. Everything is so dear, quite forbidding, and then, how am I to go in? I am ashamed to show myself in a decent restaurant." Skobeleff took him by the arm to Broffts, introduced him to his friends and treated him to dinner. When the officer returned contented and happy to his inn he found a parcel awaiting him. With it was a letter which ran, "You left behind you at dinner eight gold imperials near your plate. You should not forget your money. I send them herewith. Skobeleff."

Into Bucharest poured all the Russian officers who could get leave and who had money to spend. Now, with a general cessation of hostilities in Bulgaria, princes and grand dukes, counts and countesses, some without their counts, ladies of the theatre and opera whose troupe had dispersed itself in favour of more profitable engagements that did not strain the voice, diplomats, aides-de-camp, Polish Jews and war correspondents belonging to every European nation, jostled one another on the broad staircase of Broffts Hotel. In the restaurants and cafés, the clatter of swords on the parquet floors rose above the clatter of knives and forks, and in the seething streets the rattle of the dashing droshkies drowned the steady tramp of the fresh regiments and reinforcements marching to the war. "Bucharest was a ball-room wherein Mars, Venus and Bacchus were dancing the can-can in frantic orgies," says Forbes, who passed through on his way to London.

Around Plevna military activities were concerned chiefly with the efforts of Osman to revictual and supply his garrison, and the Russian attempt to stop the convoys from Sofia getting through to Plevna. General Toldeben did not arrive until the end of September, and for some six weeks after the Great Assault Plevna was not completely invested.

The Russian and Rumanian armies lay on three sides, and the roads from the west and south-west were only patrolled by cavalry.

Of the 56,000 men Osman had under his command on 1 September, 4,000 (3,000 on the southern sector) had been killed or severely wounded in defeating the Great Assault, and these were more than replaced by the reinforcements which accompanied the convoys in September and October, so that, by the time the town was completely invested, he had 60,000 men to feed and supply with clothes and ammunition, which required 250 wagons of food and a thousand head of cattle a week. The job of collecting supplies and getting them to Plevna, was entrusted to Chefket Pasha, the man who had presided at the massacres which had led to the war, and who, on the instigation of the English Government, had been condemned to death but had been reprieved. He was very active in collecting wagons and supplies of food and ammunition and a great convoy of 1,500 wagons left Orkhanie on 18 September, guarded by a force of 12,000 men.

General Kriloff, who had been posted on the Sofia road to prevent Plevna from being revictualled, spotted the convoy on the 20th but the Turkish guards easily succeeded in beating off the Russians who, without infantry, were unable to withstand the hail of fire with which they were assailed. A sortie from Plevna coming to the rescue, Kriloff was taken between two fires, and the van of the convoy reached the town on the night of the 22nd. Dr. Ryan, riding out on the Sofia road, saw a long train of bullock carts, stretching for a mile, winding along like an enormous snake. As he watched, a Circassian dashed up to tell the colonel with him that the tail of the precious convoy was being attacked by the Russians. By the time the Turkish cavalry reached the rear of the convoy, the Russian cutting-out party had made off with several wagons, some of which Ryan heard had contained the much needed medical supplies which he and the other doctors had been expecting.

Without drugs, Ryan knew, it was hopeless to try to save many of the wounded with whom the hospitals were crammed. Every morning when he went to the hospital, the first thing that met his eyes was a row of corpses of the men who had died during the night, awaiting burial parties. Each morning his depression deepened as he recognized the faces of men who had told him stories of their simple uneventful lives and of the wives and children awaiting them in some distant part of the Turkish Empire. Overworked and suffering from a slight wound he had sustained in a skirmish from the explosion of a shell, he began to feel that the task of trying to alleviate the horrible sufferings that met his eyes daily was hopeless. The Turkish women of Plevna attended to the wounded, Ryan found, with the devotion of a Florence Nightingale. They moved silently about in their long white robes, with only their eyes showing through their thick yashmaks. Ryan explains the hopelessness of the work of a doctor in Plevna at this time by saying that he had forty-seven compound comminuted fractures on his hands, and all were suppurating, and he had no appliances of any kind for dressing them properly.

Assisted by a sortie from Plevna, another large convoy, commanded by Chefket in person, managed to reach Plevna on 12 October without the loss of a single wagon, the last one to get through. Again, by using cavalry alone, the Russians had failed to prevent Plevna from being re-victualled, although they had plenty of warning that the convoy was going to leave Orkhanie. The mistake made by the Russians, observes MacGahan, was in trying to waylay the convoy too near to Plevna, whereas, if they had attacked it forty or fifty miles away, the greater part of it could have been smashed by artillery fire, the oxen and draught horses killed and the drivers put to flight.

With the convoy came a party of English doctors who had been sent to Turkey by the Stafford House Committee for the Relief of Suffering. Several were old friends of Ryan's, the first Englishmen he had seen for months. On the morning after their arrival the doctors waited upon Osman and asked to be allowed to remain in Plevna to look after the wounded. Osman told them that he had decided to send the majority of the 4,000 wounded men to Sofia in the returning convoy where they would receive better treatment than could be given them in Plevna. The existing medical staff would be sufficient to cope with those who remained. The English doctors made a vigorous protest at the 'gross inhumanity' and danger of sending on such a terrible journey those who were quite unfit to travel, but Osman was inexorable. "Brusque and stern at the best," Ryan says, Osman's manner became still more forbidding when the English doctors repeated their protests. They went instead to Hassif Bey, the garrison's principal medical officer, whom they told it was a disgrace to humanity and brutal to send the wounded men on such a journey in jolting carts. Ryan sided with his chief, for he knew from experience that the ones who survived the journey would have more chance to recover than they would have in the crowded and insanitary hospitals at Plevna. If Osman did not send the wounded away, he would have so many more mouths to feed.

Osman had some excuse for his ill-temper. More than two months before, he had asked the War Council in Constantinople to send him some armourers to repair the guns and rifles that had been put out of action. The men duly arrived with the convoy but no one had thought to to provide them with the implements of their craft without which not a gun or a rifle could be repaired.

Ryan asked Osman's permission to accompany the wounded who had been in his personal care, and this was readily granted, and Osman thanked him most heartily for the great services he had rendered to the army. Ryan expected to be able to get back in about a fortnight but, by the time he was ready to return, Plevna had been invested. On the night before they left, Ryan and the English doctors were entertained to supper by Dr. Robert who, again, became hopelessly intoxicated and insisted on yelling out patriotic songs in half a dozen languages until his stern faced Viennese housekeeper hauled him off in wrath and turned his friends out. Ryan never heard what happened to Dr. Robert at the end of the siege.

The convoy, each cart filled with wounded men, could only creep along at two miles an hour. Here and there a cart would stop while the driver lifted out a dead man from among his living companions and laid the body at the side of the road. There was no time to dig a grave. They reached Orkhanie in three days with the loss of only 7 per cent of the wounded, whereas, as Ryan knew, at least half would have died if they had remained in Plevna.

Before Chefket left Plevna, he and Osman spent many hours closeted together planning how the town might be

HENRY DYMOND
Morning Advertiser, with the Turks

supplied during the coming months. As a result of their deliberations a number of strongpoints with small garrisons were established on the Sofia road, in which the convoys might take temporary refuge in case of attack.

Military operations round Plevna were at a standstill, except on the Rumanian front. Visiting their lines at the end of September, MacGahan reported: "The Rumanians are pushing forward their works against the second (Grivitza) redoubt with a perseverance and pluck worthy of all praise, and which is the more remarkable as the Russians are doing absolutely nothing on their side. The rain is continuous, the mud in the trenches is fearful, and it is very cold besides, but the officers and men alike stick to their posts in spite

of this with a pluck and resolution which excites my admiration. They evidently mean to take the second redoubt, or
have a desperate try at it. They are now within sixty yards
with their third parallel, and they are just beginning the
fourth parallel, which they mean to push within thirty yards
of the redoubt before giving assault. At this short distance
the terrible Turkish fire is reduced to a minimum, as the
Turks will not be able to fire more than two rounds before
they come to the bayonet. The Rumanian soldiers seem to
be stout fellows, and I think they are sure to get this redoubt.
Were the Russians advancing as rapidly on their side, Plevna
would fall before two weeks."

Meanwhile the Russians, according to MacGahan, were
completely at sea. They had no plan, no idea, no lead and
did not know what to do next. "I think history offers no
such example of a splendid army in such an utterly hopeless
condition," he declared. On 19 October the Rumanians
assaulted the Bash Tabiya with scaling ladders to climb the
thirty-foot high walls, but the Turks battered their heads
in with rifle butts, axes and spades and the attack was
repulsed with the loss of 1,000 men.

In the middle of October, winter set in with heavy snow
and torrents of rain, making the roads impassable, a serious
matter for the Russians who were dependent on ox-carts to
bring their supplies from Sistova. The Russian engineers had
built excellent bridges across the Danube, but no one thought
of constructing a metalled road from there to Plevna, and,
as a result hundreds of wagons and teams became bogged
down in the mud. In the Russian army, now drawing its
flanks round Plevna, 20,000 men were sick and there was
talk of abandoning the siege, and retreating across the
Danube until the spring. But the Czar would not hear of it.
For the Russians to retire and set Osman free would be to
confess they were unequal to the capture of a hastily fortified
town. The loss of prestige both within and outside Russia
would be too great. Plevna must be taken, he told his
officers. Its supplies must be cut off and its army starved
into submission.

As Kriloff had proved powerless to stop Osman's convoys

General Gourko was placed in command of all cavalry detachments west of the Vid. Plevna was not yet completely circled with Russian troops, but to blockade Osman it was necessary only to cut the south-west road to Sofia between Plevna and Orkhanie, which was held by Chefket Pasha. The village of Gorny-Dubnik, about twelve miles due west of Plevna, was chosen as the point at which to cut the road. It was one of the strongpoints established by Chefket and Osman, and its two redoubts were garrisoned by seven thousand to eight thousand men with four guns under the command of Hifzi Pasha, the officer who had brought the first convoy to Plevna.

Not only were the Turks in a strong position, but the Russians had to fear the possibility that Chefket might come up with his twenty battalions from Orkhanie, and Osman make a sortie, in which case they would be taken on both flanks. As it turned out Osman was kept occupied by a heavy bombardment and a feint attack, and Chefket, fearing for his neck if the Russians caught him, did not stir; the little garrison of Gorny-Dubnik were left to face sixteen battalions of the 2nd Infantry Division of the Imperial Guard, four battalions of chasseurs, sixty cannon, two squadrons of the Czar's private escort and two groups of the 4th Regiment of Don Cossacks, or about 35,000 infantry and 10,000 cavalry. The attack was fixed for 24 October. The Imperial Guard which had recently arrived from Russia, was confident of success and, despite the warnings of their comrades who had experienced the desperate resistance the Turks were accustomed to make, they marched towards Gorny-Dubnik thinking that the job of ousting a few Turks was an easy one. Their temerity was to cost them dear.

The Turkish positions were to be attacked by three columns of infantry, the right column from the north-east commanded by Major-General Ellis, the centre column by Major-General Baron von Zeddeler and the left column from the south by Major-General Rosenbach. A fourth column, under Colonel Tcherevine, took up position on the west, so that the Turks were encompassed by a formidable

circle of fire, and were shelled by sixty cannon. The bombardment opened at 8 a.m. and by 10 a.m. the commander
of the Grenadiers of the centre column judging that the
assault had been sufficiently prepared, launched his attack
on the eastern redoubt, and, after a fierce struggle, drove
out the Turks. But when his men tried to pursue them to
the second redoubt they were hurled back by a withering
fire. Supposing that the signal had been given for a general
advance, the three major-generals gave the order to attack,
independently and without co-operation. As the Russians
surged up to the redoubt on three sides, it vomited fire with
such murderous effect that the Russians were thrown back
in confusion. Nearly all the officers, including two colonels,
who led the columns were killed and Generals Zeddeler
and Rosenbach were wounded.

While this had been going on at Gorny-Dubnik a further
column, which had been sent against Telis, another strongpoint on the Sofia road, to prevent Chefket Pasha from
coming to the assistance of Gorny-Dubnik, had been crushed
by the Turkish defenders who had followed the fleeing
Russians and slaughtered the two to three hundred wounded
left on the ground. The Russians had lost a thousand men
and with his flank exposed to a sortie from Orkhanie,
General Gourko was now in a dangerous position. He decided
to push home the assault on Gorny-Dubnik and try to
secure the village before help could arrive. To this end
he issued the most careful instructions to the column
commanders so that the assault should be launched simultaneously, but the prearranged signal was not observed and
the three columns again made isolated attacks, all of which
were halted by the murderous fire of the Turks. General
Gourko ordered his men to lie low and wait for nightfall.

During this pause the men who held the small redoubt
captured in the morning crept by way of a ditch, and under
cover of a little house which the Turks had unwisely left
between the two redoubts, right up to the ditch in front of the
larger redoubt. They could not be reached by the Turks
without exposing themselves on the parapet above, and the
two opposing forces carried on a warfare of stones, lumps

of earth and pebbles, under cover of which the Russians cut steps in the wall of the redoubt.

At 5 p.m. a column of Guards, 5,000 strong, were sent against the redoubt. "Conquer or die," they shouted as they marched forward as if on parade and a great cheer arose from their comrades as they advanced firmly in the face of death. At the same time all sixty Russian guns poured a deadly shell-fire in to the redoubt. In a few seconds the redoubt was a scene of indescribable horror as a vast column of flame, smoke and dust arose against the scarlet tints of the setting sun. The men sheltering below the parapet leaped up the steps they had made and were followed by the guardsmen in an irresistible stream. Although they fought magnificently the Turks were overwhelmed and at about 6 p.m. Ahmed Hifzi hoisted the white flag. Three thousand five hundred Turks lay dead and 2,235 were taken prisoner, but another 5,000 made good their escape. For eight hours the Turks had held their own against more than three times their own number of the finest battalions of the far-famed Imperial Guard and they had taken toll of 4,000 Russian lives. A few days later Telis surrendered and the blockade of Plevna was complete. With the clearance of the Turkish strongholds on the west of the Vid, the Russian flanks could close round Plevna and, by completing its encirclement, start its investment.

As October drew to its close, 150,000 Russians and Rumanians tightened the band of steel round the beleaguered town. Except for an occasional shell, the Russians, occupied with their lines of investment, left their opponents in peace.

CHAPTER FIFTEEN

NIGHT ATTACK

ONE day early in November MacGahan paid a visit to Skobeleff's lines. Things had been quiet for some time and he rode to the southern sector hoping to find something to vary the monotony of the siege. Skobeleff, he learned, was preparing to advance his lines and push the Turks back from a dangerous salient. After the September assault, he had been ordered to fall back and abandon the Green Hills. Now, he proposed to re-establish his position on the Lovtcha road.

As MacGahan rode up, he could see Skobeleff, dressed as usual in a white uniform and mounted on a white charger, galloping in front of the Turkish skirmishers who were pouring a hail of fire at him. Skobeleff pulled up his horse and stopped to examine the position, the bullets whistling about him. Then, having seen what he wanted to, he rode leisurely back, lost in thought.

"Why do you expose yourself so wantonly?" an officer asked him reproachfully. "I must show my men that the Turks don't know how to shoot," replied Skobeleff. Many of Skobeleff's men, MacGahan could see, were fresh-faced boys from Russia, recruits sent to fill the gaps torn in the regiments at Krishnin, and officers were few, for the veterans had not been replaced.

The night of the attack was thick and foggy, just what Skobeleff wanted to cloak his advance for, under cover of the fog, he could creep to within 100 yards of the Turkish trenches, near enough to dash forward before they had time to rouse up and fire more than a round or so. MacGahan was there to see the detachment move off.

"All the forenoon the troops were moving in small detachments towards the place of concentration near the

Lovtcha road, and everyone knew that an attack was arranged for five o'clock in the afternoon. The fog effectually concealed the hostile lines from one another and the batteries were silent. To us who were waiting this silence was ominous, for it was broken by the muffled tramp of the men and words of command as the detachments went by in the fog. At three o'clock the ragged red and yellow flag was taken from its place by the side of the door of the low mud hovel occupied by General Skobeleff.

"It was a most picturesque and romantic cavalcade that filed out of the yard and followed the young leader out to certain danger, and possibly death. General Skobeleff, alike heedless of cold and damp and whizzing missiles, was the only one who was not bundled up in overcoats and mufflers. He led the way through the narrow alleys of the village, mounted on a white horse—the soldiers look for the white horse as much as for their beloved Commander—confident, cheerful, inspiring to look upon. Behind him a motley of retinue: Circassians, with long surtout and silver-mounted harness and weapons; blond youths already scarred and covered with decorations; correspondents in civil dress, Cossacks half hidden in their grey coats and hoods, and in the middle of the group a picturesque Circassian on a white horse bearing the tattered banner, quite like an old Crusader with his quaint arms and curious dress.

"The flag, too, is quite mediaeval in appearance, and completed the illusion to perfection. It is a square silk banner, fastened to a Cossack lance, and has on the one side the white Cross of St. George, and on the other the letters 'M.S.' standing for Michael Skobeleff and the date 1875 in yellow on a red ground. The tattered silk was carried through the Khorand campaign, and has fluttered in all the hard fights which have made the young General so famous."

The troops, after losing their way a dozen times, were halted and drawn up in order near an encampment of straw huts, each man carrying a rifle and a spade, and well supplied with food and ammunition; at the rear stood a group of stretcher-bearers, and a battery of mitrailleuses, bundled up like so many human beings to keep out the damp. In front, a little body of picked men, those who were to make the first rush, use the bayonet, and then throw it aside for the spade, and endeavour to dig-in before the Turks returned. To MacGahan the scene was dramatic and impressive. Men and horses stood out in exaggerated relief against the background of grey mist which was so thick as to make objects invisible the length of a company front. The square masses of determined men stood with their eyes fixed on their general, as he rode along the ranks.

"Well, comrades, what do you say? Are we going to win today?"

"We will try to, your Excellency."

"You won't disgrace yourselves?"

"Why should we, Excellency? We are glad to go."

"Remember one thing, my men. Don't tear along. We are not going to take Plevna tonight. We are only going to turn the Turks out of their trenches. Remember, this is not a matter of bravery as of discipline and obedience. When your officers cry 'Halt', you've got to halt, however much you want to charge the Turks, and they are nothing to be afraid of."

"We are not afraid of them."

"That's right, comrades. Do you remember Krishnin, and how we thrashed them there?"

"Yes, your Excellency."

"Do you remember how we ran after them?"

"They ran like rabbits," a smiling fellow replied.

"Were you with me there? You are one of the old ones, I think?"

"I was with your Excellency when we took that redoubt."

Skobeleff moved along the line, greeting old comrades, talking over old battles, chaffing one man, complimenting another: the band he told them would play a waltz in the Turkish lines tomorrow. Turning to a staff officer, he whispered, "I am fidgety about the young soldiers. It is a risky business, a night attack in fog. Even an old hand may lose his head. I shall not remain with the reserves as I intended. I will lead the attack myself."

'Surely,' thought MacGahan to himself, 'a finer lot of men never went into a fight;' young, healthy, devoted and confident, every face wore an expression that was proof of courage and earnestness and even of religious zeal. Skobeleff reined up in front of the regiment: he took off his cap and crossed himself, and the air seemed to rustle as officers and men followed his example. For a moment each man was alone with his thoughts. MacGahan bared his head.

"Close-up; shoulder arms," came the order. MacGahan could see the perfect confidence of the soldiers inspired by the presence of their infallible leader, their protector, their beloved friend. "Close-up. March!" Skobeleff disappeared into the gloom, already far in advance. As the men followed him, MacGahan took his place beside the battery which was to give the signal for the assault. When the opening salvo shook the air, the hot breath of sixteen guns scourged his face and in a minute the air was filled with the zing and swish of bullets. Looking round he could see the supports lying in the dirt, rifles in hand, anxiously trying to find something to shoot at. From the front the rattle and roar of the rifle-fire sounded like the surging of a storm. Beside him the battery kept banging away, deafening and blinding him with the flashes. Shells came screaming past, exploding with a sharp ringing sound. From the impenetrable darkness a couple of stretcher-bearers loomed up, dodging and jumping to avoid the bullets. Down in the hollow below came spitting flashes of lead.

As the chain of men moved forward, the general's figure in front grew more and more indistinct. The Turks, thank God, had not heard their approach: a sentinel's rifle fires: the men halt in their stride, their hearts beating violently. Another shot, a third, and then silence. No reply came from the advancing Russians. Perhaps the Turkish outposts were firing only at shadows. Dead silence reigned, to be broken by the ringing voice of Skobeleff: "Children, follow me," he called, and his voice was drowned in the roll of drums and the cheers of the men, and a deafening volley from ahead, as the Russians sprang forward. "Where's Skobeleff?"

someone shouted. "He's in front, in the enemy's lines," another replied. "He does not care; he fears nothing."

Skobeleff was through the outpost line; behind him charged his men. In a moment they were in the Turkish trenches, bayonetting and stabbing the defenders, for the the Russians were too few to take prisoners. But some of the young Russians had faltered and thrown themselves down on the first Turkish volley. In a moment their panic was over and they were in the trench with the others, and followed them to the next line, chasing the flying Turks. Behind the Russian assault force, barely a hundred in number, followed ten Companies of the Vladimirsky Regiment with spades to throw up parapets in the rear of the captured trenches.

The Turks were mustering for a counter-attack, their bullets coming like buzzing bees, whistling round the ears of the men digging for dear life. Skobeleff was far ahead. "He fights like a soldier," one of the digging men remarked. "And he does not hide himself like a general," replied another. Now and then, a soldier gave a groan and, dropping his spade, sank to the ground. His place was quickly filled by another and the work went on, and the parapets grew. In an hour the job was done, the position secure.

By 2 a.m. the Turks had been reinforced and the counter-attack grew in earnest. Volley after volley came pouring into the Russian lines and from behind their breastworks the Russians replied in kind. Standing on the parapet Skobeleff encouraged his men and cheered them to fresh efforts. In moments of comparative calm, he moved up and down the trenches, inspecting the work, making a suggestion or ordering the men to close-up or open out. "The enemy will attack us very soon," he told them, "I shall be on the left. You must fight like men. Die at your posts but do not give in."

In a moment of quiet, Skobeleff galloped to the rear to write a dispatch to headquarters, announcing his success, but scarcely had he time to dictate a couple of words before a wave of firing burst out in front. In a moment he was off back to the threatened position. While he had been absent the enemy had crept round the flank and had opened an enfilade fire on the men digging communication trenches to connect the front and second lines. Two companies of raw troops had taken fright and had thrown down their guns and run; they ran straight into Skobeleff. With quick perception, Skobeleff took the situation in at a glance. Threats, he knew, would have no effect on a panic-stricken multitude; hard words would only demoralize them more.

"Good health, my men!" (the usual greeting of a Russian general inspecting a parade) shouted Skobeleff, cheerfully, even joyfully. The fleeing men came to an abrupt halt; some even returned the usual reply, "We wish you good health," but the voices were half-hearted and doubtful. "Thank you, my eagles, for your service. You have fought like heroes today," returned Skobeleff. The men, who but a minute before were a disorganized rabble, began to draw themselves up and fall into something like a line. "I am proud to command you," Skobeleff announced. "Finer fellows than you I have never come across." The men had now completely recovered, and were in excellent line. Skobeleff pretended to discover that they were without their rifles. "What does this mean? Where are your veapons?" he asked. The men looked down sheepishly, not a word was said. There was a painful silence. Skobeleff changed his tone, "What have you done? Thrown away your rifles? You are cowards. You have run—and from Turks! It is a disgrace: it is shameful. You miserable wretches, all of you. I won't command such scum. Be off, get out of my sight." The men, quite humiliated, stood transfixed.

Skobeleff stood eyeing them for a moment, "March after me," he called. The men followed as he led them back to the front. At the place where they had thrown away their rifles, he halted them and bade them pick up their arms. "Shoulder arms," he ordered. The command was obeyed, but not confidently, not well. Turkish bullets were singing round the men. "That won't do," cried Skobeleff, taking his stand on the top of the trench. "Stand at ease. Now then, shoulder arms." This time it was better done, but Skobeleff would not relent. "Once more. Nothing but parade drill will do. Shoulder arms!" This time it was splendidly done. "Present arms," he ordered. As the men stood with 'arms presented', Skobeleff walked up and down the line until satisfied at last, he let them take cover. The lesson had been learned.

The trenches were still too narrow and Skobeleff ordered them to be widened. As the officers passed along the lines, they were forced to expose themselves to the enemy's fire. Captain Kuropatkin, Skobeleff's chief of staff, drew his attention to the skirmishers who were still lying out in front. Leaping on the parapet, Skobeleff called to their commanding officer, "Captain Dombroffsky, you will be good enough to bring back your men." "I will do what I can," replied Dombroffsky, touching his cap; but while he was in the act of lifting his hand, something whistled between Skobeleff and Kuropatkin, and Dombroffsky lay stretched on the ground, a bullet through his temple.

The pale streaks of dawn were marking the sky: for that night at least the Turkish counter-attack was over. They had attacked both flanks of the new Russian position but had been beaten back. Skobeleff threw himself down in the captured trench to snatch a few hours sleep. His men made themselves as comfortable as they could, eating their biscuits and thinking of the hot breakfast their comrades were enjoying in the rear. From out of the mist came the rattle of wheels and in among the hungry Russians came a Turkish transport wagon, its driver calling to them to clear the way as he was bringing their breakfast: before he could discover his mistake he was pulled off his wagon and, with peals of laughter, the Russians set to to examine the contents of the Turkish pots and kettles.

The slope on which MacGahan spent the night watching, or rather, hearing the battle, was continuously swept by bullets zipping through the twigs of the breastwork round the guns. Skobeleff had given him the treat he had promised and there was more to come.

In the trenches the men of the Vladimir Regiment boiled their tea in cans suspended over fires of brushwood. Skobeleff lay asleep in a little hole, dug for him in the centre of the trench. He had been up and down several times since dawn, inspecting the entrenching work, at times seizing a spade and showing the men how to work. "You see," he pointed out, "that sapper's training was some use after all!" The trench was now a broad path in which three men could walk abreast, and the breastwork so high and broad that a grenade could not penetrate. Each gun pointed through an embrasure. The banquettes were long and wide enough for a whole regiment to stand upon. But Skobeleff was not satisfied: "Push up a battery here and make embrasures and a breastwork for it at once," he ordered. "When will it be ready?" he asked. The men were much fatigued, but they set to work at once, promising it by midnight. "Don't you think it could be done before?" urged Skobeleff. "The enemy will try to recapture these trenches tonight, and we must receive them with bombs and grape-shot."

"We will try to have it ready by ten o'clock."

"What is the name of the sergeant who will superintend the work?"

"Mitrophan Koltzoff."

"Point him out to me."

A handsome sergeant of sappers is brought to Skobeleff.

"Was it you, my friend, who dug the trenches under yesterday's fire?"

"It was I, your Excellency."

"Well, look, my fine fellow, if you finish the batteries for me by tonight, and throw up some earthworks on our left flank during the night, you shall be a Knight of St. George tomorrow."

"I will try."

"Very well, remember your promise."

"If I am not killed, I will do it."

"And if you get killed, you will die honourably for your country."

"I will do my duty, your Excellency."

The space between the new trench and the enemy's position consisted of a deserted strip of withered bushes of small oak, the dry leaves of which fell off at the slightest touch. Into these trees Turkish snipers had climbed to shoot into the trenches, where the Russians watched to shoot the 'game' as they called it. No sooner was the flash of a Turkish sniper seen, than a hail of lead whistled through the leaves and, more often than not, a body fell from the tree's branches. Those killed in the trenches were buried at once. A prayer was read over the bodies, the hole in the ground was blessed with the sign of the cross, and nothing remained except the memory of a man for whom tears would one day be shed in some little hamlet where his family vainly await his return.

As night approached Skobeleff ordered the sentries: "Don't fire on any account if you see the Turks coming: give the alarm by word of mouth. The nearer they come the better. If they get on the parapets, give them the cold steel." As the evening fire grew heavier and heavier the men wanted to reply, but Skobeleff would not allow it. "Let them waste their ammunition," he said. The fog grew denser and denser and it was very cold. Sitting on their banquettes or leaning their backs against the breastwork, the men dozed fitfully, looking like clumps of grey earth on the ground. The fire from two or three hundred yards away alone indicated the presence of the enemy. Sometimes a rustling was heard in the bushes, indicating the presence of a Turkish sentry. It grew darker and darker and the Turkish fire grew fainter and fainter. Not even the leaves on the trees rustled. In the trenches the camp-fires had gone out. The Russian sentries peered into the darkness. Something seemed to scrape against the breastwork; footsteps could be heard, stealthily. The sentinel aimed his rifle in their direction, listening with beating heart as he groped in the darkness with his eyes.

"Don't fire," came a voice from outside, "I am a scout. Don't fire. Wake the general. The Turks are leaving their trenches and forming for action." "To arms," the sentinel whispered, but Skobeleff was already at the breastwork. He had heard the faint noise in his sleep and had awakened in time to hear the whispered conversation. "To arms, my men. To the breastwork," he called. Silently the men lifted themselves up and pushed their rifles through the loopholes.

"I knew the Turks would come tonight," whispered Skobeleff. "Now, gentlemen," he said, turning to the officers, "to your posts. If the enemy gets up the breastwork give him your bayonets. I am afraid the Turks will break through our line somewhere. Of course we shall chase them out but we may have a bad half hour."

Suddenly, the death-like silence becomes alive with noise and tumult as the advancing Turks fire, disclosing that their line was a mile in length. A thousand bullets buzzed over the Russian trenches. Some lodged in the earth, others struck trees with a hissing sound resembling the pouring of molten lead into water. No Russian fired in reply. The Turks could be seen about seventy feet distant, dark, menacing masses visible in the red light of their volleys. Above the rattle of rifle-fire, wild cries of "Allah!" could be heard. "Battalion—fire!" yelled Skobeleff. From the trenches belched the fire of a thousand rifles. "Don't give them time to recover," ordered Skobeleff. "Fire in platoons." From behind, the Russian batteries lifted their voices, and the Turkish guns bayed in response. Crash, crash, roar the Russian volleys; the Turks are now within forty paces. Death had played havoc in their ranks, but they came on undaunted. In the trenches the flashing volleys throw a red glare round the men, immersed in smoke. Bullets fly everywhere. Skobeleff's voice rises above the din, but his words are lost. For a moment chaos reigns, and then the Turks are gone. "Thank God, we have repulsed them," cries Skobeleff.

By seven o'clock the men were tired out and dispirited after the excitement of the night. It was damp and cold and the field smelt of blood. "I'll wake them up," exclaimed Skobeleff, and he ordered up the band. The men cheered up and the effect was wonderful. The national anthem was played to the accompaniment of volleys from the Russian batteries, shots from the sentries and the loud applause of grape-shot, the sound of which is very much like the applause on a first night at a theatre. As the hymn came to its close, it was followed by vociferous cheering, which drowned the noise of the guns, and the band broke in to the 'Plevna March', a tune not unfamiliar to Skobeleff's men. "We have lost the art of war," Skobeleff said to one of his officers. "Our fathers were better military psychologists and knew the influence of music on soldiers. It raises the spirit of an entire army. Napoleon—the God of War, knew this well, and led his men to the charge to the stirring sound of a march."

Skobeleff remembered the request and promise he had made the day before. The embrasures had been completed, and the sergeant of the sappers had earned his St. George.

Inquiring for him, Skobeleff learned that Koltzoff had been sent to the rear on duty, so he made the cross up in a parcel with a letter addressed to him, but, by the time it was written Koltzoff had reappeared. Skobeleff hung the cross round his neck and shook him by the hand.

That night Skobeleff complained that the scouts were badly posted and declared that he would go out and move them himself. His men's hearts sank as he cleared the parapet, and they were angry that their young general was wantonly exposing himself within a few hundred yards of the enemy. For half an hour they were beset with anxiety. "His life is enchanted," says one soldier. "Yes, it was charmed at Khiva," replies another. "For nine days and nine nights he did not eat or drink and a Khivite muttered his spells over him. And now his life is charmed so that bullets pass through his body without doing him any injury." "Let us cure the general of his love of exposing himself," suggested a staff officer. "How are you to do that?" another asked. "Have you not noticed," pointed out the officer, "how he hates people to stand by his side on exposed ground? Every time he jumps on the ramparts, we'll jump after him." When Skobeleff returned from posting the scouts, he turned and stood on the parapet, in the face of the fire. In an instant he was surrounded by a crowd of officers and men.

"What are you standing there for, gentlemen? Have you come to meet your bullets?" Skobeleff asked in an irritated tone. "We have the honour to belong to your Excellency's staff," an officer replied, putting his hand to his cap. Skobeleff understood and laughed, and returned to his cubby-hole, where his table was covered with maps and plans.

In a moment he was up again. In the captured trench

there had been piles of Turkish telegraph wire. Where was it? It was found and brought to him. Throw it in front of the trenches, he ordered, and it will entangle any of the enemy who try to creep up at night. But Skobeleff was not satisfied; the enemy might advance under the shelter of the trees and bushes which covered the ground between the Russians and the Turks. They must be cut down, he ordered. After a time Skobeleff went out to see how the men were getting on. He met them returning. "Have you finished?" he asked. "No, the Turks are firing," came the reply "they are everywhere." "You are afraid," shouted Skobeleff. "Close up. About face. Back to your work and quickly too or I'll put you through your paces in front of the Turkish trenches." The men were gone and soon the sound of axes could be heard. When they returned Skobeleff met them. "Well," he asked, "have you finished the work completely? Have you any wounded?" "Not a single man," came the reply.

In the morning Skobeleff saw the menacing profile of a newly constructed Turkish redoubt. "They must be chastised for their insolence," he declared, and called a council of war. "Sit down in a circle, my men," he told them. The officers and non-commissioned officers sat close around him, the men in an outer circle. All listened eagerly with their eyes on the general. "Look here, my men," he said "we are going into action tonight, and I must explain it to you, so that there will be no muddle. I am very much dissatisfied with this division," he began, "it is quite changed from what it used to be." "There are many new hands, Excellency," replied the old soldiers, "they are not yet used to the work." "Your business is to teach them their work," he ordered.

"Tonight," he told them, "the force of which you will form a part will march up to the trenches as noiselessly as possible. As you come within twenty paces of them, cheer, and the drums will beat the assault. Then throw yourselves into the trenches, bayonet everyone you come across, drive the Turks away and capture as many rifles as you can. I will give three roubles for every gun taken. Take the enemy's guns and they are no longer soldiers. If you kill a

Turk and leave his gun they will find another man to take his place. When you see the Turks coming on in large numbers, jump over the ramparts and lie down. Don't fire until you are ordered. If there are too many of them, you may retreat, but retire slowly firing on them as you go. Remember that the Turk hates volleys. When you retreat, you must not only bring your wounded back with you, but your killed as well. Remember, if you leave but one man behind, you had better not show yourselves to me. I won't look at you. You must fight like devils. Prove that you are the same fellows with whom I took Lovtcha and the redoubt at Plevna."

That night the fog cleared. By eleven o'clock everyone felt nervous. Skobeleff looked out over the ramparts. "Forward in God's name," he whispered. "Form in line," he told them, "march elbow to elbow, so that each soldier may feel his comrade by his side." The advance guard disappeared. After a time there came a cheer and a volley of firing; and then some of the men came back. "All are dead; we alone have escaped," they declared. The panic extended itself to the men in the trenches. Another group came climbing over the breastwork. The affair had miscarried and now the Turks were advancing to attack in their turn. Shouting and yelling like wild beasts, the Turks came charging against the Russian trenches. The men who but a few minutes before had retreated in panic, now stood coolly waiting to receive the shock of the enemy's charge. "Battalion fire," cried Skobeleff. The Turks were not twenty paces away. A thousand bullets sped into the charging mass; from the darkness came screams and groans. The Turkish wave receded. Five minutes later they came on again. "They may break the ramparts this time," cried Skobeleff, "be ready." The Turkish bugles sounded 'Storm' and again the mass hurled itself forward, again to be shattered by the Russian volleys. Firing wildly, the Turks retreated.

"Oh," exclaimed Skobeleff, putting his hand to his side. "What has happened?" an officer asked. "Speak less loudly," whispered Skobeleff, "I am severely wounded," pressing the palm of his hand against his side. The officer supported him;

"No, let me go. This won't do. The men will see us," Skobeleff whispered. "Good cheer, my men," he shouted as loudly as he could, "I congratulate you for beating the enemy so well." "Glad to please you," was shouted back. "Mind, stand honourably. If he falls on us again, we will send him back a third time. Whatever may happen, stand together, and remember, sooner die in the trenches than give them up." The men gave a cheer. "You had better retire to your tent," urged the officer. Skobeleff insisted on walking unaided. In the tent his coat was removed and Captain Kuropatkin searched for the wound. "Where is it?" asked Skobeleff. "Why there is no wound at all," Kuropatkin joyfully exclaimed. "It is a contusion. The bullet struck you and glanced off."

Skobeleff was soon back in the trenches, encouraging his men in repelling a third and last attack on the new position. The Turkish assault was not renewed and the Russians were left in undisputed possession of the new position which shortened their lines of investment by nearly two miles.

CHAPTER SIXTEEN

THE INVESTMENT

ON a circle thirty miles in circumference the Russians waited for the plum to drop into their laps. They knew, and Osman knew, that it was now only a matter of weeks before the Plevna garrison was starved into surrender or attempted to break out, either on its own or in conjunction with the promised army of relief. Osman put a brave face on it, and when a message was sent in to ask if he would take the prisoners captured at Gorny-Dubnik and Telis into Plevna, he stated in his refusal that he had supplies for eight months, and he hoped the Russians would not be too uncomfortable in their wet and soggy trenches.

General Todleben's plan of investment was complete. Plevna was gripped in a circle of steel by an army of 180,000 men, divided into six sectors:

		Batts.	Sqds.	Guns
North	General Tchernat 3 Rumanian Divisions	28	28	78
East	General Krudener IX Corps	18	4	80
South-East	General Zotoff IV Corps	13	4	48
South	General Skobeleff ('Skobeleff's men' as they proudly called themselves)	27	6	96
South-West	General Kataley Guards Corps	16	2	54
West-North-West	General Ganetsky Corps of Grenadiers	30	22	126
At Lovtcha	General Karzow	34	4	136
Facing Orkhanie	General Gourko	38	84	76

Comprising, 204 battalions, 154 squadrons of cavalry and 694 guns.

The Russian plan was twofold: once the investment was complete the Russian and Rumanian lines of circumvallation were slowly drawn tighter and nearer and nearer to the Turks by trench and sap, by Todleben's 'pick and shovel campaign' as some of the Russian officers contemptuously called it, and exercises were carried out for the quick concentration of troops should Osman try to break out through any particular sector. All the sectors were connected by telegraph and news of any Turkish move could be flashed round the lines in a few seconds. General Gourko lay to the south-west of Plevna to prevent the advance of the army of relief from Sofia. Osman's men, too, were kept busy with picks and shovels and by November the circle of defence round Plevna had been completed and the garrison could face attack from any quarter.

Now the Russians and Rumanians could sit and wait for the irresistible advance into Plevna of an ally more powerful than they. Starvation and disease would, they knew, defeat Osman's heroic army at no further cost to themselves. In due time, patience would bring the reward which impetuosity had failed to achieve.

General Skobeleff's night attack on 10 and 11 November was the principal event of the investment of the doomed town. Much to his chagrin, Skobeleff had been ordered to retire from the position he had won prior to 11 September, on the ground that it was too dangerously exposed, and, on his falling back, the Turks had pushed forward and erected new redoubts and trenches, forming a projection into the Russian lines which both seriously impeded communications between Generals Skobeleff and Zotoff, whose sectors were now separated by the impassable ravine of the Tultchenitza, and constituted a weak point in the circle of investment. By his successful assault on the Green Hills, Skobeleff gained access to a lateral road which cut out the long detour to Zotoff's sector, and he secured a vantage point from which he could look down into the Turkish lines.

In Plevna, the news of the fall of Gorny-Dubnik and Telis

and the realization that the supply line to Orkhanie was cut, led to despondency, but the spirits of the defenders cheered up when they recalled the Sultan's promise that a great army would be sent to their relief. Mehemet Ali was, they knew, at Sofia collecting men and supplies for their succour. To the Turks, the apparent failure of Skobeleff to push on to the capture of the Krishnin redoubts was hailed as a victory, for they did not know that his object was limited, and they thought that his night attack was a prelude to a fresh assault on Plevna.

On the day following the repulse of Skobeleff's attack on the new Ghazi Osman Tabiya, a *parlementaire* was brought into Plevna, summoning Osman to surrender:

The Grand Duke's letter read (translated from the French):

General Quarters, Poradim.
30th October 1877.
Russian date.

"Monsieur le Maréchal,

I have the honour to state to your Excellency the following facts:

The Ottoman troops of Gorny-Dubnik and of Telis have been taken prisoner. The Russian armies have seized the positions of Osikovo and Vratza. Plevna is surrounded by the Army of the West, strengthened by the brigade of the Imperial Guard as well as by the Grenadiers; the communications are cut, one must not count any more on any more rations.

In the name of humanity and to prevent further bloodshed, for which your Excellency alone will carry the responsibility, I request you to cease all resistance, to name a place where we can negotiate the conditions of the capitulation.

Please accept Monsieur le Maréchal the assurance of my high esteem."

Nicholas.
Commander-in-Chief of the Russian
armies in Europe.

To His Excellency Marshal Osman Pasha at Plevna.

While Osman wrote his reply, the six Cossacks who had escorted the flag of truce were given, in order to impress them with the wealth of the supplies in Plevna, an ample meal.

To the Grand Duke's letter, Osman replied as follows (translated from the French):

> General Headquarters of Plevna.
> 12 November 1877.
> Western date.

"I have received your letter dated the 30th October which your Imperial Highness has kindly sent me.

The Imperial troops under my command have never ceased to show proof of courage, perseverance and energy. In all the battles up to now they have been victorious; because of this His Majesty the Tzar has been forced to bring as reinforcements the brigade of the Imperial Guard as well as the Grenadiers. The defeat of Gorny-Dubnik ana Telis, the capitulation of the troops who were there, the breaking up of the communications, the occupation of the main roads are not sufficient reasons for me to be forced to surrender my army to the enemy.

My troops are not in want of anything and they still have not done all they must do to safeguard the Ottoman military honour. Up to today we have given our blood with joy for our country and our faith; we will go on doing it rather than surrender.

As to the responsibility of the bloodshed, it belongs in this world as well as in the world beyond to those who have instigated this war.

I present to your Imperial Highness the assurance of my distinguished esteem."

> Ghazi Osman.
> Commander of the Army of Plevna.

To His Imperial Highness,
The Grand Duke Nicholas at Poradim.

The texts of the letters were circulated to the officers of the garrison, and Lieutenant Herbert says that Osman's noble and dignified language was applauded, particularly the phrase which brought home the responsibility for the bloodshed to the guilty. Herbert continued to be stationed on the Janik Bair and he did his turn of duty in the redoubt close to the one held by the Rumanians, where, much to the anger of the Russians, the Turks and Rumanians entered upon an unofficial cessation of hostilities. During a temporary armistice for the burial of the men who had fallen in the recent Rumanian assault, he found the Rumanians were getting tired of the petty slaughter constantly going on between the two redoubts. He had a long conversation and a smoke with a Rumanian officer who, in broken French and with comical gestures, told him several stories with equivocal meanings, the point of which was somewhat lost in the telling, and, on several Rumanian officers' joining them, they sat down to a meal on the thin carpet of snow. Even the dirty, cowardly and furtive mongrel dogs, which infested both camps, Herbert noticed, seemed pleased to enjoy the truce and rolled together placidly on the frozen ground.

Guard duty in the Bash Tabiya was so severe that the two battalions who formed its garrison had to be relieved every twenty-four hours. The enemy were only the width of a road away and a merciless fire was directed at the slightest sign of movement, so that the redoubt could be relieved only during the hours of darkness. Under a ceaseless hail of shells and bullets, cooking and washing were impossible and during their term of duty the men lived on biscuits, maize bread and melted snow. So dangerous was the duty considered that a man commanded to the Bash Tabiya bade farewell to his friends and made his peace with God. Eventually, the sniping became so wearisome to both sides that an unofficial truce was declared when each redoubt was relieved, and sentries were posted. So friendly did the Turco-Rumanian friendship become that the Russians took over the Grivitza redoubt and after that there were no more truces. Dozens of rifles were fired at every black speck which looked as though it belonged to a garment and, at a distance of 120 yards, few shots failed to find their mark.

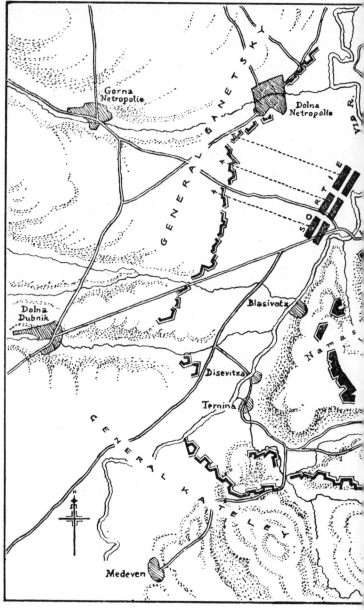

PLEVNA. T

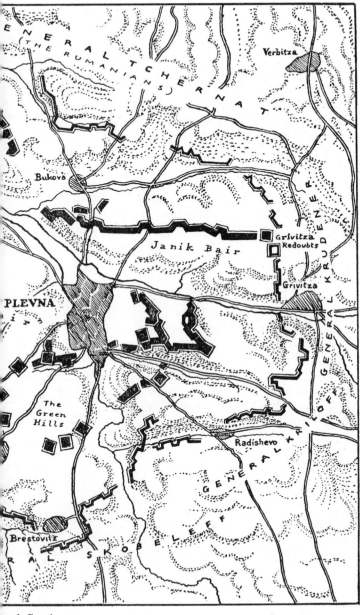

The zone in between the two redoubts became a maze of trenches as both sides tried to counteract the temporary advantage gained by the other, and each resorted to devices to deceive the enemy. Life-sized fully dressed figures, some with movable limbs, were exposed to draw the other's fire. The Rumanians, before they left, erected a white sheet with a fire burning behind it, and a shadow drama of a very thin man and a woman of monstrous proportions was enacted for the amusement of the Turks.

As the rigours of the Bulgarian winter became more and more severe, sentry duty round the Turkish redoubt was reduced from four hours to two, and then to one hour, and even so, sentry duty was looked upon as the last refinement of torture. Standing in a hole four feet deep the upper part of his body was exposed to the bitter blasts of the icy wind, and the lower part froze. Any attempt to move about brought a fusillade of shots. Insufficiently fed to withstand the cold, the sentries were compelled to keep a ceaseless watch for the enemy who might suddenly spring upon them, and to struggle against the dangerous drowsiness brought on by a temperature of ten degrees below freezing point.

The Russian bombardment, which was kept up for a few hours each day and occasionally at night, was chiefly directed against Plevna itself, and the civil population and the sick and wounded were the main sufferers. Every few minutes would come the boom of one of the great Russian siege-guns, the giant shell could be heard approaching like a railway train, followed a few seconds later by the roar of its explosion and the crash of crumbling masonry if it struck a house. Sometimes the shell, exploding in the street, caught a group of women and children, or it might strike one of the many houses sheltering the sick and wounded. As the shelling continued, the civil population, both Turkish and Bulgarian, took refuge in mosques and churches. Mattresses and blankets were strewn on the floor and cauldrons of soup steamed where once the smoke of incense had risen. At night candles illuminated the places of refuge with a thousand flickering flames casting eerie shadows, as the Christian shells spread death and destruction throughout Plevna.

Plevna was one vast hospital. Plague stalked its streets and hideous diseases reigned unchecked for there were no drugs or medicines to combat them. Each house contained its quota of sick and wounded soldiers; the hospitals overflowed, and the doctors and surgeons without drugs and without lint could do little to alleviate suffering. Linen rags were treasured as priceless; fresh wounds could be bandaged only when a man died. In the streets, night or day made little difference for the dead had to be buried at all hours, and the mortality from shell-fire and disease became so great that a death excited little comment and no feeling. Gaunt figures with hollow cheeks and desperate burning eyes scuffled over heaps of offal for a grain of food, and above all rose the stench of abomination, the smell of rotting corpses and decomposing carcasses. In the ruined starving town men called upon their Maker in hopeless despair to relieve them of their sufferings; little children cried aloud in agonies of hunger, and women huddled together in tearless misery.

The weather was bitterly cold. Wood ran out and to keep themselves warm and to cook their food the men in the trenches and redoubts crept out on the slopes and hills and tore up all the vines but, soon, all the vineyards had been uprooted and there was nothing left to burn. Rations were reduced to half a pound of bread, half wheat half maize, and less than half a pound of meat of wretched quality for each man. There was no tea or coffee, and in the Turkish army no alcohol to warm the body, and benumb the mind. Tobacco was almost non-existent and a cigarette cost 1s. 1od. Cigarettes and biscuits were staked at dominoes and chess. Sugar in the black market sold at 10s. per lb. Herbert paid a Jew twenty-five piastres for a 4 oz. tin of execrable tinned beef and he bought a cup of Liebig's meat extract for the same price. An egg cost ten piastres. Trafficking in articles of consumption was strictly forbidden, and no one was allowed to kill a horse or ox, as they might be needed for a break-out. There was no soap, and the soldiers' clothes were in tatters, their feet bound up with rags. Anything was seized for warmth, women's petticoats, and trousers, and many soldiers wore Russian and Rumanian uniforms under their greatcoats. But during those dreadful weeks, not more than 200 regular soldiers deserted, and those who left the camp were chiefly Circassians. Quarrels, says Herbert, were rare and with one voice the garrison cried 'No Surrender', and each man longed for a chance to break out through the iron ring.

In the middle of November, five Turkish prisoners were sent into Plevna by the Russians with copies of *The Times* and the *Daily News*, containing news of the complete defeat of the Turkish armies in Armenia, and the fall of Kars. These English papers, which were sent so that Osman would have no doubt of the authenticity of the news, stated also that the army of the Quadrilateral was unable to advance and that the Shipka Pass was blocked with snow, thus preventing any Turkish offensive from the south. Osman sent the Russians a message thanking them for the newspapers which would, he said, help to pass the long winter evenings! So that Osman's garrison should not be left unaware of the Turkish disasters, the Russians affixed placards on poles, written in misspelt, ungrammatical Turkish, facing the Turkish lines which read: "Kars has been taken, and Mouktar Pasha's army has surrendered. You are surrounded on all sides, and cut off from every possibility of escape and succour. Your Sovereign wishes to make peace: it is only Osman who retains you here. Surrender and preserve your lives for your families. If you do not you will die of starvation. You have done your best and nothing more can be expected of you." That night Skobeleff errected an illuminated sign stating that Kars had surrendered. These signs were shot down by the Turks.

On 13 November another *parlementaire* came into the Turkish lines with a second letter from the Grand Duke Nicholas. It informed Osman that he was completely surrounded and begged him in the name of humanity "to give up resistance and the useless shedding of blood". In his answer Osman replied, "I recognize the motives of humanity which have prompted the invitation addressed to me; but I do not consider that I have exhausted all means of resistance

which my situation commands me to employ." Five days
later he sent a *parlementaire* with a lettter to the Grand Duke
expressing his readiness to surrender, but only on condition
that he should leave the town "with all the honours of war",
and that his army should retire, without arms, to either
Sofia or Widdin, as he should choose. After a short deliberation, the Grand Duke replied that the proposition could not
be entertained, more especially as the capitulation of the
army of Plevna, without any conditions, was now only a
question of time.

For weeks the Plevna garrison had comforted themselves
with the thought that the Army of relief would soon arrive;
great reliance was placed on the sworn word of the Sultan
that Plevna would be saved. The coming of Mehemet Ali
was watched for and prayed for daily: sentries and outposts
at Krishnin when they returned to their lines were eagerly
asked, "Any news? Have you seen any smoke on the Orkhanie
road? Have you heard guns on the south?" Many were the
false alarms and bitter disappointments. "They must be here
tomorrow, they cannot tarry any longer," the men said to
each other, and when the morrow came and with it another
day of dreary waiting, the sentries looked towards the south
with ever increasing anxiety and suspense. "Why don't the
English help us?" some asked. "We have been told they
would, and now they have left us in the lurch. Are they
afraid of the Russians?"

At the end of October the Military Council at Constantinople suddenly woke up to the fact that they were about
to lose their best army at Plevna, and Mehemet Ali, the
German born, French educated, Turkish general, who had
been relieved of the command of the army of the Quadrilateral, was dispatched to Sofia with orders to collect an
army for the relief of Plevna. Other armies were denuded of
men, and troops were hurriedly brought to Sofia whether
or not they were suitable for such an undertaking. Shivering
Arabs and sturdy Anatolian peasants were herded together
into regiments with the remains of a Bosnian division that
had been through the fiery ordeal of the Shipka. Lacking in
cohesion and unity, the bulk of the army consisted of a rabble,

an utterly imperfect instrument for such an adventure. A man of energy and determination, Mehemet Ali advanced his army to Orkhanie, still held by Chefket Pasha, where he arrived on 22 November. Learning of this movement, General Gourko hurried towards Orkhanie. To the inexperienced and disorderly rabble of Mehemet's command the mere sight of the Russians was enough, and they fled in confusion and panic, and that was the end of the hoped for relief of Plevna.

"What will Osman do?" was the question asked on all sides in the Russian lines of investment. It was known from deserters that the Plevna garrison was suffering severe privations from hunger, cold and disease, and that supplies were dwindling. In a matter of a week or so Osman would have to decide whether to surrender or try to cut his way through the Russian lines. The Russians knew that a man of Osman's calibre would not surrender and they prepared for every eventuality. Meanwhile MacGahan found little to observe. One day he watched the families of several Bashi-Bazouks being escorted by guards to Plevna to which they were being sent as a retaliatory measure for the hundred Bulgarian families Osman had ejected. He noticed that they were being treated with great kindness by the Russian officers who gave them food and money, in spite of the fact that one of the women had recently shot a Russian sergeant.

Many of the war correspondents who had followed the Plevna campaign had left in despair of anything happening. MacGahan, Millet and Frederick Villiers stayed on and early in November they were joined by Irving Montagu, the war artist of the *Illustrated London News*, who had been in the Asiatic theatre of war for many months, and Coningsby of *The Times*. Montagu and Coningsby took up their quarters in a hut at Poradim, and an incident of their sojourn there was described by Coningsby at a press dinner in London after the war.

"Never, under any circumstances, gentlemen," he warned his listeners, "should you become a war correspondent, go to a war with a war artist: they are dangerous to a degree on the war-path, I can assure you.

"Some of you may remember a picture in the *Illustrated London News*," he went on, "representing Montagu and myself attacked by wolves in our encampment at Plevna. The true story of the origin of that sketch has never been told; you shall have it now." Coningsby described how one night they were disturbed by the howling of wolves outside the tent. There was, he knew, only one way to get rid of them. "If there was one thing in this world calculated above all others to scare those wolves, it would be a sketch by the

Mr. Coningsby
The Times, with the Turks

special artist of the *Illustrated London News*; so without much ado I rushed into Montagu's tent, seized one of his latest productions, and, rushing out into the open, displayed it by the light of the moon to those noisy intruders. The effect was magical: with a howl I can never forget they frantically tore away, far, far out into their dreary Balkan retreats. But, gentlemen, there is a terrible sequel to this, which proves, beyond the shadow of a doubt—how dangerous a travelling companion your war artist is."

About an hour afterwards, he explained, those persistent wolves actually came back in redoubled numbers. "It was a terrible vengeance on me," he said. "Montagu came

flying out of his tent. He startled me. Had one of the brutes
got hold of him? I asked myself. He came in breathless haste,
saying, 'There is but one thing now left to us, otherwise we
shall be devoured: it is a terrible resource, but extreme cases
call for extreme measures,' and with that he rushed forward
and seized my last manuscript for *The Times*. The next
moment I found him outside facing a crowd of those lean
beasts, reading aloud to them one of the paragraphs from
my last article. It was more than enough for our four-footed
enemy. They disappeared in less than no time; indeed I have
been told that they have not been seen in Bulgaria since."

In Constantinople, notwithstanding Osman's success,
signs of dissatisfaction and dissension were increasing daily
as the populace learned from English newspapers the
imminence and certainty of the fall of Plevna, which, according to their own newspapers was about to be relieved at any
moment. All Turkish newspapers were warned that they
would be suspended if they published 'false news' that is,
news unpleasant to the Turks, or, in the words of the official
warning, "of a nature to trouble men's minds", which made
the public believe that the news was worse than it actually
was. Most Turks had begun to believe that, in spite of the
bravery of their soldiers, there was nothing to be gained by
the war, and they were convinced that the European Powers
would never let the Russians take Constantinople. The sight
of the last reservists, men over forty, being marched up to
the Seraskierate, the War Department, to draw their uniforms, did little to reassure the people, and throughout the
Empire farms were going to waste, their harvests ungathered
for want of men. The terrible casualties, for Turkish warfare
was always conducted with wanton disregard of life, were
having their effect, and every one was war-weary. In con-
sequence, the 'peace party' with whom the Sultan was
believed to be in favour, grew in strength, in opposition to
those who, usually in their own interests, demanded a
continuation of the unequal struggle.

On 1 December Osman Pasha summoned all officers
commanding divisions, brigades and regiments to a council
of war. Before they left their commands each was instructed

The correspondents' camp attacked by wolves
(Montagu of the *Illustrated London News* and Coningsby of *The Times*)

Storming the Grivi

(The Great Assault)

Colonel Wellesley and the correspondents of the *Scotsman* and *Weekly Graphic* in the captured Grivitza redoubt

The Shipka Pass: General Radetzky's Dragoons to the rescue

Night attack: General Skobeleff resting in the forward trenches

The Tu

uced from a fifteen-square-foot supplement to the *Illustrated London News* of February 2, 1878)

Plevna

Osman Pasha on his way to be received by the Czar

Osman Pasha en route to Kharkoff
(presented with a bouquet in Bucharest)

to sound their men on two questions: "Shall we remain in Plevna until food is exhausted and surrender when there is nothing more to eat?" or "Shall we make a desperate effort to force the lines of investment?" When the commanding officers came to the council they stated that the overwhelming desire of their men was to try to break through the Russian lines. Osman himself said that he was in favour of a sortie, but many of his officers shrank from taking upon themselves the responsibility for the frightful bloodshed which must occur. "Let no man deceive himself," Osman said, "as to the chances of success of such an attempt. They are infinitesimal but I think the honour of our country and the fair name of our army render it incumbent upon us to make a last and supreme effort." The council decided unanimously in favour of the sortie.

Osman outlined his plan. The Orkhanie road to Sofia barred by Gourko's army corps, he said, offered not the slightest chance of success. He proposed that the Plevna garrison should cross the Vid at the bridge on the north-west of the town, and force its way through the Russian lines and, if successful, push off in the direction of the River Isker with the object of reaching Sofia by a long detour. If the venture succeeded, the armies of Widdin, Sofia and Plevna would be united, and one hundred and fifty battalions would be at the Sultan's disposal. The sortie was fixed for 10 December.

When the news of the impending battle became known in the garrison the prospects of action, and escape from the living death of Plevna, had a magical influence on the men. They became intoxicated with the hope of success; those who had despaired became merry and cheerful; sick men recovered miraculously and wounds that had refused to yield to treatment began to heal. Men who had sat glowering at each other in silence for days, burst into excited chatter about nothing in particular.

There was much to be done, and, as far as was possible, it had to be kept from the Russians. Stores had to be distributed and the men slowly withdrawn from their lines and brought to the concentration point on the plain by the bridge over the Vid, which was to be augmented by two further bridges. All this required much going to and fro, and to deceive the Russians, who from their artillery spotting observatories could look down into the Turks' lines, the march of detachments, artillery and wagon trains were made at night. Strict orders were given to all outposts and sentries to keep a watch for Bulgarians who might try to pass through the lines, it being well known that the Russians would reward handsomely information about any attempt at a sortie.

Apart from the organization of the break-out, which required minute detailing as to the disposition of the forces which would lead the assault on the Russian lines, their supports, and the marshalling of the wagon train of supplies, Osman had two other great problems to face, the fate of the Turkish residents and of the wounded and sick which he could not carry with him.

The Turkish civilians were determined to go with Osman: he shrank from hampering his army with five hundred Turkish families in ox-carts. Of the two evils, the danger and hardship of a forced march in winter through the Russian lines, which was certain to be pursued, if it succeeded; or the revenge of the Bulgarians, the Turks feared the latter more than the former. The leaders of the Turkish community, granted a hearing, threw themselves at Osman's feet, imploring him with tears in their eyes to save them from the Christians. At first Osman peremptorily refused to fetter his army with such a cumbersome burden. The Czar, he pointed out, who had shown his humanity by liberating the serfs, would not allow the inhabitants of a conquered town to be ill-treated. The Czar, the Turkish leaders urged, would be too late: the fury of the Bulgarians and of the Cossacks would be let loose directly Osman evacuated the town, some hours before the Czar could enter it. Eventually Osman gave way. He knew too well the cruelty of race and religion.

The sick and wounded who could not travel would have to be left behind. To ensure their safety, Osman summoned before him the Elders of the Bulgarian community and the Christian priests and made them swear on the Bible and on the Crucifix that no outrage would be committed upon the helpless inmates of the hospitals. The Bulgarians solemnly swore in the name of Jesus Christ that no harm would befall those left behind.

As the day of the attempted break-out approached, rifles were inspected, taken to pieces, cleaned, oiled and tested and, if found to be damaged, were replaced: each officer was issued with a Winchester repeating carbine; each man was given one hundred and thirty cartridges and six days' biscuit. Bayonets were sharpened and lances dealt out to the Circassian cavalry from the stock of captured Cossack trophies. Wagons were filled with ammunition, water, forage, tents, tools, blankets, and each battalion was allotted sixty pack-horses and twelve ox-drawn carts. Cart wheels, and gun-carriage wheels, were greased and bound with straw to deaden the sound of their movement. The last remaining supplies of food, salt, sugar and quinine were distributed and boots and sandals and linen rags for bandages were dealt out to the most needy.

Each battalion was ordered to send three officers to familiarize themselves with their designated route to the concentration point. Dummy figures were made to place in redoubts and trenches to make the Russians believe that they were still manned. By the doctors, six thousand convalescent wounded or sick, all who could walk, were selected to act as wagon drivers and orderlies. Those whose condition was hopeless, those who had lost legs or feet, and those suffering from infectious or contagious diseases were to be left behind. A thousand of these unfortunates were collected in the larger houses and put under the care of foreign surgeons. Three hundred carts were allocated to the Turkish civilians and a staff officer was appointed to see that they were not piled up with household goods and furniture. As the wagons and carts were packed they were sent to the concentration point on the plain on the east of the River Vid, which was screened from the gaze of the enemy by the hills.

During the morning of the 9th Osman Pasha's 'Order of the Day for the Sortie' was read to the troops. This gave detailed orders and times for the movement of each battalion and regiment. The army was divided into two divisions, each of three brigades, and a brigade was allotted to protect the convoy. The First Division was to attack the Russian lines, and the Second Division was to remain in support. On the conclusion of the reading of the Order, the men cheered lustily and cried "Allah Akbar" and "Yok tesslim", "No Surrender". As dusk fell, the soldiers quietly left the redoubts they had defended for so long and marched towards the northwest of the town. It was freezing cold and in the east dark snow clouds were massing. The stillness of the evening air was broken only by the suppressed sounds of moving men, carts and gun limbers, as the last rays of the sinking sun glinted for a moment on Plevna's domes and minarets. As the light died, flakes of snow began to fall.

William Herbert had a last farewell to make. During the siege he had become friendly with a young Turkish girl who, contriving to elude the vigilance of her family, always had something for him at the place of tryst, a cigarette, a drop of brandy or a loaf of bread. Years later he was to write that this ill-educated Turkish girl of seventeen was one of the only two women he had met who fulfilled his ideal of womanhood. The other was a Jewess whom he knew at Widdin. The Turkish girl was to accompany her family next day on the trek from Plevna, and Herbert, not knowing if they would meet again, took leave of her in a corner of her garden, by the dogs' kennel, the inmates of which had died of starvation and, unburied, were sending forth a stench which attracted a crew of carrion crows and croaking ravens who refused to be disturbed from their ghastly meal. As they talked, the contents of a bloody pail were thrown from the window of a neighbouring house, in use as a hospital, and they could hear the screech of the surgeon's saw as it worked its way through the bones of a leg or an arm. Herbert and the girl never met again, for she was killed next day with her family by a Russian shell.

At the concentration point the blackness of the night was lit by sparse fires which threw monstrous shadows as the gaunt men and lean beasts passed by the flickering flames. On the fringe of the bivouac, which occupied an area of two to three square miles, huddled the Turkish residents, the fat trader with his well-stocked harem, and the lean, hollow-cheeked labourer with his wife, child and donkey, the men preoccupied, the veiled women sobbing, and the youngsters playing at hide-and-seek around the carts and camp-fires. In the feeble light of lanterns the wagon trains and battalions moved silently into the light of the fires, an endless procession of soldiers taking up their appointed places.

Herbert walked through Plevna for the last time. Officers were going round placing notices on the houses where the wounded lay. Herbert helped them to place many of these signs which read:

Il n'y a que des
blessés dans cette
maison

As he went on his errand, Herbert thought: 'Desolate, dead, God-forsaken Plevna; it is no more like the thriving and pretty Plevna of July than the decaying corpse of an old hag is like the living body of a young girl in the full vigour of youth.' In the empty unlighted streets, here and there slouched an outcast, like a starving beast of prey; or a woman huddled in a shawl slipped by him. Surrounded by dark, silent, white-roofed houses, not a chink of light to be seen anywhere, the metallic ring of his footsteps on the frozen ground broke the silence of death. As he moved from house to house, tripping over a corpse in the gutter, from one came curses and screams. Pushing open the door, Herbert saw, in the feeble light of an oil lamp, men without feet, without arms or hands, fighting and struggling for a scrap of food one had found in a disused cupboard, a morsel which a dog or cat in a civilized house would consider itself insulted at being offered. As he stole away, a man leaped out of the darkness, trying to snatch the pot of paste, which he thought to be food, from his hand. Herbert belaboured the face he could hardly see with the brush and rammed it down the man's spluttering throat.

Finishing his bill-sticking, Herbert went to help the staff officers in the town-offices clear up and pack official papers. While he was there, Osman Pasha rode up, preceded by a torch bearer and escorted by a troop of Saloniki cavalry. Herbert had not seen him since the September battles, and as the torch-light fell on his face he saw that his features were drawn and care-worn, his cheeks hollow, and his fore-head lined, but his eyes were lit with the light of angry determination.

Herbert said good-bye to Plevna and went to his con-centration point, where he threw himself down listening as he dozed to the steady tramp of the men of the First Division who were moving over the bridges to take up their position for the morrow. Around Plevna, the redoubts and trenches lay silent and untenanted. To possess them, the Russians had expended 30,000 lives, and to defend them 10,000 Turks had died.

CHAPTER SEVENTEEN

THE BREAK OUT

AT 3.30 a.m. Skobeleff was awakened by an officer. A spy, a Polish Jew, had come through the lines; Osman had issued three days rations and a pair of sandals to each man and the army of Plevna was gathering on the plain by the bridge over the Vid; the redoubts and trenches in front of Skobeleff's sector were deserted. Would he lead a party of volunteers to the Turkish lines which he said were abandoned, and risk being bayoneted if his words were untrue? the spy was asked. He consented at once and the reconnaissance set off. They stealthily approached the Turkish lines; they stopped and listened. Not a sound could be heard. The party crept on. They reached the first line of trenches; they were empty, so were the second and third lines. Now they stood by the Krishnin redoubt. There was no sound of life, and they climbed inside. Its garrison of a thousand men were gone. Hurrying back the men told Skobeleff "The Turks are gone!" Skobeleff immediately telegraphed the news to the Grand Duke at Bogot and to General Todleben, and in a few minutes the drums were beating the alarm round the Russian lines of investment. Todleben, informed by the Rumanians that they had seen lights moving to the north-west of Plevna, warned General Ganetsky that the break out would probably be attempted against his sector, and he ordered a concentration of troops to support Ganetsky.

A burst of cannon-fire, instantly followed by the rattling crash of rifle-fire, warned the Russians that Osman was about to attempt to break through the toils. As the light of the winter's morning grew stronger, General Ganetsky's men could see that the plain and slopes of the heights over against them were covered with moving men and carts. Thick masses of Turkish infantry were pouring over the

199

bridges of the river, and advancing under cover of a long line of wagons. In a moment the baggage train is scattered and halted by the fire of a hundred cannon and 5,000 Berdan rifles.

The last battle of Plevna had begun. In between the advancing Turks and the Russians is a wide open plain, into which the gorge from Plevna opens like a funnel. On the Plevna side the plain is bounded by steep, rocky, bluffs or cliffs, at the foot of which runs the River Vid. From these cliffs now burst in quick irregular succession, angry bursts of flame which flashed and disappeared and flashed again. A thick pall of smoke rises against the heavy snow clouds banking on the horizon, and through the smoke the Russians catch glimpses of bodies of men, horses, cattle, carriages and wagons, pushing out across the plain. Above all rises the crashing roll of rifle-fire and the deep booming of the guns.

To MacGahan, watching from the Russian lines, it was a terrible and sublime spectacle, as 20,000 Turks advanced across the plain, thick lines of skirmishers in the lead, and on their heels another 20,000 men ready to protect their flanks and to support their charge. Behind came 500 wagons. So impetuous were the Turks that they were close to the Russian lines before their own guns had had time to fire more than a few rounds. As the heroes of Plevna advanced in silence at double quick time, they were greeted with a hail of fire. At their head rode Osman himself on a superb chestnut stallion, a present from the Sultan. As the long lines neared the Russian trenches, the bugles sounded 'Storm', and with cries of "Allah" thousands of Turks swept like a tornado into the trenches manned by the Siberian regiment. In a few minutes the Siberian regiment had been annihilated, and the Turks swept on to the batteries behind where, with desperate heroism, officers and men stood to their guns until they were hacked to pieces. The Turks had won the first round; they had broken the first lines of the circle that hemmed them in, but, before they had time to charge the next line of defences, the Russians had rallied. It was now 8.30 a.m.

While the Turks gathered for another charge, the 2nd Division of the Russian Grenadiers flung themselves furiously on the Turks with a loud cheer, and as 50,000 Turks and Russians fought hand to hand the battle swayed in the balance. But the overwhelming numbers of the Russians began to tell; Osman had delayed the advance of his 2nd Division too long, and the men of the 1st Division were thrown back, and the trenches recaptured. As the Turks hung in a hesitating mass the Samogitie Grenadiers, coming up on their flank, drove them back at the point of the bayonet. It was the moment of crisis. If Osman could bring up his reserves before the Russians from the other sectors came to Ganetsky's aid, he might yet burst through the line of encirclement. But an unexpected event dashed the Turkish hopes. Osman was wounded by a bullet which went through the calf of his leg. He was seen to fall heavily from his horse, and the news spread rapidly that he was dead. For five months, the Plevna garrison had been upheld by the moral force and the authority of their leader. As the news of Osman's supposed death spread through the ranks, the Turks fell back in disorder. Streaming back like a torrent, the now panic-stricken army broke through the 300 carts loaded with the civilian refugees of Plevna, overturning them, and leaving behind a scene of confusion, as they made for the deep banks of the Vid from where they returned the Russian fire. The Turkish sortie was repulsed. For four hours the plain in front of the bridge was swept by a hail of fire.

While the battle for the Russian lines had been going on, masses of troops from the other sectors of investment had been converging on the threatened sector, and advancing through Plevna to take the Turks in the rear. The Czar had been informed of the sortie, and he and the Grand Duke arrived in the Imperial redoubt at Radishevo in time to see his troops march through the defences that had defeated them for so long. Dispatches were brought to him every moment, and his staff hung breathless for each announcement of Russian loss and gain. At 9 a.m. the Rumanians, advancing along the Janik Bair, were halted by a storm of fire from a Turkish rear-guard in the redoubts at Opanetz, but they were soon captured yielding 2,000 prisoners. Coming up from the south-west General Kataley took prisoner 120 officers and 3,734 men who were protecting the Turkish left flank.

With the sortie repulsed, the Turks were taken front and rear. Their abandoned fortifications round Plevna were occupied by the Russians; there was no retreat and no hope of advance. For three hours the deadly hail of fire was poured in upon the Turks from an ever increasing number of Russian guns, and the air was filled with the smoke and thunder of the battle on which hung not the fate of Plevna, for that was already in Russian hands, but of Osman's army.

About 1 p.m. the firing began to die down on both sides and then it stopped entirely. The rolling crash of rifle-fire and the deep mouthed bellowing of the artillery, which had filled the air of Plevna for so long, was silenced. The Turks were hemmed in on all sides. All that human valour could accomplish had been done, and nothing remained but for them to lay down their arms and surrender to their victorious enemy. Amidst the smoke of battle, and the groans of the dying, the curtain fell on the last act of the drama which for 143 days had held the world spellbound.

Almost immediately after the firing ceased a white flag was seen waving from the road near the bridge. Osman was going to surrender. From the ranks of the Russians now closing round the Turks rose a great cheer, and it was taken up by the men behind and re-echoed by the cliffs. A moment later, a Turkish officer was seen riding over the bridge with a white flag in his hand. Led by Skobeleff thirty or forty Russians and newspaper correspondents rode towards the bridge, within point blank range of the Turkish infantry if they had chosen to fire. After a moment's talk with Skobeleff's interpreter, the officer, with his eyes bandaged, was led to General Ganetsky who, on learning that he was an officer of an inferior rank, refused to see him. A quarter of an hour later another officer appeared but, as he could speak only Turkish, he was sent back with a message written in French, addressed to Osman Pasha which ran: "Excellency, General Ganetsky who commands here, begs me to inform you that he could only receive for *pourparlers* a person able to represent you personally, for he knows that you are wounded."

As Skobeleff and MacGahan, and the others, moved nearer the bridge, another officer came and told them, "Osman is coming out". At last they were to meet their great antagonist. "Osman himself is coming out," someone exclaimed. "At any rate we will give him a respectful reception," remarked another. "He has saved the honour of his country," said Skobeleff. "Osman the Victorious he is, and Osman the Victorious he will remain." While they waited, MacGahan looked about him. The moment of Osman's appearance would be an historic one, and he wished to recall every detail. All around the ground was covered with grim relics of battle. Here and there the earth had been uptorn by the explosion of shells. Nearby lay a horse, groaning and struggling in death, close by an ox silently bleeding to death, his great, round, patient eyes looking mournfully about. In front was a cart with a dead horse lying in yoke as he had fallen, and alongside a Turkish soldier whose head had been carried off. Another lay under the wagon and around it were four wounded men, lying gazing up at the murky sky, or covered up with the hood of their ragged grey overcoats drawn up over their faces. Not one of them uttered a sound: they lay there and bore their sufferings with calm, stolid fortitude. Just behind the wagon the ground was ripped to pieces by shell-fire, telling how these unfortunates met their fate. The road and its edges were dotted here and there with dead and wounded Turkish soldiers, oxen, horses, and shattered carts; and a few hundred yards north of the road, the ground over which Osman Pasha's sallying column had made their heroic charge, was literally covered with dead and wounded.

Two horsemen appeared on the bridge. "It is not Osman," someone said. "It is Tewfik Pasha, Osman's chief of staff," declared another. Tewfik rode up to the group of Russian officers, and speaking very slowly in French he said, "Osman is wounded." "Not severely, we all hope," replied Skobeleff. "I do not know," was the answer. Then there was a long silence. "Is there anybody you wish to see?" asked

Skobeleff. "To whom do you wish to speak?" No reply. "What the devil is the matter with the man? Why doesn't he speak?" interjected Skobeleff in English. But Tewfik remained impassive, gazing steadfastly before him, and giving no sign that he had heard. "We look upon Osman as a great general," observed one of the officers, but Tewfik remained silent. Fortunately, at this moment, General Stroukoff of the Czar's staff arrived, and he elicited from Tewfik the information that the Turkish army surrendered, and Osman also. As Osman Pasha was unable to come himself, added Tewfik, and was unwilling to entrust the important duty of the surrender of his army to anyone else, he very much wished that General Ganetsky would come and see him in the little house to which he had been carried. An aide-de-camp was immediately sent to General Ganetsky. The little group of Russian officers and war correspondents waited in silence; around them lay the Turks, still armed; everyone's nerves were at the highest tension, and it would take, thought MacGahan, but an accidental shot to set everyone fighting again.

General Ganetsky seemed possessed with the same fear. He galloped up and simply said to General Stroukoff, "You go," pointing at the guard house by the bridge. The young officer immediately put spurs to his horse and galloped down the road through the ranks of the sullen and silent Turks who were massed round the bridge. Riding through the midst of the crowd of soldiers, and obliged to make frequent detours to avoid the killed and wounded, Stroukoff reached the little tile-covered loam hut, around which were standing a number of Turkish officers, beys and pashas, Osman's aides-de-camp, and doctors wearing the brassard of the Red Crescent. Throwing the bridle of his horse to his Cossack orderly, Stroukoff entered the house. Inside he was faced by three doors. The first opened into a stable full of wounded men; the second into a room in which stood a number of officers conversing together in subdued tones. In the third, a wretched little room filled with smoke from the fire and dimly lit by two small windows, he found Osman Pasha seated on a wooden bench, his wounded leg resting on an empty tin cartridge box. His face was pale, his eyebrows bent, but to Stroukoff his eyes expressed extraordinary intelligence and calmness. Hassif Bey, his surgeon, was attending to his wound, and at the back of the room stood several elderly generals, whose appearance betokened respect and sorrow.

On General Stroukoff's entrance, Osman rose with difficulty, made him the Oriental salute and extended his hand. "You are wounded, I beg you to remain seated, General," Stroukoff implored him. Stroukoff stated his name and rank and Osman invited him to take a seat, but the Russian thought it more seemly to remain standing. "I come here," he told Osman, "by the order of General Ganetsky, to congratulate your Excellency on your brilliant attack, and at the same time to inform you that General Ganetsky, having received no order from His Imperial Highness, the commander-in-chief, can only offer you a surrender without conditions for you and your whole army." After a few minutes of deep thought, Osman, slowly lifting his head, remarked to his surgeon, with a gesture of fatalistic resignation, "One day follows another, but no two days are alike; one brings success, another misfortune," and then, turning to Stroukoff, he said, with a suppressed sigh and a bow, "I submit myself entirely to the wishes of the commander-in-chief of your army." "Pasha," replied the ever courteous Stroukoff, "all is in the hands of God."

A few minutes later General Ganetsky arrived at the hut. Coming into Osman's room, he removed his cap and held out his hand with the frankness of an old soldier. "I congratulate you: your attack was magnificent. Give, I beg you, the order to your men to lay down their arms." For a moment there was complete silence. No one seemed willing to pronounce the last fatal word. "Excellency," said Stroukoff looking at his watch and addressing Ganetsky, "it is already after four o'clock, it will be too late . . . would you repeat your request?" An interpreter repeated Ganetsky's words, upon which Osman made a sign to Adil Pasha, one of his generals of division, who saluted him respectfully and left the room with General Stroukoff. Osman Pasha, accepting the inevitable with a shrug, suddenly took off his sword and, after looking at it for a moment as if to say 'farewell', handed it to General Ganetsky.

Outside, near the bridge, the Russians had slowly approached nearer and nearer the Turkish army, and it was now closely surrounded. The Turks sat or lay on the ground amidst the broken carts and guns; the Russians stood in a wide circle, some 50,000 men awaiting the last act in the drama of Plevna. Adil Pasha strode up a little hill and stood on its summit, like a Mullah on the spire of his minaret calling the faithful to prayer. Waving his hand, he called upon the soldiers to lay down their arms. For a moment there was complete silence, the Turks remained motionless, then their officers moved among the men, explaining the folly of resistance, and telling them to throw down their rifles. Slowly and unwillingly the Turks cast aside their rifles, tore off their cartridge pouches and emptied the cartridges on to the ground. Some stamped on them till all the powder had run out.

While the surrender of the army of Plevna was being completed, Skobeleff and Ganetsky crossed over the Vid to await the Grand Duke Nicholas who came to congratulate the troops, and particularly the gallant Siberian regiment and Grenadiers, who had withstood the Turkish assault. He congratulated them on their brilliant victory and their heroic courage and, raising his cap, called for a ringing cheer for the Czar. Osman Pasha who was proceeding in his carriage to Plevna, hearing that the Grand Duke had arrived, turned back to meet him. As the Russian commander-in-chief rode up to the carriage, Osman raised himself up, and assisted by his surgeon, steadied himself by holding the hood of his carriage. For some moments the two leaders gazed at each other, and then the Grand Duke stretched out his hand, and shaking Osman's warmly exclaimed; "I compliment you on your defence of Plevna. It is one of the most splendid exploits in history." Osman smiled sadly and answered in a few words, which were lost in the cries of "Bravo, Bravo" with which the officers of the Grand Duke's suite saluted the hero of Plevna. Prince Charles of Rumania who came up congratulated him also, but to him Osman did not reply so warmly for to the Turks the Rumanians were rebels.

"He is a grand figure," exclaimed Colonel Gaillard, the French Military Attache, to MacGahan, "I was almost afraid of seeing him lest my expectation should be disappointed, but he more than fulfils my ideal." "It is the face of a great military chieftain," said Skobeleff, "I am glad I have seen him." By the Grand Duke, who was introducing his staff to Osman, Skobeleff was called to the carriage. For a moment he and Osman looked at each other. At first the commander of Plevna did not quite comprehend who he was, then his face relaxed into a smile, and his hand went out to Skobeleff. "One day you will be the commander-in-chief of the Russian army," he said. Each had met a foe worthy of his steel; they bowed and parted, never to meet again.

Osman was taken into Plevna, to spend the night with his doctor and servants in a Bulgarian house. The Czar also passed the night in the town and next morning he expressed the desire that Osman Pasha should join him for lunch. On the Grand Duke's orders, Osman had already started for Bucharest, but he was stopped and brought back and transferred to the carriage the Czar had placed at his disposal. As he was helped from the carriage at the gate of the Czar's house and assisted to walk up the path, a spontaneous cheer, with cries of "Bravo, Osman", broke from the two to three hundred officers assembled to welcome him. With Hassif Bey on one side, and an aide-de-camp on the other, Osman slowly made his way to the dining-room where the Czar's chef had laid out all the delicacies the Imperial cuisine could provide. As he entered the room the Czar moved forward to welcome him. Osman made to remove his sword and hand it to his conqueror, but the Czar stopped him and gave it back. Through an interpreter the two men had a long conversation, at the end of which the Czar expressed the hope that Osman would have no reason to be dissatisfied with his treatment in Russia. Before Osman left for Kharkoff, his assigned place of internment, Colonel Klioutcharoff, of the Czar's staff, presented him with a sprig of myrtle as a sign that the prisoner army, and its valorous chief, should no longer be included amongst the enemies of Russia.

The night before, finding Tewfik wandering about searching for Osman, Skobeleff took him off to his quarters. MacGahan who was with them, describes the meeting of the two men who had fought so valiantly against each other on the Green Hills where Tewfik led the counter-attack in September.

"A warm fire burning gaily in General Skobeleff's mud hut, a glass of vodka and some warm soup at once thawed out our benumbed hands and feet, and we were soon enjoying a hot dinner, with the appetites of men who had been in the saddle since daylight, with not a morsel to eat. Tewfik seemed much depressed and downcast. He spoke little, and was at first almost as taciturn as he had been on the bridge. He brightened up, however, as the meal progressed, drank a glass of red wine, a glass of sherry, and a couple of glasses of champagne, when General Skobeleff proposed the health of Osman Ghazi, and drank to the brave defenders of Plevna. A merry smile broke over his face when Skobeleff asked him who had commanded the Turks on the Green Hills, and I think it must have occurred to him now, for the first time, that his entertainer was Skobeleff, the indefatigable, restless, daring spirit with whom he had exchanged so many hard blows on the Lovtcha road and Green Hills. Nobody had mentioned Skobeleff's name in his presence, nor had Skobeleff told him who he was, but the fact that we had come out of the Lovtcha road, together with Skobeleff's question about the Green Hills, was quite enough to en- lighten him. So he said, with a smile, 'Ah, it is you who gave us such tough work on the Green Hills all this time. You are General Skobeleff.' Skobeleff laughed and said 'Yes'. 'That was a very good attack of yours that evening in the fog and darkness. Very well done. But you did not get it all.' 'No,' said Skobeleff, 'I did not want it all,' and they both laughed."

But Tewfik soon lapsed again into sadness. Skobeleff put him in his bed and went off to spend the night with some of his officers.

During the night, the Russians moved into Plevna, and at noon next day the Czar attended the celebration of a *Te Deum* in the great Grivitza redoubt, held so long and heroically by the Turks. At the entrance to the redoubt, the possession of which had cost so many lives, the Grand Duke waited: as the Czar in his carriage, accompanied by Prince Charles of Rumania, drove up, the assembled troops broke into a loud cheer, and from the cordon of guns round Plevna, came a tremendous salvo unaccompanied this time by the angry hiss and explosion of shells that had gone on for so many months. As the Czar alighted, the Grand Duke advanced and saluted; the Czar kissed him and hung round his neck the grand cordon of the Order of St. George, and Generals Todleben, Imeretinsky, and Generals Nepokoit-schitski and Ievitzki, the chiefs of staff and his assistant of the army of Bulgaria, were invested with different grades of the same order.

Within two days of the fall of Plevna, the Czar left Bulgaria and returned to St. Petersburg, but before he left he expressed a wish to lunch with Skobeleff who had been made Military Governor of Plevna. He arrived at noon, and invited the general to join him at the table. As master of the house, it was customary for the host to remain standing, superintending the meal of his royal visitor. After lunch, the Czar turned to Skobeleff, saying, "Show me your house," and to his staff, "You, gentlemen, need not accompany us." As Skobeleff showed him round, the Czar suddenly embraced him and told him, "I thank thee, Skobeleff, for all thou has done. For thy good service, many, many, thanks." The slur of June was finally erased.

On 10 December, a telegram, which came from Paris, was received by a Greek banker in Constantinople. It appeared to relate to a matter of romantic interest: "Mademoiselle Plevnice has become engaged to M. Kamaroff", it ran, and within an hour all the capital knew that Plevna had fallen. The way to Constantinople was open and once more Hannibal was at the gates. For months the Sultan had kept the bad news of the war from the people. Only the better informed had seen through the smoke screen of thanksgiving services for fictitious victories, and the popular cries of Abdul, the 'Victorious', as the Sultan paid his regular Friday visits to the Mosque. Now the Ottoman Empire faced disaster. Freed from Plevna, the Russian armies would soon be knocking on the gates of Constantinople. Would he become the scapegoat of popular fury? the Abdul asked himself. From his palace he watched anxiously to see how the people would take the news of Plevna. Nothing happened. Fate had willed it, the people said, when they learned of Osman's surrender: their anger and hatred was directed not against the Sultan but against the Christians.

All was now lost, save Constantinople itself. Somehow the victorious Russians must be halted. For 400 years the Crescent had waved over the Bosporus. Twice it had been carried to the gates of Vienna. Since 1453 Hagia Sophia had resounded with the words of the Koran: would now the Bible return? With the war now virtually lost, the Sultan turned all his energies to keep the Russians from Constantinople. He sent an urgent request to Queen Victoria asking her to intercede with Russia for an armistice as a prelude to the conclusion of peace. For a year Abdul had relied on the intervention of the Powers, more particularly Britain. Day by day he had watched the ebb and flow of British politics; who was victorious at Westminster was more important to him than who won in Bulgaria. From his garden in his palace at Yildiz, in his summer house equipped with the most modern telescope and the most up-to-date telegraphic system, Abdul sat gazing out over the Bosporus, listening to the pulse of Europe, and anxiously watching for the smoke of the British battleships which would draw an iron curtain between Constantinople and the Russians.

In Downing Street, Disraeli heard the news of Plevna. Its significance was not lost upon him. Freed at last the Russian hosts would surge forward to Constantinople. In a lecture before the Royal United Service Institute on 30 November, Archibald Forbes had said that, if Plevna fell before Christmas, and weather conditions were favourable, there would be "no serious obstacle to prevent the Russians from crossing the Balkans immediately afterwards by the

Shipka Pass". Disraeli read Forbes's opinion in *The Times* on 3 December. At a meeting of the Cabinet hastily called on 12 December, the Foreign Secretary was ordered to express "their earnest hope that should the Russian armies advance to the south of the Balkans, no attempt would be made to occupy Constantinople or the Dardanelles". Such an occupation, the Foreign Secretary was commanded to explain to the Russian Ambassador, "even though it should be of a temporary character and for military purposes only", would be "most desirable to avoid". If such an occupation "appeared imminent", he was instructed to warn the Ambassador, public opinion in Britain "might call for measures of precaution".

Public opinion in Britain left the Russian Ambassador in no doubt of its sentiments. Since June the British Fleet had lain in Besika Bay, near the Aegean entrance to the Dardanelles. "We don't want to fight," yelled the British crowds, "but by jingo if we do," they chorused, "we've got the ships, we've got the men, we've got the money too. The Rooshun Bear we've thrashed before, and while we're Britons true, THE RUSSIANS SHALL NOT HAVE CONSTANTINOPLE." And they meant it. The *Morning Post* demanded that hostilities must cease immediately, or England would declare war. The *Standard* declared that England must stand between the Russians and Constantinople. Parliament was summoned to meet on 17 January, unusually early, and it was learned that the Government proposed to ask for a Vote of Credit of £6,000,000 for the army.

In London, 'Plevna' was on everyone's lips. Sangers Circus was brought to a close with a huge military spectacle entitled 'The Bombardment and Fall of Plevna', most realistically staged, and at every music hall show some reference was made in song or patter to the topic of the hour.

In St. Petersburg, Archibald Forbes, witnessed the reception of the victorious Czar by the people of his capital, "a reception," he wrote, "the like of which for pure enthusiasm I have never witnessed." According to custom, which prescribed that the Czar in setting out for, or in returning from, any great enterprise shall kiss the glittering image of the Holy Virgin of Kazan, the Czar drove straight from the railway station to the Kazan Cathedral, where Forbes was already installed and was to telegraph to the *Daily News*:

"Its interior was a wonderful spectacle. People had spent the night sleeping on the marble floor, that they might be sure of a place in the morning. There had been no respect of persons in the admissions. The Mujik in his skins stood next to the soldier-noble whose bosom glittered with decorations. The peasant woman and the princess knelt together at the same shrine. At the tinkle of a bell the great doors were thrown wide open, and on the surge of cold air was borne a great throbbing volume of sounds, the roar of the cheering of vast multitudes, the booming of artillery, the clash of the pealing joy bells. In stately procession the Emperor reached the altar, bent his head and his lips touched the sacred image. When he turned to leave the building, the wildest confusion of enthusiasm laid hold of the throng. His people closed in about the Czar till he had no power to move."

Rescued by the officers of his suite, the Czar passed close to Forbes who could hardly recognize him as the same anxious, hollow-cheeked man he had last seen standing in a Bulgarian road. The fall of Plevna had restored him to health and spirits, and he looked, Forbes thought, cheerful and happy. Before the war started, Forbes was told, the Czar had jokingly consulted a gipsy as to its outcome, and the Oracle had replied, Forbes was assured, "Beware of Plevna".

In Plevna the heroic army of Osman was herded into captivity. The number of prisoners taken was recorded by the Russians as, 10 pashas, 130 superior officers, 2,000 subaltern officers, 40,000 infantry and artillery men, and 1,200 cavalry, in all 43,340 men. It was estimated that the attempt of Osman Pasha to break out had cost the Turks between five thousand and six thousand lives and the Russians two thousand. Seventy thousand rifles and seventy-five guns were captured. The prisoners were kept in Plevna, encamped in the open. No food was given them and no attention was paid to the wounded and sick. When the Turks asked for food the Russians told them that they had been issued with six days biscuit on the 9th. They could not drink the water of the Vid, because it was contaminated by the hundreds of bodies that had been thrown into it by the Russians. There were no drugs and no firewood, though the Russians offered to sell pieces from the broken Turkish carts at 4s. 8d. per single block. Only those who had money could live. Russian, Polish and Rumanian Jews sold bread at 1s. 10d. per loaf of 12-16 oz., clean water at 10d. per mug, cheese at 10d. per oz. and a single potato at the same price. The officers' baggage was seized and sold by the Russian privates at auction, and those who resisted robbery were killed. Even Osman's private baggage was seized, and the Turks who had been placed in charge of it were killed.

In the fortnight in which the prisoners remained at Plevna, three to four thousand died from the privations and sufferings to which they were subjected. On eight of the fourteen days, a small dole of bread was dealt out, and batches of starving, shivering men were sent through the frost and snow from one internment camp to another and back again. Many of the Russian officers, to their credit, expressed the deepest indignation at the way Osman's gallant army was treated, but no one did anything about it. "It is the fortune of war," declared the Russians with a shrug of the shoulders. Many of the horrors to which the prisoners were subjected were due to nothing more than disgraceful inefficiency. Although the Russian leaders had known for months that Osman's army must one day surrender and would be without food, no arrangement had been made to feed, clothe or provide medical attention for 40,000 men. No one had thought of it.

No one thought, either, of the Turkish wounded and sick who had been left in the town; to be more precise, only the Bulgarians thought of them. They missed some, but many, and those who had stayed to look after them, and in the end nearer four thousand than one thousand as originally intended had been left behind, were dragged from their shelters and massacred. The Bulgarian Christians had sworn in the name of their Saviour to respect the men without legs or feet, and those too sick to be taken, and in the name of their Saviour they cut their throats, disembowelled them, gouged out their eyes and kicked them to death. Some escaped and when the Russians woke up to the fact that there were at least a thousand men requiring attention in Plevna, besides those who had been wounded in the sortie, their condition was fearful. For three days they had been without food or water and their wounds had been undressed. Hundreds died, each hospital room had become a charnel-house, the air tainted with putrefying corpses of the dead and the festering wounds of those still living. One correspondent, Frank Millet, who entered Plevna with the Russians says: "The most active imagination cannot picture the thousandth part of the frightful suffering, misery, and wretchedness to be found within the narrow limits of the town, nor draw the faintest outline of the panorama of ghastly horrors, almost unparalleled since the plagues of past centuries, which were there exhibited." In the houses, which formed the receptacles for the sick and wounded, the living and dead lay together indistinguishable along the walls, behind the doors and under the windows. Considerable force was necessary, he found, to open a door, as across the entrance there lay the lifeless bodies of wretched creatures who had dragged themselves thither in the last hours of their agony in hope of succour, or at least of a breath of fresh air. When the doors were at last thrust open, putrid odours burst out, overpowering strong men and causing them to turn sick and faint. In the mosques the pavement was covered with crouching forms, some moving, others motionless and silent; while here and there the faces of the dead stood out in ghastly relief, with a fixed expression of great agony.

The dead were dragged out from the living. Fifty soldiers carried the bodies to three peasants' carts, all that were available, and the corpses were carted away and thrown into ditches. The work progressed so slowly that some Bulgarians were compelled to assist, and their brutality horrified the witnesses. They dragged the bodies down the stairs by the legs, the heads bumping from step to step with sickening thuds; then out into the streets through filthy mud, where they slung them into the carts, with the heads or legs hanging over the side, until they had a load of a score of half-naked corpses. Their conversation while they did their work was horrible to hear. Sometimes they brought out a body still warm, the heart still beating, and the flush of life on the cheek. One Bulgarian said, "He is still alive", and proposed to leave him without stopping to see if he was alive or dead. The others cried, "Devil take him! He will die before tomorrow anyway. In with him." And so the living went in with the dead, and were tumbled together into the same grave.

When the three carts had been filled, they were driven away, jolting and shaking, so that, now and then, a body fell out into the mud and was picked up and jammed in amongst the others to prevent it falling out again. All these proceedings were carried on in the full light of day when the streets were crowded with men, women and children, until the sickening sight became so common that no one heeded or cared.

When the dead had been removed, bread and water were pushed into the rooms of the sick, and the feeble wretches fought for it with their last breath. Some, propped up against the wall, slowly ate until their eyes became fixed in death. The effort of eating the long needed food was too much for them. The living seized the morsels in the dead man's hand and struggled for it, cursing each other and wrangling over the spoil, to fall dead themselves, perhaps, before they had time to eat the coveted crust of bread.

So perished some of the heroes of Plevna, victims of man's inhumanity to man.

On the same day he had been received by the Czar, Osman Pasha was escorted by a guard of honour composed of Cossacks to Bogot where he stayed in a tent for a fortnight being attended by his own surgeon, and by a German doctor and some Sisters of the Red Cross. From there he was sent to Kharkoff where he was treated with a chivalry and a magnanimity which formed a glaring contrast to the terrible sufferings his soldiers were forced to undergo on their march to Russia.

The majority of the prisoners were sent off within a week or so of the fall of Plevna. The Russians had made no provision for the thousands of starving, ill-clad men who came into their hands in the midst of winter, and the army that had fought so gloriously in the defence of Plevna was subjected to the most brutal treatment. In weather that became suddenly severe, the Turks were marched off in rags and without shoes, although along their route thousands of empty transport wagons moved in the same direction. If a man fell by the wayside, he was left to freeze to death, his body to be devoured by the wolves. Between Plevna and Bucharest, 5,000 men died; of the 43,000 men who set out, only 15,000 reached Russia, and only 12,000 returned to their homes after the war. In all, some 50,000 Turks died in Russian captivity.

Frederick Villiers made a drawing of the 'Death March of the Turkish Prisoners', the 'saddest sight' he ever witnessed. Travelling through Rumania with Colonel Humphrey Sandwith, C.B., who was in charge of funds to alleviate suffering in the war between Russian and Turk, Villiers found the route strewn with dead oxen and horses. The temperature was fifteen degrees below zero. It was bitterly cold and the countryside was one vast plain of snow, broken only by the bleak telegraph poles which traced the road. The dead stillness was broken only by the dull beating of the carrion crows as they hovered over their prey. Far off, breaking the horizon, came a long line, slowly moving in caterpillar fashion. Villiers saw it was a column of men, spiritless and broken as they trudged to captivity. They were half-starved, almost dead with fatigue and the cruel cold, many with fever burning in their eyes, mere walking bones and foul rags. Sandwith, with the keen scent of the medical practitioner, sniffed the taint of small-pox and typhus lingering around them in the frozen air. "For our lives, Villiers, we must get to windward of these poor fellows," he shouted and he drove the sleigh to the left flank of the approaching column.

As they passed the slowly moving column, Villiers saw that many of these miserable creatures were falling out of the ranks and lying down to die. One had just thrown himself in the snow at the roadside; he could go no farther. A comrade, loath to leave him, followed and tried to persuade him to struggle once more to join the line. There was no answer; he had swooned or was dead. The ghastly line of living phantoms were trudging wearily forward. A soldier of the rear-guard now came up. With the butt end of his musket he roughly pushed the living man back into the ranks; then with a brutal kick turned the head of the fallen Turk over in the snow. A wild fixed glare met his gaze. The Turk was dead. The soldier hastily shouldered his rifle and rejoined the guard.

Thousands and thousands of birds of prey whirled around, settling in front or rear of this sad procession, like sharks round a doomed ship. A few yards farther on, lying half covered with snow, was the nude body of a dead Turk, who had been stripped by his companions for the sake of the little warmth of the fetid rags he had worn on his gaunt limbs. A carrion crow had just settled on his clenched hand, and the dogs were hurrying up to their loathsome repast.

Another man lay with upturned face staring at the heavens through the slowly falling snow. He was not quite dead, although the flakes lodged on his fixed eyeballs. Dogs and swine from the village nearby were quarrelling for their share of the ghastly feast.

In the next village, Putineiu, Villiers and Sandwith found a Russian officer caring for the prisoners. He was full of compassion, but Villiers found his dress, rich sables and a gold-mounted stick, a strange contrast to that of the ragged men to whose wants he administered so kindly. After each contact with the prisoners, the Russian, Villiers observed, stripped by the stove in his quarters while his servant sprayed him with Violette de Parme, sponged his beard, and combed his hair in a jewelled mirror, which came from his gold and turquoise dressing-case, a gift from the Czar. The Russian lit a cigarette in a jewelled amber holder. "Pah!" he exclaimed. "One cannot eat suckling pig and caviare when these poor devils are starving, but one can smoke and not be ashamed, and this tobacco is priceless."

As Villiers and his companion left the village, another long black line came in sight, more prisoners tramping footsore and weary, with cadaverous faces and ice-laden beards. Some trudged along on their heels: their toes had been sloughed away in the biting frost; many were half naked, the rotten clothes having dropped from their limbs, showing great pale patches of frost-bitten flesh.

Plevna had fallen, but the War was not yet done.

CHAPTER EIGHTEEN

ONWARD TO CONSTANTINOPLE

THE Turks still had 175,000 men under arms in the European theatre of war. The war was far from lost but, after the fall of Plevna, Turkish resistance collapsed. Since the beginning of the war Turkey had lost 75,000 men fallen, and disabled by wounds and disease: another 75,000 had been taken prisoner, 150,000 men of the best blood of the Ottoman Empire, more than it could stand. The armies south of the Balkans now consisted of elderly reservists, new recruits and undisciplined Asiatic irregulars. At a council of war in Constantinople, it was urged that the armies should retire to Adrianople and make it a second Plevna. This was the right course, but it was overruled, and Suleiman, now the Turkish commander-in-chief, was allowed to execute his plan to defend the line of the Balkans, which the Turks were convinced could not be crossed in winter.

The next Russian step was not easily decided. One hundred and ten thousand men had been released by the fall of Plevna, but the Russian armies were confined by the frozen Danube in their rear and snowy mountain barrier ahead. Many of the older generals advised delay but, urged on by Gourko and Skobeleff, the Grand Duke flung caution to the winds and decided to strike a final blow while the Turks were demoralized at the loss of Plevna, and before the English could intervene. The possibility of British intervention, to prevent the Russians reaching Constantinople, was thought so likely that the Russian commanders were warned to consider as an enemy every person or body of men having a military character, even though belonging to a non-Mussulman nationality and wearing a uniform other than Turkish.

On 18 December, a winter of terrible severity, even for

the Balkans, set in and the temperature dropped to three degrees Fahrenheit. The Turks, knowing the hurricanes of snow, named the 'Kriwitza', which raged at this time of the year, in their milder climate south of the Balkans, reassured each other that the crossing of the Balkans would be impossible for months. These storms, which frequently raged for several days, blew with such terrific violence that no one ventured out while they lasted. The strongest trees were uprooted, and the roofs of houses carried away: warned of their approach, the people of the Balkans prepared for a week's siege. The Russians paid little attention to the warnings of the local inhabitants, but were soon undeceived by a series of disasters. A convoy of wounded, surprised by one of these tempests, was unable to advance a step. The ambulance carts were overthrown and the whole convoy was overwhelmed, few escaping to tell the tale. At one camp buried in the snow, the soldiers set to work to dig out their comrades, and found them dead. In the defiles of the Balkans it was impossible to face the storms. Many Russian outposts succumbed to the fury of the storm and the snow fell so heavily that it was impossible to distinguish a man at fifteen paces. When the tempests ceased, the snow remained and the soldiers wrapped themselves in old carpets and pieces of tents, to keep out the cold, and enveloped their boots in rags and pieces of sheepskin to prevent them from slipping. These were the conditions that faced the Russian columns advancing through the Balkans.

Skobeleff determined to buy up for his men all the furs he could lay his hands on, and, having as usual no money, he appealed to his father, now his junior in rank. The old man, who pretended the most fearful jealousy of his brilliant son, inquired at once, before he was even told the reason for his son's call, "How much?" "How much of what?" asked Skobeleff ingenuously. "How much money do you want? I can see through you, you know," demanded Skobeleff senior. "You are cleared out again, I suppose." "What are you thinking of? I have several thousands with me. I only want you to help me buy fur coats for my men. You know I don't understand these things. I only want your advice." The father's face lit up with a self-satisfied smile. "Of course, as though you understood anything." "How can I, without your advice?" humbly replied Skobeleff. "Without you I can do nothing." Quite thawed, father and son went off to see the Rumanian merchant. Skobeleff senior inspected each coat separately; pulled it out, smelled at it and almost tasted it to see that it was good, so that the perspiration stood in large drops on his brow, until the transaction was completed, and the wagons driven off to his son's headquarters. "Well good-bye, Father, and thank you very much," called Skobeleff as he mounted his horse. "To whom shall I send the bill?" inquired the fur dealer. "Oh, to my father! Father, pay him please. I will return the money," shouted Skobeleff as he put spurs to his horse. When General Dimitri Skobeleff died three years later, Skobeleff learned that he was far richer than he had made out. Knowing his son, the old man had never dared tell him!

The Russian advance was organized into two spear-heads, that of General Gourko on the west, from Orkhanie to Sofia, and that of General Radetsky through the Shipka, which was subdivided into three columns, those of Skobeleff on the west, Radetsky in the centre and Prince Mirsky on the east. While Gourko took the longer route via Sofia to Adrianople, which was defended by Suleiman with 40,000 men, the other three columns would simultaneously pour out of the Balkan defiles on Veissel Pasha, who had at his command another 40,000 men, and push on to Adrianople.

Faced by a narrow gorge, protected by sixteen redoubts, and impossible to carry by direct attack, Gourko determined to by-pass it by mountain paths, but no one knew of a road. Never dreaming that anyone could find an alternative route, the Turks sent no one to watch for the Russians elsewhere. Inquiring of the local Bulgarians, Gourko found a shepherd who declared he knew a mule path through the defiles, and a reconnaissance showed it to be practical. On 25 December, his men set out through three feet of snow and at a temperature of fifteen degrees below freezing point, along steep mountain paths, and by 2 January they were down on the other side in the plain of Sofia without the

Turks suspecting that their flank had been turned. Taken unawares, the Turks were routed and Sofia was occupied on 4 January.

In his Order of the Day, Skobeleff told his men, "We shall be surrounded by precipices and abysses. We are going where the wild beasts even have not penetrated." He told each man to carry a bundle of wood for making fires and he mounted his small mountain guns, all he could take, on the backs of camels he had brought from Asia. Each soldier was given six days' rations and had to carry ninety-six cartridges. So well organized was his advance that not a man was lost crossing the mountains where the snow lay in places ten feet deep and had to be tunnelled through. Over a thousand men died from frost-bite alone in the other columns. So long was Skobeleff's column that its head debouched on the southern side of the mountains before the tail had started on their journey.

On mounting the first hill, Skobeleff's men saw before them an immense wall of rock, steep, frowning and wind-swept. Scrambling and climbing they reached the summit, exhausted and out of breath to find another steep wall frowning down upon them. This one was covered with deep snow, into which they sank to their chests. Pushing forward, they wound now to the right, now to the left, then turning back again to avoid a yawning precipice. At the top they found footpaths through the forests so narrow that the men had to march in single file. The snow was so deep that each man had to strain to lift his foot out of the snow into which it had sunk. Sometimes the snow slipped under their feet, their legs spread out and they fell sprawling. In the thickets, bushes had to be bent on one side, the branches scratching the men's faces and tearing their clothes to rags. Mountain guns on sledges were pulled along with ropes. Some ascents were so steep that the men slipped down five or six times before they succeeded in reaching the top. Some fell up to their necks in to snowdrifts and had to be pulled out by their comrades making a chain, holding each other's waists. The clothes of those who fell in the snow became frozen stiff, and their hair froze into matted ice. Fatigued and weary, some of the men sat down on rocks of ice, but these immediately rolled away down steep inclines. If they threw themselves down in the snow, those that followed marched over them, tramping on their faces and chests.

Skobeleff was through it all, encouraging his men, taunting one, laughing at another, helping a third man out of a hole. When at last he lay down to rest, a cordon of men formed around him to prevent him from being trampled on. "This is an impossible undertaking," one of his officers said to him. "All the better," was the reply, "because the Turks will not expect us. A leader on the defensive should always dread so-called impossible positions." When the men reached their first night's quarters, they found a hot meal ready, for Skobeleff, throughout the march, pushed forward supplies of food. The cooks dug down until they got to the earth, made fires with the wood they had brought, and cooked the men's suppers.

Next day the same laborious march lay before them. There was no road or even the tracks of wild beasts to follow. The Cossacks were sent ahead to construct a path: they lay down on the snow and crawled along, pressing it down as they went. Then they walked up and down pressing it hard. On the right as the army passed rose a mountain wall, on the left a precipice fell perpendicularly into unfathomable depths. The abyss made men giddy: two got sick and fell to their death. Long before his army was through the mountains, Skobeleff, with whom was Kuropatkin, his chief of staff, was down on the plain reconnoitring the enemy position.

While Radetsky held the Turkish centre, Skobeleff attacked their left flank, and Mirsky threatened them on the other flank. On 9 January, before all his men were through the mountains, and with no artillery save a few mountain guns, Skobeleff attacked Veissel Pasha at Shenovo. As usual he led the assault in person; surrounded by his officers he stood on a little knoll above which flew the tattered standard which had followed him from Khiva to Plevna, and now to Shenovo. The enemy concentrated its artillery on the prominent group of officers. "Gentlemen," Skobeleff asked, "will you please stand a little more apart, distribute yourselves a little more. Otherwise we shall all be blown to pieces. Today, my life is wanted," he added in apology. "If I fall there is no one to take my place."

Skobeleff ordered the Onglitzky Regiment to advance. In a few minutes they had cleared the first trenches, and the Turks could be seen running to a wood behind. When the Russians did not follow, the Turks came out and started firing. "Send two squadrons of Cossacks to clear them out," ordered Skobeleff. Lowering their lances the Cossacks hurled themselves on the Turks who ran back into the wood: Skobeleff sent the Onglitzky Regiment in to clear them out. Amongst the trees the fight became one of bayonets and rifle butts, the Turks being chased from tree to tree and from thicket to thicket.

Two more regiments had now come through the mountains. As they marched up with bands playing and flags flying, Skobeleff exclaimed, "Now victory is certain," and launched them against the Turkish centre, into a hand to hand bayonet fight in which quarter was neither asked nor given. As the Russians and Turks thrust at each other, neither looked into the other's face, for it is a superstition that the dead man's glance will haunt his killer for life. Desperately as the Turks defended their position, they were forced back at the point of the bayonet. The Russians carried all before them. They passed through the Turkish trenches and redoubts like a whirlwind. By a quarter to two, the village of Shenovo was in their hands. Before Skobeleff reached it an orderly came galloping back to say, "Your Excellency, the Turks have hung out a white flag." "How, where?" he asked. "Surely not so soon as that?"

As Skobeleff and his staff galloped up, a procession came to meet him, doctors and hospital men, waving above their heads sheets of paper, their Geneva certificates. "Let them attend to the wounded," Skobeleff ordered. "They are doctors. They will help our fellows as well as the enemy's. They are our friends, let no one insult them." Then the staff galloped on. Riding through the wood, and passing heaps of bodies, they came out on the plain. On the left, Radetsky's men were beginning to flow out of the Shipka, under the frowning masses of the Balkans. Ahead lay a long line of redoubts, held by Skobeleff's men. As Skobeleff rode up he asked, "Where is the white flag?" "Behind us," the soldiers shouted. There on the summit of a little hill, beside a row of guns, waved the flag of surrender.

A cavalcade approaches. It is Veissel Pasha coming to surrender. Skobeleff stretches out his hand to him. "Today Turkey perishes. It is Allah's will," says the Turkish commander soberly. "You have fought splendidly, bravely," Skobeleff replies; though to MacGahan he mutters in English, "yet they were cowards to give up such a position." Turning to his men, he cries, "Thank you, my friends, thank you comrades. How many men have we taken?" "Thirty-five thousand," is the reply.

The last battle of the war is won; the last Turkish defence line broken. With the name 'Shenovo' added to his standard by the Czar's command, Skobeleff is ordered to thrust on to Adrianople. In fifteen days his men march 300 miles, and the second city of the Ottoman Empire is occupied without a shot on 21 January. On its way, his army marched and rode through a sickening panorama of death. Fleeing panic-stricken before the Russian advance, 200,000 Turkish refugees set out for Constantinople. F. D. Millet, the *Daily News* correspondent, describes what he saw personally:

"As we rode along the road, the first thing that met our eyes was a number of bodies of Turkish soldiers lying in the road crushed by the wheels of passing artillery, and trampled into the mud by the feet of many horses. Before we had gone four miles the corpses of peasants, both Turkish and Bulgarian, were to be seen lying in the snow, and some of them had already been exposed to the weather for two or three weeks. Some had blood-stains still fresh on their garments. Dead horses and cattle blocked the path at every few steps, averaging two to the distance between the telegraph posts; and as we went farther and farther the number rapidly increased, and hundreds of abandoned arabas stood in the road and choked the ditches alongside.

"The road, too narrow for the immense trains that had

passed over it in hasty flight, was now supplemented by beaten tracks through the rice fields on each side; and there were traces of bivouacs in the snow, which became more and more frequent as we proceeded, until these side paths were almost literally carpeted with the debris of camps, and our route lay between two rows of dead animals, broken arabas, piles of rags and cast-off clothing, and human bodies, for thirty-five miles of the whole of the first day's ride. We saw the bodies of Bulgarian peasants with terrible wounds in the head and neck, sometimes mutilated and disfigured; women and infants, children and old men, both Turkish and Bulgarian, fallen in the fields by the roadside half buried in the snow, or lying in the pools of water. It seemed to have been one long battle between the peasants of both races, in which the dead were counted equally for each; but while many of the bodies bore marks of violence and showed ghastly wounds the great proportion of the women and children were evidently frozen to death, for they lay on the snow as if asleep, with the flush of life still on their faces, and the pink skin of their face and hands still unblanched.

"Side by side with these, many corpses of old men, full of dignity even in death, lay stark by the roadside, their white beards clotted with blood, and their helpless hands fallen upon their breasts. From the muddy water of the ditches tiny hands and feet stretched out, and baby faces half covered with snow looked out innocently and peacefully, with scarcely a sign of suffering on their features. Frozen at their mothers' breasts, they were thrown down into the snow to lighten the burden of the poor creatures who were struggling along in mortal terror. At every step we met new and more horrifying scenes; man and wife lying side by side on the same blanket, with two children curled upon the snow near, all frozen dead; old men with their heads half cut off; some Bulgarians, mutilated as only the Turks know how to mutilate; and on each side of the road broad continuous bivouacs deserted in haste, strewn with household effects.

"For many miles we had been trampling in the mud carpets, bedding, and clothing. Now the highway was literally paved with bundles, cushions, blankets, and every imaginable article of household use. Broken arabas, too, began to multiply; and as we approached the little village of Tirali, we saw in the distance, on either side of the road, a perfect forest of wheels, reaching to the river on the right, and spreading away up the hillsides on the left. Several dead Turkish soldiers and one or two Russians, showed that there had been a little skirmish there; and we rode into the midst of the great deserted bivouac, the horses walking on rich carpets and soft draperies, all crushed and trampled in the mud. The scene was at once so unique in its general aspect, so terribly impressive, so eloquent of suffering and disaster to innocent people, that I hesitate to attempt a description of it.

"Hundreds of acres were covered with household goods. All along the river bank, following the windings of the road, over the hill, and across the fields where the road makes a sharp turn, reached this bivouac, at least three miles in extent, and of varying width. Over this great tract the arabas were standing as closely as they could, with their oxen placed together. The frames of the carts were in most cases broken to pieces. Sick cattle wandered listlessly about among the wheels. Corpses of men, women, and children lay about near every araba, and the whole ground was carpeted with clothing, kitchen utensils, books and bedding. It was a pitiable sight to see an old grey-bearded Turk lying with his open Koran beside him, splashed with blood from ghastly gashes in his bared throat. Bundles of rags and clothes nearly all held dead babies. Crowds of Bulgarians swarmed in this great avenue of death and desolation, choosing the best of the carts, and carrying away great loads of copper vessels, which lay about in profusion, and mud-soiled bedding, with no more respect for the dead than for the rags they lay on. These scavengers would drive their carts across the heads of dead women and old men, without even a glance of curiosity at the bodies."

But Millet did not, and could not, see it all. At every railway station and all along the line to Constantinople, were long trains of wagons laden with refugees, lying, sitting,

standing, and hanging on outside. Even the buffers of the
engines were occupied; the poor wretches clinging to their
precarious hold as the trains moved. Many fell off *en route*,
and a great number died of cold and exposure. The iron
luggage cages under the carriages were crammed; when the
trains reached their destination those who thus travelled
were so cramped and frozen they could not be moved.
In some places the fugitives sat for three days in the wagons,
waiting for the train to move on. No one dared alight, for
there were hundreds ready to seize each vacated place.
When the Turkish refugees reached Constantinople, they
told stories of the massacres carried out by the Bulgarians
and the Cossacks. The course of the River Maritza, they said,
had been changed by the bodies of 2,000 children cast into
it by the Russian Cossacks.

From Adrianople Skobeleff pushed on towards Constantinople, but he was halted on 31 January at Tchataldja by
the announcement that an armistice had been signed. The
Turks had thrown themselves on the mercy of the Russians,
and had agreed to recognize the independence of Mon-
tenegro, Rumania and Servia. Bulgaria was to be an
autonomous province, and Russia was to be indemnified by
a grant of territory. The war was over. Halted in their tracks,
the Russian army gazed at the walls of Constantinople,
and no one yet knew if the Russians would occupy the
Turkish capital. Britain was determined that they should
not, and on 12 February, on the pretext of protecting British
lives and property, the five British ironclads lying in the
Dardanelles were moved up to Constantinople, the Sultan
seeing at last the smoke of the British Navy which he had
so anxiously awaited. Declaring that it might be necessary
to protect the lives and property of their citizens too, the
Russians occupied San Stefano, six miles from Constantinople, and there a few days later the Treaty of San Stefano
was signed, ending the war between Turkey and Russia.
It was subsequently submitted to the Congress of European
Powers at Berlin, where the Czar was stripped of his gains
and from where Disraeli returned to London with 'Peace
and Honour'. Turkey lost 70,000 square miles of territory,

and Russia gained 3,300 square miles in Bessarabia. Britain was the only winner with the island of Cyprus. The Congress of Berlin created countless new frictions and sowed the seeds of the First World War, for in Bosnia and Hertzegovina, the two provinces ceded to Austria, stood a little town named Sarajevo, where thirty-six years later the shot was fired which set the world in flames.

Russia gained very little by the war, save the prestige that she had freed some of the Balkan Christians. If it had not been for the defence of Plevna, she might have gained more; she would certainly have been at Constantinople far sooner, perhaps in July 1877. Osman's heroic defence prolonged the war, but did it affect its result? By holding up the Russians for four months, and by defeating their assaults, he cost the Russians dear, but we must not give Plevna a significance it does not deserve. The most that can be said is that, by holding up the Russian advance, Osman bought time for the Sultan's friends to rally European fears in Turkey's favour. When the Czar's armies finally reached Constantinople, he was baulked of his prey: fearing the intervention of the European Powers he had to be content with very little. But the same might have happened if he had reached Constantinople in the previous summer. With public opinion still enraged against the Turks, it might have been difficult to stop him, and without the loss of prestige and drain on his resources brought about at Plevna, the Czar might have been more difficult to dislodge. Plevna at least saved the European Powers from an embarrassing situation, and its prolonged defence may have saved the lives of countless Englishmen. No one knows and the question is not now one of the slightest importance.

More important to us is what happened subsequently to the people whose names have filled these pages.

Of Czar and Sultan, Alexander II, fell a victim to an assassin in 1881. Abdul the Damned, as he was to be called, was deposed in 1910, and died in 1918. Osman Ghazi, released from captivity in March 1878, returned to Constantinople where he became commander-in-chief of the Imperial Guard, Minister of War (1878—85) and Grand

Marshal of the Palace. He died, aged sixty-three or sixty-eight, it being uncertain which, on 4 April, 1900.

How Januarius Aloysius MacGahan died within a week of the end of hostilities is told by Frederick Villiers. One night, Villiers travelled from Constantinople to Skobeleff's headquarters where he and MacGahan had been bidden to dinner. MacGahan, he told Skobeleff, was not well. Though not fully recovered from the exhaustion of the campaign, he had gone to nurse a friend, Lieutenant Greene, the United States Military Attaché, who was ill with typhus. He asked Skobeleff to excuse him, Villiers said. "I know MacGahan thoroughly. I fear he must be seriously ill not to keep an appointment with me," replied Skobeleff. "I am going to send a telegram to find out how he is."

While awaiting the reply, Villiers, Skobeleff and a French correspondent sat down to dinner. Villiers recalls that the conversation turned on the question of what men fought for. "The Turk fights for fanaticism," said Villiers, "he knows if he kills a Christian he passes into a world where his stomach is always full and his harem contains the most lovely *houris* imaginable." "Then what do the Russians fight for?" asked Skobeleff. "For their particular Gods—the Great White Czar and Holy Russia," replied Villiers. "Yes, that is so," laughed Skobeleff, and then turning to his French guest, he asked, "And you, Monsieur, what do you fight for?" Springing to his feet, the Frenchman posed heroically and said, "Ah, *pour la gloire!*" "Bravo!" said Skobeleff. "And now you English?" Villiers, thought a moment, "Well, probably the greatest aspiration of all." "Vat's dat?" smiled the Frenchman. "Why, British interests, of course," said Villiers.

As they finished dinner a reply was brought to Skobeleff's telegram. It read, "MacGahan seriously ill. Unconscious." Skobeleff, who as a Russian general could not ride in Constantinople without ceremony, sent Villiers galloping ahead, on his own white charger, to the succour of their friend, while he changed into civilian dress and followed by train. He was too late. When he arrived at the British hospital, MacGahan was dead of typhus. He could not, he was told, enter the room because of the fear of infection. Skobeleff, thrusting the doctors aside, burst into the room where his friend's body lay and knelt at the bedside, bursting into floods of tears. Villiers had the greatest difficulty in tearing him away. MacGahan's funeral was attended by Skobeleff, several other Russian generals and by many newspaper correspondents. Five years later his body was taken back to the United States in a warship and reburied in an Ohio grave, and a statue to his memory was erected in Sofia.

Skobeleff did not long survive his friend. Promoted a full general, he returned to Russia a national hero. In 1881 he commanded the Russian army in Central Asia where he conquered the Tekke-Turkomans, and was made Governor of Minsk. On 7 July, 1882, while staying at the Hotel Deseaux in Moscow he died at three o'clock in the morning, it being said, from a heart attack. It is supposed that his heart had been affected by the fragment of shell which struck him at Plevna during the night attack in November. He was thirty-nine years old.

When the news of Skobeleff's death became known all Russia wept. "I am deeply shocked and affected," wrote the Czar to Skobeleff's sister, "at the sudden death of your brother. His loss to the Russian army is one it is hard to replace, and it must be deeply lamented by all true soldiers. It is sad, very sad, to lose men so useful and devoted to their mission." When the news spread in Moscow, immense crowds collected outside the hotel. "Skobeleff is dead," whispered the crowd. "God is angry with Russia," murmured an old soldier. "Skobeleff is dead," said the old soldier to one of Skobeleff's veterans. "Nonsense, it is impossible," the other replied. "I tell you he is dead." "There must be some mistake. It is impossible for Skobeleff to die." Skobeleff's man went on his way. Meeting a friend he told him, "How foolish people are. Someone has just told me Skobeleff is dead. It must be some other fellow, not our Skobeleff." Skobeleff's Requiem Mass was attended by the Grand Dukes Nicholas and Alexis, the Minister of War, and the Governor General of Moscow, and when his body was taken to his country estate for burial, the streets of Moscow were lined with soldiers.

Archibald Forbes went as a correspondent to only two more wars. He was in the Afghan War of 1879, and he travelled straight from there to South Africa where the British were fighting the Zulu Chieftain Cetewayo. Forbes missed the massacre of Isandhlwana, but he witnessed the defeat of the Zulus at Ulundi, and, after the battle, he rode 120 miles through country infested with hostile Zulus to Landmanns Nek to put his story on the wire to London where it was read out in the House of Commons, as the first news to be received of the decisive battle of the campaign. Forbes did not go to war again. He lived in London until his death, after a long illness, aged sixty-two, on 30 March, 1900, five days before Osman Pasha died in Constantinople. Three days before Forbes died, his old friend Robinson, the manager of the *Daily News* went to see him. He found Forbes in delirium, his face pale and emaciated, his eyes staring wide open, and calling out, "Those guns, man, don't you see those guns? I tell you the brave fellows will be mowed down like grass." His unconscious mind may have been recalling those terrible scenes he witnessed at Plevna.

Dr. Charles Ryan, unable to return to Plevna in October, went to the Asiatic theatre of war instead. On the conclusion of hostilities he returned to Constantinople where he was welcomed by Osman Pasha and decorated with the Medal of Plevna. Thirty-eight years later General Sir Charles Ryan returned as the Principal Medical Officer of the Australian Forces in the First World War, wearing, by special permission, his Plevna ribbons. After the war he returned to his house in Melbourne in the garden of which bloomed, and may still bloom, the lineal descendants of the seeds he gathered at Plevna. His descendants cherish, one hopes, those souvenirs he gathered of the great siege in which he played such a noble part. Ryan died on 23 October, 1926.

Of the ultimate fate of William Herbert, I have no knowledge. He may have returned to the commercial career broken by his quixotic enlistment in a foreign army, and his gallant work at Plevna. He and Ryan do not appear to have met in Plevna, and Herbert speaks of Ryan as one of the English doctors who paid a brief visit to Plevna in October 1877.

F. D. Millet, the newspaper correspondent who after the war became an artist, died on the *Titanic* in 1912.

Frederick Villiers lived to sketch many scenes of battle in all parts of the world.

Irving Montagu, the war-artist, tells two anecdotes of Plevna. The night before Osman's attempted break-out Montagu saw the spy at Skobeleff's headquarters who brought the news of Osman's preparations. After the war, he saw the man again, selling postcards in the Caledonian Road in London.

In 1879 Montagu read the following news item in a Bristol newspaper: "Thirty tons of human bones, comprising 30,000 skeletons, have just been landed at Bristol from Plevna." Those who sacrificed their lives in the assault and defence of an obscure Bulgarian town ended their careers as fertilizers for the soil of England!

To my inquiry about Plevna now, the Committee for Friendship and Cultural Relations with Foreign Countries, The Peoples' Republic of Bulgaria, has courteously informed me that Plevna is an important industrial and commercial centre with a population of 60,000. A mausoleum was built by the people of Bulgaria in memory of the Russians and Rumanians who fell in the great siege, and traces of the earthworks and of the Grivitza redoubts remain. On the south lies Skobeleff Park, overlooking the "Valley of Death", and the great redoubt Skobeleff captured and lost has been restored.

Though the scars are now healed, I like to think of Plevna as Forbes and MacGahan saw it, its gallant defenders hurling defiance at its no less heroic besiegers. From its slopes and hills now rise sounds no more lethal than the roar of tractors and harvesters, but, I think that if we stood on the Radishevo Ridge, or on the Green Hills, we should see Forbes and Villiers peering through the cannon smoke, or MacGahan watching his friend Skobeleff riding his white horse and leading the assault on the great Krishnin redoubt. To our ears would come wafted on the breeze the shouts of men bent on victory or death, rising above the sharp crackle of rifle-fire and the deep booming of the guns. Who these men were now does not matter. They belong to a past age, the battles and sieges of which are now of no importance. But the deeds of the gallant Skobeleff and the heroic defence of Osman the Victorious in the great siege of Plevna serve to remind us that courage, devotion to duty, inspiration and pertinacity are not the prerogative of any particular nation, colour or creed.

APPENDIX

PRINCIPAL OFFICERS OF THE PLEVNA GARRISON

As the text is filled with strange names I have omitted mention of those of the Plevna garrison. To repair this injustice, I list Osman's principal officers.

Commander   Musir (Marshal) Osman Pasha

The July Assault:

Chief of Staff	Brigadier Tahir Pasha
Staff	Lieutenant-Colonel Hairi Bey, Lieutenant-Colonel Raif Bey
Principal Aide-de-Camp	Lieutenant-Colonel Talahat Bey
Commander of Artillery	Colonel Ahmed Bey
Commander of Cavalry	Colonel Osman Bey
Surgeon-in-Chief	Colonel Hassif Bey
Commander 1st Division	General Adil Pasha
Commander 2nd Division	Brigadier Hassan Sabri Pasha
Commander Reserve	Brigadier Sadik Pasha

The September Assault and Investment.

The same as for July except that a third division was commanded by Brigadier Tahir Pasha, and the Reserve by Brigadier Rifa'at Pasha. Colonel Tewfik Bey, afterwards Pasha, who had been at Lovtcha, returned to Plevna and led the counter-attack against Skobeleff. He is said to have been the engineer-officer in command of the fortifications erected between 20 July and 6 September. At the sortie on 10 December, the First Division which made the assault, was commanded by Brigadier Tahir Pasha.

BIBLIOGRAPHY

OUTSIDE PLEVNA

BAKER, VALENTINE *The War in Bulgaria*. 2 Vol. 1879.

BOYLE, FRED *Narrative of an Expelled Correspondent*. 1877.

COOKSON, FIFE *Armies of the Balkans*. 1879.

FORBES, ARCHIBALD *War Correspondent of the* Daily News, 1877–8.

    Glimpses through the Cannon Smoke. 1880.

    Souvenirs of Some Continents. 1885.

    Barracks, Bivouacs and Battles. 1895.

    Camps, Quarters and Casual Places. 1896.

HUYSCHE, WENTWORTH *The Liberation of Bulgaria*. 1894.

MONTAGU, IRVING *Camp and Studio*. 1890.

NEMIROVITCH-DANTCHENKO, V. *Personal Reminiscences of General Skobeleff*. 1884.

VILLIERS, FREDERICK *Pictures of Many Wars*. 1902.

WELLESLEY, COL. THE HON. F. A. *With the Russians in Peace and War*. 1878.

INSIDE PLEVNA

GAY, DREW *Plevna, the Sultan and the Porte*. 1878.

HERBERT, WILLIAM VON *The Defence of Plevna*. 1895.

RYAN, DR. CHARLES *Under the Red Crescent*. 1897.

MILITARY AND POLITICAL

GREEN, F. V. *The Campaign in Bulgaria, 1877–8*. 1903.

HARRIS, DAVID *Britain and the Bulgarian Horrors of 1876*. 1939.

HOZIER, CAPT. H. M. *The Russo-Turkish War*. 5 vols.

MACGAHAN, J. A. *The Turkish Atrocities in Bulgaria*. 1876.

MAURICE, MAJOR F. *The Russian-Turkish War*. 1877.

PEARS, SIR EDWIN *Forty Years in Constantinople*. 1915.

SCUDAMORE, F. *A Sheaf of Memoirs*. 1925.

WIRTHWEIN, WALTER G. *Britain and the Balkan Crisis (1875-8)*. 1935.

WITTLIN, ALMA *Abdul Hamid. The Shadow of God*. 1940.

INDEX

DATE DUE

NO 26 76			